DISCARD

D1055322

FOUNDATIONS OF VOCATIONAL EDUCATION

RUPERT N. EVANS
University of Illinois
at Urbana-Champaign

CHARLES E. MERRILL PUBLISHING COMPANY
A Bell & Howell Company
Columbus, Ohio

THE MERRILL SERIES IN CAREER PROGRAMS

Editorial Board: Director, Robert Taylor, The Ohio State University; Theodore Cote, Temple University; Aleene Cross, University of Georgia; Louise Keller, Colorado State College; Mary Klaurens, University of Minnesota; Carl Schaefer, Rutgers–The State University; Robert Warmbrod, The Ohio State University.

Copyright © 1971 by CHARLES E. MERRILL PUBLISHING COMPANY, Columbus, Ohio. All rights reserved. No part of this book may be reproduced in any form, electronic or mechanical, including photocopy, recording, or any information storage and retrieval system, without permission in writing from the publisher.

International Standard Book Number: 0–675–09227–2

Library of Congress Catalog Card Number: 73–146317

8—76
Printed in the United States of America

FOREWORD

Throughout its history vocational education has enjoyed a vigorous eclectic philosophy. This pragmaticism has its roots in many disciplines and in the warp and woof of our schools and society. Dr. Evans explicates some of these linkages, their rationale and some of their strengths and limitations.

He has identified critical problems and issues and most importantly, their interrelationships. He also discusses alternative solutions and their consequence for many facets of vocational education. The book is thought provoking. It extends horizons and perspectives and, as its title implies, provides the kind of insights and understandings essential to building "foundations" for vocational education.

Dr. Evans is eminently qualified to author such a text, having been intimately involved in vocational education through several decades in a variety of roles. His experience as a local vocational teacher, a university professor, a college of education dean and as an eminent researcher, member of national boards, councils and advisory groups cumulatively provide him with a unique and rich background which he has brought to bear in this text.

Robert E. Taylor
Editorial Director
Series in Career Programs

PREFACE

This book is designed for vocational educators and those planning to enter the field, who are pursuing a program of personal development which will insure competency in that specialty. A complete knowledge of vocational education and its relationships with society is essential to effective performance. With this in mind, the book concentrates on basic principles affecting all of human resource development.

In the United States, vocational education has come to mean education for any occupation which normally requires less than a baccalaureate degree for the beginning worker. It is used in that sense in this book, and covers all such education, whether public or private, in school or out of school, and regardless of the source of funds which pay for it. The distinction between vocational education and education for the professions is an arbitrary one, and a term is needed to refer to the full range of education for work. In this book "occupational education" is used to cover all educational programs for work, regardless of the occupational level.

The first section of this book is devoted to the goals of vocational education. It describes how these goals have shifted to an emphasis on human resource development, and away from a narrow concern for meeting the needs of local employers. The second section presents an overview of the contributions of four social sciences toward these goals and toward the means of achieving them. The third section is concerned with present programs of vocational education and trends which are likely to affect the ways in which we achieve our goals. It is organized, not in terms of subject-matter areas within vocational education, but rather in terms of social organizations which conduct programs of vocational education. This is followed by a section on methods of preparing personnel to conduct programs of vocational education. The final chapter looks at the future of vocational education and its part in the development of all of occupational education, with particular attention to the role of occupational education in underdeveloped areas of this country and the world and its role in the development of every individual's full human potential.

Any book of this type is written by many people other than the "author." Particular acknowledgement is due, however, to Professors Willard Hill and Harry Belman of Purdue and to my father, Loren Evans, who inducted me into the mysteries of vocational education; to the College of Education of the University of Illinois, which has employed me while I learned more and which provided the sabbatical leave which allowed the bulk of writing to be done; and to staff of the Center for Research and Leadership Development in Vocational and Technical Education at The Ohio State University who invited me to join them during the period of the leave and assisted me in many other ways. And I thank my wife and daughters for their forbearance and for their patience in proofreading the manuscript.

The following persons have read portions of the manuscript and have offered many suggestions for improving it:

Joseph Arnold, Robert Campbell, Ulrich Ernst, Donald Lux, William Nelson, Robert Taylor and Robert Young of the Ohio State University; Harry Broudy, Joe Burnett, Bernard Karsh, Ernest Robinson, Hazel Spitze, Jacob Stern and Robert Tomlinson of the University of Illinois; Howard Rosen of the Department of Labor; Jack Willers of Auburn University; Ronald Stadt of Southern Illinois University; Garth Mangum of the University of Utah; and Dale Riepe of the State University of New York at Buffalo. Final responsibility, of course, rests with the author, and many of the suggestions which have been offered have not been included. The result is a personal document in many ways. Its success should be judged in terms of its effect in suggesting ways in which vocational education can better serve the needs of youth and adults. Vocational education has no other reason for existing.

Rupert N. Evans

CONTENTS

Part I   OBJECTIVES OF VOCATIONAL EDUCATION

Chapter 1 INTRODUCTION

In its broadest sense vocational education is that part of education which makes an individual more employable in one group of occupations than in another. It may be differentiated from general education, which is of almost equal value regardless of the occupation which is to be followed.

According to the previous definition, foreign language study is vocational education for those students who plan to be interpreters, and driver-education is vocational education for the broad range of occupations which require persons to be able to drive an automobile. And education in *any* specialized field is vocational education for those persons who plan to teach in that field. Algebra and higher mathematics, and advanced foreign language are not general education subjects, because they are not needed by everyone regardless of the occupational field which the person plans to enter.

While the intent of each student has a great deal to do with determining whether or not a particular subject is vocational education for him, it is possible, by choosing subject matter and methods of presenting that subject matter, to insure that a subject has little or no vocational value for any of the students enrolled. However, all general education subjects could be taught in a way which would emphasize their occupational value and relevance to society as a whole.

The term "vocational education" is often used, especially in federal legislation, to include only instruction which is designed to enable persons to succeed in occupations which require less than a baccalaureate degree. While this distinction is useful in subsidizing educational programs which tend to be neglected by schools controlled by individuals who emphasize only the preparation of students for the professions, it has little utility outside this realm. Vocational education and general education are intimately interwoven. In most instructional situations some students are there for vocational purposes. Every general education course can have occupational value, and awareness of occupational goals leads students to see the relevance of certain content which otherwise might appear highly irrelevant.

BASIC OBJECTIVES

There are three basic objectives in any public school vocational education curriculum. Listed in chronological order of their acceptance as goals, they are: (1) meeting the manpower needs of society, (2) increasing the options available to each student, and (3) serving as a motivating force to enhance all types of learning. A few vocational education programs sponsored by employers have these same three goals, but most do not. Very often they are designed only to meet the short-term manpower needs of a single employer.

Not all public manpower development programs attempt to reach all three of these objectives. For example, most Manpower Development and Training Act (MDTA) programs include no general education component except for the occasional teaching of reading to students who are functionally illiterate. When the adult MDTA trainees see that reading is essential for success on many types of jobs, they acquire reading skills rapidly. The same type of facilitation could apply to other general education subjects, but these are rarely taught concurrently with vocational skills in MDTA programs.

The managers and stockholders of profit making organizations rarely see justification for using their moneys and facilities to train more people than they need. Nor do they wish to educate personnel in ways which will increase the probability that they will change employers. On the other hand, they are interested in providing education programs which will increase employees' options within their own company, increase the job satisfaction of their employees, and meet the company's current and anticipated needs for skilled manpower.

Profit-making vocational schools are seldom interested in providing training to persons who are unable to pay the cost of training (though this objection disappears if the federal government will pay these costs).

If they plan to stay in business for a long time, they will try to recruit students who are easily employed and avoid students against whom employers often discriminate. They prefer offering programs in occupations where the demand is greater than the supply, and they avoid programs where enrollments are apt to be small and placement of graduates difficult. Since their students are interested in securing employment as rapidly as possible, general education courses are not included in the curriculum unless they are masked by names which indicate to the student that they will help employability, e.g. "technical report-writing" for engineering technicians. Because their teachers rarely have tenure, and because the managers of private schools tend to measure efficiency in terms of repeat business, their instruction tends to be more up to date than in some public school programs. It would appear then that private vocational schools are (1) interested in increasing the options of some students but not indigent or disadvantaged ones, (2) interested in helping to meet some of the nation's manpower needs, (3) not at all interested in designing instruction to increase the intelligibility of general education, yet (4) are relatively effective in achieving their limited goals.

Vocational education programs which require students to pay more than nominal tuition usually practice a considerable amount of de facto segregation by socio-economic levels. Vocational high schools, area schools, and technical institutes which are operated on campuses separate from college preparatory programs also promote socio-economic segregation. In contrast, comprehensive high schools and community colleges can provide integration of socio-economic classes through the general education portion of their curricula which enroll students from all types of backgrounds for a significant portion of the school day. Gradually accumulating evidence indicates that socio-economic segregation impedes the achievement of the goal of increasing individual options. Despite the many obstacles imposed by their institutional roles, teachers in public vocational schools and vocational departments in comprehensive public schools usually have all three of the basic objectives in mind and work toward their achievement. It seems reasonable to assume that teachers who strive to achieve all three goals are more likely to reach all of them than teachers who strive for only one or two.

SPECIFIC OBJECTIVES OF THE INSTRUCTOR

In addition to the three basic objectives which should apply to all of vocational education, each course has its own objectives. Moreover, the instructor may have developed objectives which apply only to certain of his students in that course. These specific objectives should be in accordance with all three basic objectives.

Too often, specific objectives are warped by the goals and structure of the sponsoring organization, by personal prejudices of the instructor, and by the availability of unneeded equipment and unavailability of needed equipment. More frequently, they are distorted by instructors who lack competence in certain needed phases of instruction, and therefore substitute other instruction which is not as essential. The worst situation occurs when instruction is offered by an individual who has no specific goals or no means of achieving the goals which he does have.

SPECIFIC OBJECTIVES OF THE STUDENT

Surprisingly little is known about student objectives in vocational education programs. It is believed that students frequently seek vocational goals in courses that teachers believe to be nonvocational in nature. For example, a student who wishes to be a writer may take elective English composition courses and may attempt to shape the character of the assignments which he receives in ways which will further his vocational aspirations. One may infer that this is frequently the case by examining data from "Formal Occupational Training of Adult Workers" (2, p. 11), which indicates that 37.7 percent of adults over age twenty-two who have less than three years of college say that they have had vocational courses in high school. Since courses in which instructors have vocational objectives are not offered to this proportion of students, it would appear that as adults, some of these persons saw vocational value in nonvocational courses. Whether or not they saw these values when they were students is open to question.

Similarly, the instructor may have a vocational objective while the student does not. This probably occurs most frequently when students have strong avocational interests such as in increasing the performance of automobiles and enroll in vocational automobile mechanics courses to further their avocational rather than their vocational interests. Since, however, such students are almost invariably excluded if their lack of vocational interest becomes apparent to the instructor, these discrepancies between instructor and student goals are very often concealed.

TAXONOMIES OF EDUCATIONAL OBJECTIVES

As we study the objectives of instructors and students, it is helpful to have a means of listing and describing them. Bloom (1), Krathwohl (3), and Simpson (4) have developed taxonomies for classifying educational objectives in the cognitive, affective, and psychomotor domains. Each of these three taxonomies provides a classification scheme which enables one to develop a hierarchy of objectives. Thus, within the psychomotor domain, objectives having to do with perception (sensory stimulation, cue selection and translation) come first in the taxonomy. This is followed by set, (mental set, physical set, emotional set), guided response (imitation, trial and error), mechanism, complex response (resolution of an uncertainty and automatic performance), adaptation, and origination. Perception is necessary before guided response can be accomplished, and complex response is necessary before adaptation or origination can occur.

By using the taxonomy, the instructor can determine whether or not he inadvertently is setting objectives early in the course which should be preceded by the attainment of simpler objectives. A second use of the three taxonomies is as a check list to enable the instructor to determine whether or not he is concentrating too much of his instruction within the cognitive, affective, or psychomotor domains and to determine whether or not he will move the class toward sufficiently high goals within each of these domains.

BEHAVIORAL OBJECTIVES

There has been considerable controversy about the desirability of specifying objectives in behavioral terms. An objective which is specified in behavioral terms identifies precisely the types of behavior the student should be able to exhibit at the end of the instructional program. Proponents of the use of these objectives feel that more general objectives are of little value in guiding an instructor's actions from day to day and are of little value to students in determining whether or not an objective has been achieved. Opponents feel that the use of behavioral objectives tends to tie the hands of the capable instructor by restricting him from taking advantage of chance opportunities (unusual events in the community, a series of questions which show that students are particularly interested in an unusual topic, and the like) which can facilitate learning markedly. Moreover, they feel that many worthwhile outcomes of education, especially in the field of values, are difficult if not impossible to state in behavioral terms. This controversy is far from being resolved.

Conflicts in Objectives

A vocational education program which is designed to help meet national manpower needs may actually decrease individual options and vice versa. For many years nurses aides, orderlies, and even practical nurses and professional nurses have been markedly underpaid compared to other individuals performing work of a similar level and requiring similar amounts of intelligence and education. Clearly society needs workers in these fields, so in order to help meet the nation's manpower needs, vocational education should establish programs to prepare workers for these positions.

At the same time, one of the obvious reasons for manpower shortages in these fields has been their relatively low pay and poor working conditions. If the shortages of skilled workers in these fields become severe enough, wages are almost certain to rise and working conditions to improve. The extent to which vocational education provides programs which meet the nation's manpower shortages determines the number of individual options its trainees will have. These options will be decreased if the students have been prepared for an occupational field which does not produce as much income as another might. Moreover, the options of current workers are decreased if too many trainees are produced. On this basis, some economists have argued that federal funds should not be spent for vocational training for fields in which wages and working conditions are substandard.

On the other hand, failure to produce skilled workers to meet society's manpower needs may also decrease individual options. Obviously a person who is denied any sort of vocational training suffers because he does not have skills which are saleable. Equally important but less obvious is the fact that when a particular occupation lacks enough skilled workers, employers seek ways to substitute workers in other occupations to meet their needs. Thus, the shortage of terrazzo workers has virtually eliminated the use of terrazzo floors in many parts of the country and has provided employment for cement finishers, tile setters, and carpet layers who were trained to produce or install alternative types of floor coverings. Thus, a shortage of skilled workers not only raises the price of that skilled labor in the short run, but it may in the long run succeed in pricing the entire occupation out of the market. Obviously this decreases the options of workers in that occupation.

A vocational program which concentrates too heavily on achieving one of the basic objectives is certain to neglect the other two. Thus, a program offered by an employer may contribute markedly to meeting the manpower needs of the nation (though it set out to meet the manpower needs of the employer), but completely neglect the goal of making general education more meaningful. More often, a program with a single goal achieves that goal, and in the process accidentally achieves the other two in part. It seems clear, however, that a program which is designed deliberately to meet all three of the goals of vocational education is more likely to meet all these goals in substantial measure than is a program which achieves one goal on purpose, and two by accident. Though there are instances in which there are conflicts in basic goals, in the great majority of cases, the three goals complement each other. The next section of this book looks at the three basic goals of vocational education in greater detail.

REFERENCES

1. Bloom, Benjamin S., *et al. Taxonomy of Educational Objectives: Cognitive Domain*. New York: Longmans, Green and Co., 1956.

2. *Formal Occupational Training of Adult Workers*. Manpower/Automation Research Monograph No. 2. Washington, D.C.: U.S. Department of Labor, 1964.

3. Krathwohl, David R., *et al. Taxonomy of Educational Objectives: Affective Domain*. New York: David McKay Co., Inc., 1964.

4. Simpson, Elizabeth J., "The Classification of Educational Objectives, Psychomotor Domain," *Illinois Teacher of Home Economics*, X, No. 4 (Winter, 1966-67), 110-144.

Chapter 2 MEETING THE MANPOWER NEEDS OF SOCIETY

The earliest and most widely accepted objective of vocational education is to provide a mechanism for meeting the manpower needs of the local community. Today it should be recognized that the needs of the nation and of society as a whole are as important or more important. Industry, government, the church, the schools, and indeed every institution of society requires trained people if they are to survive. While the needs of the family are almost invariably ignored in statements of manpower needs, society is gradually recognizing that consumer education, sex education, and some form of homemaking education are essential to the survival of the family as well. If specially educated personnel are needed for the survival of each of these institutions, some mechanism must be found to provide these people. The history of society is interwoven with more or less successful attempts to meet these needs.

While the need for trained personnel has been recognized throughout history, the problem of providing such personnel has become increasingly difficult as the rate of change in manpower needs has accelerated. When an individual could expect to spend a lifetime in the same occupation and could expect to transmit to his children in essentially unchanged form the skills, knowledges, and attitudes which he had learned, the need for institutionalizing vocational education was much less than it is now, when few people can expect to engage in exactly the same productive activities for even a year.

History

The oldest method of meeting manpower needs was for the father to pass on to his sons and for the mother to pass on to her daughters the occupational information they had acquired from their parents, plus what they had learned by trial and error during a generation of productive work. But when a technological revolution such as the substitution of agriculture for hunting or the substitution of bronze for stone tools occurred, transmission of the family heritage was no longer a satisfactory educational program for workers in the newly generated occupations.

ON-THE-JOB TRAINING

While training by the parent was accomplished almost entirely at the place of work and was carried out simultaneously with productive activity, the next type of on-the-job training included a new element. The instructor was a worker who was not necessarily a member of the family. On-the-job training (OJT) by persons other than parents occurred whenever members of more than one family were engaged in a productive activity. It had the advantage of providing for the orphan, and allowed the new worker to learn from more than one instructor, but it had the disadvantage that the trainer did not have a vested interest in seeing that the new worker was fully trained. OJT continues in occupations from the simplest to the most complex, but in most vocations, it probably will involve teaching only those skills and knowledges which are unique to a particular employer and hence are not suitable for more institutionalized types of vocational education.

APPRENTICESHIP

OJT has always been relatively haphazard. The new worker observes, practices, learns by trial and error, and occasionally receives direct instruction, if the experienced worker does not feel threatened by the potential competition. There is no guarantee that the new worker will learn everything about the occupation. Instead he probably will learn only a portion of what is practiced in a particular place of employment at a certain time.

Apprenticeship attempted to combine the best of family instruction and OJT by having an experienced worker agree to teach the full range of an occupation, acting in lieu of the parent. In return the trainer received the services of the apprentice for a certain time span—often ten or more years. The method of instruction was similar to that used by the family, and by on-the-job training, but was more complete because the trainer agreed not to withhold any of the mysteries of the craft as was (and is) so commonly the case in OJT. For this reason apprenticeship has always been a practical necessity for a cadre of workers in highly skilled occupations which could not be learned efficiently through on-the-job training.

Apprenticeship reached its peak in Europe just prior to the beginning of the industrial revolution in the seventeenth century. At that time, it was the primary means of instruction for most skilled and semi-skilled occupations. It was highly formalized, and graduates of the apprenticeship system were the only persons licensed to practice in many occupations. Apprenticeship continues today, though in this country it is largely restricted to the construction crafts, certain highly skilled metal working occupations, and certain occupations in the printing industry. The principal changes have been that apprentice-ship begins later in life, lasts for a shorter period (often three to six years), and instruction is guaranteed by a group of employers or employ-ees, rather than by a single craftsman.

SCHOOLS

The newest device of society for providing occupational skills is the school. Originally schools had a vocational purpose only and were insti-tuted for the priesthood, which was regarded as being so highly skilled that apprenticeship would not suffice. The school required the presence of several novices who could be given nearly indentical instruction in the theory and practice of an occupation. Schools for the priesthood began more than three thousand years ago.

As time went on other occupations acquired sufficient importance and content to warrant the development of special schools to meet man-power needs. By the middle ages, instruction in bookkeeping and algebra were provided in formal schools, and by 1900 almost every professional occupation had one or more schools devoted to it. At present, almost every skilled, technical, and professional occupation inducts at least part of its workers through formal school programs offered in high schools, community colleges, universities, and private occupational schools. In addition to their occupational purposes, schools are now used as a means of imparting knowledge which is useful to all citizens, regardless of occupation. Unfortunately they also serve to provide instruction which once had occupational value for the gentry, but which now is largely irrelevant for anyone.

PRIVATE AND PUBLIC SCHOOLS

Usually, new occupational education programs are introduced in the private schools first. Later, if a program thrives, it is introduced into the public schools.

Most private schools are more flexible than public schools in adapting to changed manpower needs. They depend on tuition for financial support, and if they cannot attract students, they must go out of business. Students are influenced to a certain extent by salesmanship, and by the availability of training in glamorous occupations; however, a private vocational school which does not place its students in good jobs will die eventually. Public schools, on the other hand, too seldom are concerned with placing their students, or even with attempting to attract students who can profit from vocational education. One of the major factors which enables private schools to cope rapidly with changing manpower needs is the fact that their instructors are rarely on tenure. This means that if an instructor is no longer needed, he can be discharged with no difficulty, while many public schools prefer to continue an unneeded vocational program until the death or retirement of an existing instructor. Moreover, public schools are afraid to enter new occupational training programs until the long-term necessity for such training is clearly established, for they do not like to be saddled with unneeded teachers.

The principal incentive for the establishment of a public school occupational education program in a particular field, when an existing private institution could expand to meet manpower needs, is the shifting of the cost of instruction from the student to society. The tuition charge in a private vocational school is approximately the same as the total educational costs per individual in public schools. Since a major part of this latter cost is paid by society, obviously, tuition costs which are paid by the individual are much lower in the public school setting.

Local advisory committees can be of marked assistance to school programs in providing education which meets local manpower needs. A mechanism is needed for providing information from employer and employee groups, government, and lay citizens on improvement of vocational education on a state and national basis. The establishment of state and national advisory councils who will annually evaluate vocational education programs clearly seems to be a step in the right direction.

PLACEMENT OF GRADUATES

There is no perfect method for determining whether or not a particular vocational education program is helping meet the manpower needs of the nation. Most job placements are local rather than national, and are affected markedly by local labor market needs, which may be at considerable variance from national needs. In addition, both local and national manpower needs may be affected sharply in the short run by current economic conditions which have little significance in terms of long-range manpower needs of the nation, but which do have marked effects upon placement rates. Eninger (4) has shown clearly that schools which operate placement offices for their students have better vocational education programs than schools which do not offer such a service. The most likely reason for this finding is that the placement office serves as a feedback mechanism for adjustment in the content and methods of the vocational training program to meet local labor market needs.

INDUSTRY OPERATED SCHOOLS

Not all schools, of course, are operated by public institutions or by private profit or non-profit making educational organizations. Many large industries operate schools of their own. Less publicized schools are operated by trade associations in fields such as baking, cleaning and dyeing, restaurant management, manufacturing engineering, water plant operation, etc. This extremely important part of vocational education is covered in detail later.

INSTITUTIONALIZATION TRENDS

With the exception of a few very recently developed occupations, instruction in almost every field has progressed through the various types of occupational education institutions in the same order in which society invented them. Thus the practice of medicine was first taught by physicians to their children, then was taught on-the-job, then through apprenticeship, and only in the late nineteenth century became an accepted part of formal instruction in the schools. Generally, the older and more highly skilled the occupation, the earlier it made the transition through these various institutions to become part of the school curriculum.

Shifts in the method of providing instruction occurred gradually. Thus, in the late nineteenth century one could find physicians being prepared in every institution of society devoted to occupational education. Only recently have all practitioners of medicine been required to go to school. At the present time, most occupations outside the professions are still in the process of transition, with gradually increasing proportions of workers being prepared in the school and gradually decreasing proportions being prepared through the family and on-the-job training. With few exceptions, the semi-skilled vocations have not reached the point where they are included in school curricula.

None of society's means for providing occupational instruction has ever been discarded totally. Instead, the simplest means of instruction have tended to become devoted to the simplest occupations. However even in the most complex fields, e.g., medicine, OJT continues as a means of teaching content which applies only to a particular place of employment. New jobs which have developed, and technical occupations which have split off from existing vocations, tend to start farther up the hierarchy of vocational education institutions. Thus, new workers in the field of engineering technology have seldom if ever been prepared through family instruction, and were taught only briefly through on-the-job training or apprenticeship. Instead, the bulk of such occupational preparation has from the beginning been provided in schools. Indeed, the availability of schools has been the primary limiting factor in the development of these occupations. Without schools to develop trained workers, the occupations within engineering technology can not flourish.

Why We Are Not Meeting Manpower Needs

During the nineteenth century, the United States met many of its manpower needs through the immigration of skilled workers from Europe. This delayed the establishment of significant public vocational education programs in this country until the start of World War I. Many developing countries have used a similar labor pool, but it seeems likely that soon they will be faced with a demand that native workers be trained and employed rather than reserving the best positions for foreigners. Clearly we cannot depend on other nations to meet our manpower needs. Indeed we have obligations to help under-developed nations train their own people to meet manpower needs abroad. Yet how can we do this when we are not meeting our own needs?

During the decade of the fifties, the population in the United States increased 19 percent, and the number of households increased 20 percent. During this same period the number of electricians and plumbers increased 10 percent, or half as much as the number of households, and the number of carpenters actually decreased. During the following decade of the sixties, the resulting shortage in the construction trades led to very rapid wage rate increases as construction contractors in most parts of the country attempted to attract skilled workers. This, in turn, resulted in increased costs of conventional housing and was a major factor in the more than 20 percent annual growth rate of the mobile home industry (1, p. 4).

It has been argued that the failure to train enough construction workers is because these trades are tightly unionized. Certainly at times the unions (and employers) in the construction industry, like almost every other occupational association from the American Medical Association to associations of morticians, have acted to restrict the entry of new workers. What is overlooked in this criticism is the fact that during the fifties, the number of cars and trucks in the United States increased by 50 percent, while the number of automobile mechanics increased by only 3 percent (2, p. 68). Since this is a field which is not tightly unionized, and since this example in the repair fields can be duplicated in occupation after occupation, the argument that restrictive union practices have produced our shortage of skilled workers is not very sound. Indeed, one can argue that if the construction workers' unions had not been the nation's leaders in fostering apprenticeship programs, the shortage of construction workers would be far greater than it is today.

The problem is more basic, and lies in the attitudes of the public toward certain occupations. John Gardner (5, p. 86) stated the problem well when he said, "An excellent plumber is infinitely more admirable than an incompetent philosopher. The society which scorns excellence in plumbing, because plumbing is a humble activity and tolerates shoddiness in philosophy because it is an exalted activity will have neither good plumbing nor good philosophy. Neither its pipes nor its theories will hold water." If we assume that these attitudes can be changed, we are still faced with the problem of learning what we as a society should do in vocational education to meet the manpower needs of the nation. Manpower needs are changing to the point that it has been said that "There is no place in the world of work for the uneducated person or the educated person who has not learned how to work" (8, p. 124). It might be more accurate to say that times have changed so that unless a person has learned to work, he is not educated.

Changes in Manpower Needs

LONG-TERM TRENDS

The proportion of the labor force which is made up of unskilled workers has decreased sharply and steadily for over one hundred years. Except for interruptions caused by war, pestilence, and governmental or religious suppression of innovation, this proportion probably has decreased since the beginning of recorded history. Mechanization is selective in its effects, and during the last century it has been easy to replace unskilled manpower with power from sources such as coal, petroleum, falling water, and atomic energy. Certain types of skilled labor can also be replaced by machines, but when this is done, other skilled labor is needed to manufacture, install, adjust, and repair machines. Once unskilled labor is replaced, it is no longer needed.

A second long-term trend has been a continued decrease in the proportion of the labor force involved in producing goods. Agriculture which produces materials such as food and fiber has become one of our most mechanized and efficient industries. While decreasing proportions of the labor force are required to produce our food and fiber, the knowledge and skill required of those who do produce them has increased. Similar effects are taking place in the manufacturing industry. These effects became apparent earlier in agriculture, however, because the demand for agricultural products is relatively static, while the demand for manufactured goods can be increased considerably. Despite increases in demand, the proportion of the population employed in manufacturing has declined for at least the past fifty years, with only the production of war goods temporarily reversing the long-term trend. As in agriculture, the skills of the labor force required for manufacturing continue to increase. Along with the decrease in the need for unskilled workers and the decrease in the proportion of the labor force involved in the production of goods, there has been a corresponding increase in employment in service occupations and in clerical work. In the mid fifties, the United States became the first nation in history to have less than half its workers employed in producing goods and more than half in white collar activities, especially in service and clerical work.

Many routine clerical activities are being replaced by electronic hardware such as computers, with the net effect being an increase in the skill level of the clerical occupations which remain. During the late fifties, computer corporations, which were rapidly expanding in certain manufacturing and clerical fields, predicted that they would soon be able to replace a large portion of the labor force through a revolution which would mean the end of work as we have known it. The result would be a large portion of the population doing no work at all, and the remainder working two or three days per week.

This prospect generated a great deal of unsophisticated writing and discussion. Among the predictions was that all mankind would be reduced to the status of button pushers and gauge watchers. Since button pushing and gauge watching are among the activities which are most easily automated, these predictions hardly merited notice. But they were noticed, and vocational education was provided for smaller proportions of the adult population and the male school population, on the grounds that vocational education would soon be obsolete.

YOUTH UNEMPLOYMENT
During the thirties, youth unemployment was one and a half times as high as adult unemployment. By the sixties, the youth unemployment

rate was more than three times as high as the adult unemployment rate. Among industrialized nations, only the United States has a severe youth unemployment problem. Those who have attempted to explain this anomaly have cited:

A. *Effects of minimum wage laws.* The hypothesis is that since many employers are forced to pay youth a minimum wage which is higher than their productive capacity, these employers choose not to employ youth. Folk (3, p. 92, ff.) points out that youth unemployment has not increased more rapidly following the imposition of higher minimum wage standards.

B. *A belief that youth no longer want to work.* This explanation usually ignores the definition of unemployment, which includes among the unemployed only those persons who wish to work but are unable to find work. A few more sophisticated persons, who know how unemployment is measured, hold to this belief, claiming that some youth reject the types of jobs open to them.

C. *Effects of education.* Students are more likely than adults to seek part-time or summer work. Parnes (10, p. 65) found that both white and black students had unemployment rates more than three times as high as the rates for comparable nonstudents. This would suggest that the long-term increase in youth unemployment might be associated with the long-term increase in the proportion of late teenage youth enrolled in school. However, Labor Department figures quoted by Folk show student and nonstudent youth unemployment as being at about the same level.

A fourth factor which may be related to education and youth unemployment is the probable effect of education causing youth to want to work only in occupations which have better working conditions than inexperienced youth can command. Since graduates of high school vocational programs have considerably lower unemployment rates than graduates of other curricula, bring more saleable skills to the marketplace, and command higher wages, this explanation seems plausible. Moreover, emphasis in the college preparatory curriculum on professional occupations, which most high school graduates are not equipped to follow, may lead to unrealistic expectations on the part of graduates and dropouts from this curriculum who seek employment without collegiate training.

CYCLICAL CHANGES

About once each generation the United States suddenly recognizes that it faces a critical shortage of manpower capable of performing well in semiskilled, skilled, clerical, sales, and technical occupations. These are the occupational fields with which vocational education is most concerned. Recognition of these shortages leads to sharply increased federal, state, and local expenditures for vocational education in the public schools. And in the forties and sixties it also brought about the creation of non-public school institutional mechanisms for meeting these shortages. In the forties this took the form of the establishment of war production training programs which were operated largely by public schools. In the sixties, the additional mechanisms included Manpower Development and Training Act programs operated by the United States Labor Department and Neighborhood Youth Corps training programs controlled by the Federal Office of Economic Opportunity.

During the periods of recognized manpower shortage, vocational education is hailed in the nation's press and in the educational literature as vital to the nation's welfare. Half a generation later, when the most acute of these manpower shortages have been met and the remaining shortages have been forgotten, vocational education is either ignored (as in the late twenties and early thirties) or sharply attacked as a waste of the taxpayer's money (as in 1952-54). There are two parts to this problem. One is related to the nation's manpower needs themselves, and the other is related to our perception of the nation's manpower needs.

Although the long-term trends noted earlier in this chapter continue with little change, there are sharp short-term trends which are affected by expansion or contraction of the total job market. When employers and consumers are optimistic, the job market expands rapidly and demands many more workers than have been employed in the past. Until recently, these new workers could be employed on unskilled jobs, so the transition to full employment was relatively painless. People were removed from unemployment rolls, part-time workers took on full time jobs, and people who had not been working for pay at all accepted full time employment. But the long-term trends make it clear that fewer and fewer unskilled workers will be needed. This means that with every successive expansion in the total economy, the process of adjustment becomes increasingly difficult. People want to work, but do not have the necessary skills and knowledge to participate in a technologically oriented labor force. Training periods for skilled workers are far longer than for unskilled workers, so training costs to employers rise, and employers thus are more likely to demand public assistance in meeting their training needs. This means, among other things, that they will demand more vocational education programs supported by public funds.

However, vocational teachers cannot be created overnight. Some experienced workers who are naturally good teachers are recruited to become teachers of vocational education. Along with them are recruited many workers who are unqualified as teachers, and a few workers who are unqualified both as teachers and as workers. The net result is a dilution in quality, but an increase in the quantity of vocational education offered. In about the length of time that it takes to create a good vocational teacher, employer and consumer optimism ebbs, the total labor force needs begin to decline, and the well trained new teachers have difficulty in securing suitable employment.

When the total labor market needs decrease, the age group which is hit hardest is the youth group, which has no employment experience. Three million of these youth are ready to enter the labor market every year. Seniority systems guarantee that present workers receive first consideration in employment. Once their needs are met, employers turn to experienced workers who are most likely to be immediately productive. Youth, who have neither work experience nor seniority, are most likely to suffer. Middle class youth secure jobs through the influence of family and friends; lower class youth who have saleable skills acquired through vocational education come next; and lower class youth who do not have saleable skills find employment almost impossible to secure. Ironically it is at this very time that vocational education begins to appear as a needless luxury to many laymen. They suggest that the solution is to keep youth off the labor market inexpensively by enrolling them in general courses with large classes and little or no instructional equipment. It seems reasonable to assume that youth who are conditioned by education (both general and vocational) to expect meaningful employment will not react passively to denial of the right to work. Moreover, in the future youth are less likely to come in large numbers from families where the major wage earner is unskilled and accustomed to low wages, seasonal unemployment, and the lack of material goods. Rising youth expectations for employment could make a sharp decrease in the size of the labor force a national disaster.

CYCLICAL CHANGES AND VOCATIONAL EDUCATION

Until the early sixties, vocational education had the meeting of the nation's manpower needs as its principal objective. So long as this was the case, vocational education should have had no alternative but to expand and contract in accordance with the perceived manpower needs. In practice, however, vocational education, as does any bureaucracy, fought reductions in support and managed instead to secure constant levels of appropriations during periods of labor surplus. On the other hand, when the nation's manpower needs were perceived to be great, vocational education profited from sharply increased appropriations.

The principal casualty of cyclical changes in perceived employment needs was the development of teachers, administrators, researchers, and other leadership personnel in vocational education. Not only did these personnel development programs suffer from a double acceleration effect (see chapter seven), but by the time such programs were put into effect, the need for their graduates had largely disappeared. This mean that leadership personnel in vocational education came almost entirely from the ranks of those trained on-the-job as vocational teachers and administrators during periods of rapid expansion in vocational education.

Perceived Manpower Needs

Actual manpower needs are changed by expansions and contractions in total labor force needs and by shifts in demand from one occupation to another. The public perception of these needs, however, is often quite different from reality. Public perception responds to "shortages" and "surpluses" reported by the press. During the early fifties, the popular press was full of articles stating flatly that we no longer needed large numbers of engineers. By the time this began to affect youth enrolling in engineering colleges, we were faced with a critical need for engineers and low enrollments in the freshmen year of engineering. Probably these scare headlines of the past will keep engineering enrollments low for a generation. There is such a lag between professional awareness of imbalances, publicity about imbalances, and public action in response to this publicity that often the public acts in the opposite direction to the way they should.

Another factor which creates a disparity between real and perceived manpower needs is the tendency of employers to hoard highly skilled workers in anticipation of future expansions. Extremely capable skilled workers have always been very difficult to find. If an employer expects to increase his need for such workers in the near future, he will probably retain all the highly skilled personnel he can and recruit additional skilled staff beyond his immediate needs. This tends to create an illusion of a greater shortage than actually exists. When the employer no longer anticipates immediate expansion, he will release these excess workers temporarily creating the impression of a widespread surplus of skilled workers. Since unskilled and semiskilled workers seldom are hoarded in any significant quantities, and since the long-term trends suggest that they will be a continually decreasing proportion of the labor force, it appears that hoarding will become an increasingly important factor in creating a discrepancy between perceived and real manpower shortages.

Manpower Forecasting

For vocational education to serve the manpower needs of society effectively, a system of long-term manpower forecasting is needed. The manpower forecasting which exists now is highly inaccurate even in the short-term. Indeed, many labor economists are of the opinion that given the present state of knowledge, long-term manpower forecasting with any degree of accuracy is impossible.

Attempts have been made to ask employers what their anticipated employment needs will be. The results have been highly inaccurate partly because employers have not practiced manpower forecasting for their own needs except to judge the quantity of managers and supervisors they will need. However, the problem involves more than the lack of practice in forecasting by employers. Several attempts have been made to learn employers' current job vacancies. This would appear to be less complicated than trying to predict future vacancies. Nevertheless these studies also have proved to be inaccurate, because employers redesign jobs to adjust to the presence or absence of skilled persons. Overnight changes in worker selection criteria are common, and training programs to adapt present and new employees to meet critical job vacancies are started and stopped on short notice. In short, employers do not know how many personnel of each type they need now, let alone how many they will need in ten years. This and the reluctance of some employers to let possible competitors know of their plans, create a discouraging manpower forecasting situation. Fortunately new approaches to forecasting (which avoid asking employers about their probable needs) are promising.

Vocational education's need for accurate manpower forecasting varies according to the proportion of workers being prepared through that system. Virtually the entire supply of military airplane pilots must come through training programs operated by the armed forces. If the need for pilots is underestimated, and the programs are kept small, the effect could be disastrous to our national defense. Similarly, if the need for pilots is overestimated, several tens of thousands of dollars will be invested in each of the pilot trainees who is not needed at the end of the training program. Instead, the program will have produced many dissatisfied officers who are not allowed to fly airplanes. Production of almost the entire supply of manpower by a single training source leads to demands from that training source for high accuracy in manpower needs projections. High accuracy is also required if there are multiple sources of trained manpower and if the graduates of each training agency are equally preferred by employers.

On the other hand, if the graduates of training system "A" (e.g. public school practical nurse training) are generally preferred to the graduates of training system "B" (e.g. on-the-job practical nurse training), the preferred training system can tolerate vast errors in manpower forecasting so long as it is preparing considerably less than the total number of trainees needed by employers. If the need for skilled workers has been underestimated, the shortage will be made up through OJT. If the need for workers is overestimated, the graduates of the vocational training program will still be able to secure employment, and personnel who have been trained through OJT will suffer. When there are multiple types of training activities for a certain occupation, and each trains less than the total number of personnel needed, the graduates of the preferred training program will be less affected by errors in forecasting than will graduates of the less preferred programs.

For the less preferred training system, however, manpower forecasting is extremely critical. Moreover, the less preferred system must have knowledge of the output of the preferred system. For example, in the construction industry, apprenticeship is the preferred training program for skilled workers, so vocational programs in most construction occupations must depend both on accurate manpower forecasting and on knowledge of the apprenticeship program output. On the other hand, because vocational training is preferred over OJT in clerical occupations, correct forecasting for this group of occupations will not be critical for vocational education until output begins to be nearly as great as demand.

MANPOWER DEMANDS

Despite the enormous difficulties involved, the Bureau of Labor Statistics, U.S. Department of Labor, prepares estimates of annual manpower needs which extend five to ten years in the future. Two hundred and forty occupations, slightly more than half of all employment in the United States, are covered. Professional and technical occupations and skilled crafts, all of which require long periods of education or training, are covered extensively. For example, estimates have been made for the annual average labor demands in occupations which cover 95 percent of employment in technical occupations, 93 percent of employment in health occupations, and 81 percent of trades and industrial occupations. However, projections of annual demand cover occupations which account for only 22 percent of employment in distributive occupations (occupations which have to deal with wholesaling, retailing, and transportation). No estimates are available for agriculture, agriculturally related occupations, or home economics related occupations, or for the numerous occupations which employ the remaining half of the labor force. In the field of distributive occupations such large occupational groupings as general merchandise sales (over three million employees), industrial marketing (over one million employees), and food distribution (one million employees) are completely omitted. In contrast, the glaziery trade is included, though it employs only six thousand people and has an expected annual need for only four hundred more.

Preparation of estimates of annual need for each occupation requires that the following variables be considered: (1) employment by age and sex, (2) demand for each type of product or service produced, (3) production requirements in each industry generated by this demand, (4) employment required to reach these levels of production, (5) trends in occupational requirements resulting from technological change, and (6) job openings resulting from retirements and deaths. In addition, estimates must be made of the growth and changing character of the economy, the gross national product, and the national income and its distribution. Errors in any of these estimates can result in errors in estimated annual demand for workers in an occupation. No assessments are made of shifts of workers from one occupation to another, so this introduces a further source of possible error. Not enough is known about occupational mobility to be able to determine its extent. There has been little success with paying people to move from areas of high unemployment to areas of low unemployment. Consequently, it seems desirable to shift away from the current policy of providing training at home and encouraging mobility after training, to a policy of encouraging mobility *prior* to training. Experience in the practical nurse training field indicates that not only do trainees move prior to training, but when instruction is provided in a geographical area where jobs are available, trainee graduates tend to settle in that area.

MANPOWER SUPPLY

Adequate manpower forecasting requires a knowledge not only of the demand for workers of a particular type but also of the supply of such workers. Knowledge of the supply side of this equation is even more inadequate than knowledge of the demand side. Workers learn the skills necessary for success in an occupation in a variety of ways:

A. Vocational education in secondary and post-secondary schools
B. Apprenticeship
C. Manpower Development and Training Act programs
D. On-the-job training
E. Proprietary vocational schools
F. Military training
G. Correspondence schools
H. Trial and error, observation, and other informal methods.

No systematic method exists for collecting information on the output of these types of training.

Attempts are now being made to secure information on the number of graduates from in-school vocational education and Manpower Development and Training Act programs. Some estimates are available on the number of apprenticeship and military technical training program graduates. However, a complicating factor is the problem of how to count dropouts from training programs. Some persons drop out of a training program because they have lost interest in the occupation or they fear they cannot succeed in it. However, a significant proportion of dropouts, particularly in adult vocational programs, is due to the fact that when sufficient levels of saleable skill have been achieved, many trainees leave the program to go to work in the occupation. This has been particularly true in the Manpower Development and Training Act programs. Since the goal of the program is to secure employability, and these trainees drop out to go to work, the goal of the program has been achieved. Many adults who enroll in community college programs meet their personal educational goals without completing an associate degree program. Since the time of a trainee is valuable, the cost effectiveness figures for dropouts who achieve employability skills before completing the program may be higher than for those who continue through graduation.

Another problem in determining the supply of persons prepared to enter an occupation is the matter of quality. Most training programs produce some graduates who are not qualified. Since few fields have established quality standards for vocational education programs, the number of such persons is unknown. Moreover, the number of persons considered to be unqualified for entrance to an occupation depends considerably upon the state of the labor market. If trained workers are in short supply, a person who otherwise would be considered ineligible may be employed immediately. Conversely, when the labor market is tight, only the most qualified, or those who have friends or relatives in influential positions may be employed.

OCCUPATIONAL SHIFTS

Many laymen think of vocational education as being a secondary school or community college program. However, approximately half of the vocational enrollment is made up of adults who are securing training to enable them to shift from one occupation to another or to enable them to cope with changes within an occupation. All authorities agree that employees change employers frequently, and that within an occupation, job titles and content change quite rapidly. Most authorities are of the opinion that the rate of such changes is increasing. A common statement is that an individual will hold seven "jobs" during his working lifetime. Unfortunately, this figure is not of much help in planning vocational education. A change in job may mean that the employee moves from one employer to another. Under this criterion, a nurse or a bricklayer may change jobs many times during a year. Yet if the knowledge, skills, and attitudes required by each employer are essentially the same, then there may in effect be great job stability. However, a steel worker may, during the course of a year's employment by one company, change occupations from yard worker to hand trucker to power trucker. The job content of these three occupations is quite different. But since one cannot normally enter employment for a steel company except as an unskilled laborer, and since promotions are based on seniority, the implications of increased rapidity of shifts from one occupation to another in the steel industry have little or no significance for vocational education which is designed to prepare youth for an entry job. (It may, on the other hand, have considerable implications for adult vocational education which is designed to make the transition from one occupation to another more painless.)

Proponents of nonspecialized education commonly use the statistics on job changes without recognition of their complexity, and suggest that because one will change jobs frequently, preparation for an entry job is not needed. "Our education is designed for a lifetime," they say, "while vocational education will be of value for only a few years." This argument overlooks the rate of change in all of knowledge, which seems to be expanding at a considerably greater rate than the frequency with which a person changes his occupation. Moreover, the same individuals who downgrade vocational education generally support education for the professions, where the rate of change is almost certainly greater than in the occupations with which vocational education is most concerned. Yet no one has suggested seriously that schools stop training people for the professions.

SLIPPAGE

All graduates of an occupational education program seldom enter the occupation for which they were prepared. Not all law school graduates become lawyers, and not all graduates of carpentry apprenticeships become carpenters. Indeed, information on a number of professional schools indicates that slippage may be as high as 50 percent. In the case of apprenticeship, it is very common for approximately one-third of the graduates to enter the occupation, one-third to go into supervisory and management positions, and one-third to become technicians of various types associated with the occupation. Any attempt to balance supply and demand in a particular occupational field must take this slippage into account. Unfortunately our knowledge of the amount and direction of this slippage is very limited.

EFFECTIVE PLANNING

An example of a type of manpower planning which partially meets the needs of vocational education is shown in Table 2–1. This table shows the approximate annual needs by occupation from 1966 to 67. The information may be deficient in that some persons who completed academic programs may not have been included. Moreover, persons who learned on the job, who were immigrants from foreign countries, and persons who shifted from other related occupations are not shown. Probably for these particular occupations, the numbers of persons not shown would be relatively small, though in other types of occupations, with less specific academic requirements, the unknown numbers might be quite large. Quality of graduates is not specified, but since the health occupations are leaders in specifying quality standards, they may be assumed to be adequate.

These data indicate that in the field of dental hygiene the eighteen hundred known academic completions in 1966 to 67 almost match the two thousand persons needed per year on the average from 1966 to 75. For the other occupations on the list, however, the total of known academic completions is much smaller than the numbers of persons needed per year. This would suggest that new health occupations training programs might better be started in fields other than dental hygiene. Much more planning of this type needs to be done. As nearly as can be determined, Table 2–1 represents the only such data now available for an occupational cluster.

Meeting Society's Manpower Needs as an Educational Objective

Not all educators see the meeting of manpower needs as a desirable objective of education. Haskew and Tumlin feel that, "The talents of people are now viewed as instruments of corporate welfare, as tools for advancement of mankind's triumph over nature (including human nature), as resources to be exploited fully, lest the economy collapse" (7, p. 66). While this may be the way some people view the talents of people, it is also true that the talents of people are important in each of these enterprises. These talents should be exploited fully with the goal not only of avoiding the collapse of the economy but also of providing each individual with a sense of control over his environment and a sense of having markedly increased individual options.

TABLE 2–1

Approximate Annual Needs in Selected Health Occupations

		Average Annual	Known Academic Completions 1966-1967		
	Office of Education Instructional Program	Openings 1966-		Voc. Educ. Post-	
Code	Title	1975	Total	Secondary	Other
7.0101	Dental Assisting	7,700	2,200	903	1,297
7.0102	Dental hygiene	2,000	1,800	452	1,348
7.0103	Dental Lab. Technology	1,700	250	189	61
7.0203& 7.0204	Medical laboratory assisting, hematology	8,400	1,800	749	1,051
7.0301	Nursing (associate)	61,000	38,237*	2,056	36,171*
7.0302	Practical (vocational) nursing	39,000	27,644	16,420	11,224
7.0501 and 7.0502 and 7.0503	Radiologic technology (X-ray, radiation therapy, nuclear medical)	6,300	3,827	383	3,444

*Includes graduates from diploma programs (27,452), baccalaureate degree programs (6,131), and associate degree programs which do not use vocational education funds (2,598).

Source: See reference 9, p. 13.

REFERENCES

1. *America's Industrial and Occupational Requirements, 1964-75.* Bureau of Labor Statistics. Washington, D.C.: U.S. Department of Labor.

2. "The American Repairman—A Vanishing Breed," *U.S. News and World Report.* (September 13, 1965), 68.

3. Folk, Hugh N., "The Problem of Youth Unemployment," *The Transition from School to Work*. Princeton: Industrial Relations Section, Princeton University, 1968.

4. Eninger, Max. *The Process and Product of T. and I. High School Level Vocational Education in the U.S.* Pittsburgh: American Institute for Research, 1965.

5. Gardner, John W., *Excellence: Can We Be Equal and Excellent Too?* New York: Harper & Row, Publishers, 1961.

6. Hall, Oswald and Bruce McFarlane, *Transition from School to Work*. Ottawa: The Queen's Printer, 1963.

7. Haskew, Laurence D. and Inez Tumlin, "Vocational Education in the Common School," in *Vocational Education*, ed. Melvin L. Barlow. 64th Yearbook of the National Society for the Study of Education, Part I. Chicago: University of Chicago Press, 1965.

8. Lindman, Erick L. and Edwin L. Kurth, "Dimensions of Need for Vocational Education," in *Dimensions of Educational Need*, eds. Roe Lyell Johns, *et al.* Gainesville, Fla.: National Educational Finance Project, 1969.

9. *Manpower Requirements and Occupations for which Vocational Education Prepares Workers*. Bureau of Labor Statistics. Washington, D.C.: U.S. Department of Labor, 1969.

10. Parnes, Herbert S., *et al. Career Thresholds,* vol. I. Columbus: Ohio State University Center for Human Resources Research, 1969.

Chapter 3 INCREASING INDIVIDUAL OPTIONS

Academic educators feel that vocational education decreases individual options. Perhaps this is true in some vocational courses for some students. But for most vocational students, options are markedly increased by the availability of vocational education, and as more vocational educators accept the increasing of individual options as a basic objective, the proportion will increase.

Our best information about increased options in vocational education comes from Project TALENT, which tested and followed up 5 percent of the students in United States high schools in 1961. It showed clearly that the general curriculum, which many educational philosophers *claim* offers the greatest number of options to students, really offers the least. The general curriculum allegedly prepares a student for any activity in life, and it enrolls 25 percent of the students who are a good cross-section of United States high school students. Yet this curriculum produces 67 percent of the high school dropouts, and its graduates rank behind both the college preparatory and vocational curricula in: (1) proportion who go to college, (2) annual earnings, (3) job satisfaction, (4) length of unemployment, (5) frequency of unemployment, and (6) almost every other measure of success.

The Nature of Individual Options

Some people have more options than others, that is to say, they have more opportunities for choice as they go through life. The person with many options can choose from several places of residence, can choose several ways of spending a substantial part of his income, and can choose from among several different occupations. The person with less options has fewer opportunities for choice as he goes through life. He may be restricted to renting a modest home or apartment; may be forced to spend a large portion of his limited income on food, shelter and clothes; and he may be forced to accept whatever employment is available by chance, for he has few saleable skills.

While the process of choosing among alternatives may occasionally be difficult, it seems clear that the person who has options or choices is in a far more enviable position than the person who does not. Ideally, a person in retirement could look back over a life which was filled with options, and feel that he had had many opportunities for significant choices, rather than being buffeted entirely by forces outside his control. He could also look forward to further options during his retirement.

Income beyond the amount required for subsistence generally increases an individual's options as does athletic ability, verbal intelligence, manipulative skill, and almost every attribute which is valued by society. Options are decreased by prejudice, poor education, social isolation, poor health, and many other factors. Some of these factors are under the control of society or of the individual, and some are not. It should be a major goal of society to strive to bring more of these factors out of the realm of chance and put them under control of individuals and groups of individuals.

The Role of Education

There is a horrible example in history of what the Educated Society might easily become . . . It is the destruction of one of the world's greatest and most creative civilizations, the China of the T'ang and Sung periods, by the imposition of a purely intellectual, purely analytical education on man and society, the Confucian Canon. Within a century this commitment to the purely intellectual in man destroyed what had been the world's leader in art as well as in science, in technology as well as in philosophy. We are today in a similar danger (4, p. 93).

This type of education not only decreased individual options but destroyed a civilization. But education, properly conceived, can not only increase options, but do so more effectively than other institutions.

In this country education appears to be the only social institution which has the increasing of individual options as a major goal. Even the family, which wants the best for its sons and daughters, often prescribes its definition of "best" in terms which severely limit the individual options of its members. Too often, the remaining institutions of society work toward maintaining the occupations of the son and the daughter at the same level as the father and the mother. Even certain educators, who view the school primarily as a transmission agent for our culture, also act as a force for maintaining occupational levels at the same point from generation to generation. This view is slowly losing ground, as gradual acceptance of the revised protestant ethic has created a revolution of rising occupational expectations, and as society has turned to education as an institution which could satisfy these rising expectations.

Institutions other than education undoubtedly increase certain individual options, but in every case outside of education, the increasing of individual options is at best a secondary goal. For example, work experience in industry often increases individual options, but this is never a primary goal of industry. If an institution has the increasing of individual options as a primary goal, it should be able to achieve this goal much more consistently than could an institution where this goal is subordinate. A screwdriver can be used as a hammer, but if serious hammering is to be done, it should be done with a tool designed for this purpose.

Not all education is designed to increase individual options. Sometimes it seems to be designed to increase knowledge, as in some of the major universities. Sometimes it seems to be designed to maintain the status quo, as in occupational education programs designed to meet the needs of local employers or in "social studies" courses which are designed to perpetuate the existing economic, political, and religious structures. Sometimes it appears to be a bureaucracy designed to serve the needs of the incumbent bureaucrats. In education as in other institutions, if the increasing of individual options is a subordinate rather than a primary goal, this goal is less likely to be achieved. Education which has the increasing of individual options as a major goal must also have the increasing of individual *occupational* options as an explicit goal.

Educational programs can be categorized roughly into three general types:

A. Those programs which have no occupational emphasis at all. These are generally based on the education of the past which was designed for an elite and emphasized leisure time activities and the performance of civic duties, with the implicit understanding that occupational preparation would be provided by the family business. These programs became ineffective for an increasing proportion of students as schools assumed the responsibility of education for all, but they continue in use, perhaps because they still work well for a small but influential proportion of the population.

B.   Separate occupational education for certain students through college preparatory programs in the high school followed by baccalaureate and graduate school programs; other students attend separate vocational schools, public and private.

C.   A combination of general education and specialized education (including occupational preparation) which reinforce each other. Occasionally the programs are deliberately designed to reinforce each other, but more commonly the reinforcement occurs in a less planned way as the individual student sees relatedness between the two types of education.

Educational theorists often see the combination of occupational and general education as being superior. Quarrels arise, however, as to the type of occupational and general education that should be provided. The principal difficulty arises in the fact that many people see specific occupational education as actually decreasing individual options. They argue that the preparation of an individual for a specific occupation inevitably ties the individual to that occupation, and even if this were the occupation of his choice, he might later change his mind, or the economic need for that occupation might decline, thus leaving him with no place to go. They argue that the school should provide a program which prepares an individual for *all* occupations, since this would enhance the individual options of all students.

This argument is fallacious on two grounds. While on-the-job training by employers and education in certain proprietary schools is limited to preparing an individual for a single occupation, this rarely, if ever, is the case in public school vocational education. Instead, vocational education in the public schools prepares an individual for a family of occupations. A machine shop course prepares a student for at least two hundred different occupations in metal work. A distributive education course prepares a student for an extremely large family of occupations in wholesaling, retailing, and transportation.

Secondly, no educational program has yet been devised which prepares a student adequately for entrance into and progress in all occupations. Undoubtedly if such a program could be devised, and if it appeared relevant to students, educational efficiency would be raised. But the fact remains that such a program has not been devised. In its absence, many schools provide a "general curriculum" at relatively low cost, with occupational education deferred until after the end of formal schooling when an individual can be given specific occupational preparation through on-the-job training or can purchase occupational education in a proprietary school. It is a complete anomaly that those who are most vehement in their condemnation of vocational education in the school as decreasing individual options want to leave occupational education in the hands of employers who are assumed to be able to provide this education more economically. They point out correctly that the occupational education provided by employers often benefits only employers and hence should be paid for by employers. But they neglect the fact that when education is designed to benefit employers, it sometimes takes a form which decreases individual options.

VOCATIONAL EDUCATION AND INDIVIDUAL OPTIONS

The content of vocational education ranges from that which is specific to a particular employer or enterprise to that which is useful in almost any enterprise. An example of the former would be instruction in how to operate a unique piece of equipment found only in a particular firm and requiring skills and knowledges which are present in no other occupation. At the opposite extreme is content from occupations in the clerical field which is present in almost every enterprise. There is general agreement that the responsibility of training for those jobs which are enterprise-specific should be placed squarely on the shoulders of the employing firm. Because of the operation of internal labor markets, a person who was trained on the outside for such a job would often have no opportunity to gain access to it. Moreover, because of economies of scale, training on the job would probably be the most efficient method of learning such an enterprise-specific skill. But perhaps most important, the benefits of training for enterprise-specific jobs clearly accrue in major part to the employer. Therefore, he should be responsible for providing the necessary training.

Vocational education for jobs which are found in many enterprises is considerably different. First, economies of scale in training programs suggest that vocational education which is not enterprise-specific should be provided either through vocational schools which serve a large number of employers, or in very large establishments which have enough need for training that they can provide large enough groups of trainees to make training economical. But if a particular firm provides training which is useful outside that firm, labor turnover is almost certain to transfer some of the benefits to other firms which have not helped to finance the training. This suggests the need either for public financing of training (inside or outside the firm) or for joint financing by all firms which could conceivably benefit from the training through shared training costs on the British Industrial Training Act model. The case for publicly conducted vocational education is strengthened by the finding of Doeringer and Piore that when individual firms provided instruction in reading and writing, their employees often were taught to read only those symbols and to perform only those calculations required by their present jobs. This narrow training perhaps reduced labor force turnover, but it certainly was not in the best interest of the trainees and may even have encouraged learning habits which would later impede the worker's ability to acquire additional training. Doeringer and Piore state that training in more general occupational skills "like literacy training, ... tends to be excessively narrow" when provided by the enterprise "and may, therefore, yield unnecessarily high adjustment costs in the long run" (3, p. 119). They suggest that federal subsidies to employers might encourage broader training programs, but this seems unlikely unless the subsidies are contingent on the provision of broad training. The recent federal contract with a chicken rendering plant for employee instruction in reading suggests that we should raise the further question of the competence of certain employers to provide broad educational programs.

TRAINING FOR SECONDARY LABOR MARKETS

It has long been recognized that jobs differ in desirability. Similarly, workers differ in their desirability to employers, since they differ in age, amount of education, verbal test scores, etc. It is easy to imagine a queue of young workers who have no vocational education and no significant work experience. If these youths were arranged in order according to their desirability to employers, and if available jobs were arranged in order according to the judgments of the potential workers as to their desirability (based on pay, opportunities for promotion, working conditions, etc.), one would expect that the most attractive workers would seek and would be employed in the most attractive jobs. In fact, this is what seems to happen. These attractive job vacancies constitute the "primary labor market."

In the "secondary labor market," which is made up of the less desirable job vacancies, no such order seems to exist. Employers spend little time screening applicants but hire almost anyone who appears at a convenient time. The relative desirability of jobs within the secondary labor market is quite uncertain in the minds of employees. Moreover, employment tends to be less secure so workers drift into and out of employment frequently, thus blurring the line between the employed and the unemployed. The worker who changes jobs seldom improves his lot, but ends up with a job which is as low or lower on the job desirability scale as the one he had before.

An employer is likely to be involved almost entirely in the primary labor market or in the secondary labor market. However, almost every employer has a few jobs (such as manager) which are clearly in the primary labor market, and a few jobs (such as sweeper) which are clearly in the secondary labor market. A few employers, such as hospitals, have significant numbers of employees in each of the labor market types, e.g., physicians and hospital administrators in the primary labor market and nurses aides and orderlies in the secondary labor market.

Federal manpower training programs (and to a certain extent, vocational education) have been placed in the unenviable position of being asked to give job training to the less desirable workers, while having their efficacy measured in terms of the proportion of these less desirable workers who secure employment. In a number of cases this has led to training for the secondary labor market because it is in this market that these less desirable workers match the availability of jobs to the satisfaction of employers. Some critics of manpower training programs and vocational education have suggested that the federal government is involved in an undesirable subsidy to the secondary labor market and has, particularly in the health fields, artificially depressed wages and working conditions by providing a flow of trained workers who are being employed at substandard wages. There is probably some truth to this argument, but the remedy is not clear. If all publicly supported training programs for health occupations were to be stopped, the cost of health care would increase dramatically, and the public would be asked to bear costs which might be far larger than it now pays for vocational training. Moreover, during the period of market adjustment, the cost in human life and suffering would be staggering.

It should be remembered that the secondary labor market varies in character from country to country and from time to time. Job vacancies for slaves and coolies have largely been eliminated in western industrial economies. As the availability of a well trained labor force increases, it is possible to invest capital effectively in equipment and procedures which move more and more jobs from the secondary to the primary labor markets. This should be one of the primary goals of vocational education, for this should markedly increase individual options.

Factors Which Affect
Individual Options

CAREER LADDERS AND THE INTERNAL LABOR MARKET

A career ladder is a succession of jobs which is available to an individual worker with each job in succession offering increased responsibility and pay and more desirable working conditions. Job career ladders may involve few steps, e.g., apprentice-carpenter, journeyman carpenter, and carpenter foreman; or many, e.g., from yard laborer in the steel industry through twenty-nine labor grades to "roller." Progression through some career ladders may be accomplished in a short time, e.g., the transition from probationary assembler to assembler may take only sixty days, while the progression from medical student to diplomate psychiatrist may take twelve years or more. Because of different aptitudes, motivations, and opportunities, a given individual may progress only part way along the career ladder, he may progress through the entire range of the career ladder, or he may even progress through the entire range and then drop back one or two steps if he finds that the increased responsibilities of a job on one of the top steps on the ladder are too pressing.

Successive steps in a career ladder are normally related in job content, with the lower steps being prerequisites to advancement to higher steps. This is not necessarily always the case, however, for there are often alternative routes to a particular stage in a career ladder. For example, a technician may come from the ranks of skilled workers or he may enter technician status from a school vocational program, having had no experience as a skilled worker. One of the primary functions of education and of vocational education in particular is to enable the individual who completes the educational program to enter a career ladder at a higher step, and to progress further along the career ladder than would be possible without the educational background he has received. Some employment situations, however, are structured so that vocational education can have little effect upon the career ladder. The example most frequently cited is in the field of the health professions, where a person who receives vocational education as a practical nurse can go no further. In most states, if she desires to be a registered nurse, her only alternative is to begin an educational program which does not take into account her previous training and experience. Similarly, a registered nurse has only a slightly longer career ladder, and if she desires to become a physician, must begin completely anew. Presumably this situation could be corrected through job redesign and changing of licensure procedures, but once having been established, it seems to be extremely difficult to change.

The internal labor market provides a completely different approach to career ladder development. In the internal labor market, a person secures employment at an "entry port." He then progresses to broader and broader career opportunities, based almost entirely upon his seniority with that company. The amount of vocational education he received before or during employment has almost no effect upon his career ladder progression. Moreover, if the firm stagnates so that retirements and expansions of production do not provide openings higher on the career ladder, he has no opportunity to transfer his seniority to another firm which may have an almost identical career ladder structure. Indeed, he may find his career ladder within a single firm obstructed because the department within which he accumulates seniority has stagnated, while other employees with less seniority move up the career ladder in other departments within the same company.

The literature in vocational education and in career development has almost completely neglected the type of career ladder which is developed through internal labor market agreements and has concentrated upon career ladders which are not tied to a particular company or to a department in that company. Recent studies which contrast the career development of college professors who owe their loyalty to a discipline rather than to an institution are a notable exception. Further studies of this type in a variety of occupational fields should throw much more light on this pervasive problem.

Efforts of the school to increase individual options of students are of little avail if a large proportion of entry-level occupations lead to dead-ends. (Since entry-level occupations are the only occupations open to recent graduates.) Moreover, society has an obligation to provide a range of individual options to persons of all ages, not just to youth. The first step in increasing individual options for all is the development of additional career ladders so that any person who enters an occupation at an entry port has opportunities to progress toward occupations which provide increased responsibilities and challenges.

The availability of career ladders is greater among large employers than small employers, mainly because there are more occupational areas covered by an existing promotional scheme. But even large employers often subdivide their operations so that promotion is possible only within one department or within one technical sub-specialty. Where this situation exists, the effect on career ladders is the same as if the large employer were really a series of unrelated small employers. Not only should the employee have an opportunity to progress as far as he is capable within a career ladder, but he should also have the right to stop at any point along the career ladder without substantial penalty. In some occupations, to refuse "promotion" is to invite discharge or other punitive action. A full range of individual options includes an option to refuse promotion as well as the opportunity to accept one. It should also be possible to shift from one career ladder to another without excessive penalty. (Where such horizontal shifts are feasible, we say that a "career lattice" exists.) Reasons for wanting to shift from one career ladder to another may be quite diverse, ranging from physical disability to changes in interests. Another common reason is that opportunities for promotion may be blocked in one career ladder, but are available in a closely related career ladder.

Education should have two types of roles to play for adults in enabling them to move from one career ladder to another.

A. It should serve an instructional function which enables the person to utilize his past experience wherever this will be of value in the new career, and it should provide instruction at a significantly high level so that as a person moves to a new career ladder, he is not forced to drop back to an entry level wage.

B. It should serve a validating function by certifying to prospective employers that the graduate, whether youth or adult, has the necessary skills, knowledge, and attitudes to succeed in the new career.

In addition, by providing a flow of trained and re-trained individuals, education should enable the employer to redesign jobs and families of jobs in ways which will enhance career development and individual options. The school as a part of its general education function should convey to all citizens the fact that career ladder restrictions based on race, sex, or religion are highly undesirable and counter-productive. Simultaneously, it should convey the message that employers and employee groups have responsibilities to all citizens and not just to themselves.

YOUTH ORGANIZATIONS IN VOCATIONAL EDUCATION

The Smith-Hughes division of occupations into occupational fields influenced the structure of youth organizations for vocational students. Thus we have the Future Farmers of America, Vocational Industrial Clubs of America, etc. These clubs have done a great deal of good by providing opportunities for leadership development and education outside the school. It is interesting, however, that the youth organizations of vocational education have proved much more resistant to change than have the vocational education programs which gave birth to them. Pitched battles have been fought over whether to change the name of FFA to indicate that it includes students who are interested in agricultural occupations other than farming. There have been numerous discussions as to whether or not Future Homemakers of America includes the wage earning aspects of home economics.

These battles are being fought on the wrong grounds. If a major goal of vocational education is to increase individual options, and if youth organizations assist in achieving this goal, it is undesirable to exclude students of general agriculture or students of general education industrial subjects (industrial arts) from vocational education youth groups. Moreover, programs of each of these organizations should give students an opportunity to learn about occupations which are not included in the original youth group charter. Ideally, there should be a national vocational education youth organization, with parallel state and local school groups concerned with all of occupational life. Then, if students change occupational goals, they could move from the equivalent of an intramural basketball team to an intramural football team. A youth organization devoted to all of vocational education could more efficiently provide programs which develop skills in the commonalities of vocations as well as in their specialties.

INCOME AND SOCIAL CLASS

Children of most middle class families receive considerable financial assistance as they progress through school. There are many costs associated with school which the student must pay, including costs of books, paper, pencils, art supplies, and, especially in vocational education, because of the relatively high cost of instruction, there commonly are charges for materials used. Moreover, the student must pay for such items as transportation to and from school, clothes which are in a style acceptable by the peer group, and minor luxuries.

In the lower-class home not only may there be insufficient funds to provide for these necessities and near necessities, but there may be considerable pressure for the student to contribute to the finances of the family, so that the parents and other children may have items which they regard as necessities. Middle class families which have accepted the values of the protestant ethic are not only more likely to transmit this ethic to their children, but also to accept the desirability of foregoing current pleasures themselves in order to enable their children to persevere in their education. Self-denial helps little, however, when income is very low. Modest housing, food, and clothing more than consumes the income of a family at the poverty level, and leaves nothing for education. Table 3–1 shows the correlation of education and poverty. It indicates that the equation "inadequate education causes poverty" is true and reversible.

Students who need money for their own needs or for the needs of their families often try first to secure it by part-time employment. They frequently are unsuccessful in this, because they lack saleable skills. If we remember that an unemployed person is defined officially as a person who is looking for work but has been unable to find it, we can attach considerable significance to the findings of Parnes. He found that while only 52 percent of students are interested in working, in contrast to 96 percent of youth out-of-school (7, p. 50), the rate of unemployment for those in school is almost three times as high as the unemployment rate for those who have dropped out of school (7, p. 66). Obviously, both sets of figures must be considered for one alone is misleading.

TABLE 3–1

Education and Poverty

Educational Attainment of Family Head	Percent of Families Below Poverty Level		
	All Families	White	Black
Less than 8 years	25.2	21.1	40.1
8 years	11.2	10.1	24.1
1 to 3 years high school	10.7	7.9	29.8
High school graduate	5.4	4.6	16.9
1 to 3 years college	4.4	4.0	8.9
Baccalaureate	2.0	2.0	1.1
Average	9.7	7.7	27.8

Source: Derived from reference 8, p. 5.

If students do find work, over 15 percent work more than thirty-five hours a week, and well over half work more than fifteen hours per week (7, p. 91). This amount of work is almost certain to have detrimental effects on school achievement unless the student is well above average in verbal intelligence. The result is likely to be less interest in school and more interest in income, even though the occupation in which the student is engaged is very likely to lead to a dead end. This emphasizes the need for financial assistance which goes beyond scholarships or fellowships which pay for tuition (if this is charged) to include work-study programs and direct financial aid. After the student reaches age sixteen, the best possible solution seems to be a part-time cooperative education program which not only provides income, but relates the material the student learns in school to what he is learning in his occupation. Manpower Development and Training Act programs have always recognized the need for financial assistance to the adult trainee.

SEX

Citing experience in Canada, Hall and McFarlane point out that "... the girl has a much greater likelihood of climbing above her parents (occupationally) than is the case for the boy" (6, p. 49).

> Over 60 percent of the boys from the families of non-manual workers are themselves employed in non-manual occupations,

whereas 90 per cent of the girls with a similar background are in non-manual work . . . two-thirds of the girls whose fathers or guardians are manual workers have found work in non-manual fields, . . . (while) two-thirds of the manual workers' sons are engaged in manual occupations . . . (6, p. 59).

Not only is this true of the world of work, but also of school.

The school world . . . turns out to be, fundamentally, a feminine world. It provides an academic atmosphere in which girls thrive and boys fail . . . it is a world to which girls adapt with relative ease. Boys appear to reject it, and eventually it rejects them. Moreover, the school is a feminine world in the vocational sense. It prepares them admirably for their careers in the work world . . . Especially is this true for those who continue to university, those who prepare for school teaching and nursing, and those who enter clerical occupations . . . our society provides much more in the way of specialized training facilities for girls than for boys (6, p. 65).

In part, the design of educational facilities which serve girls better than boys has come about accidentally. Girls seem to be attracted to white-collar jobs, and the college preparatory programs of schools provide a greater degree of occupational preparation for white-collar than for manual occupations. Girls more than boys are willing to enter low paying occupations, and teaching has been one of these occupations. This has led to the development of teacher education programs which cater largely to women and to the development of common school staffs heavily populated by women. School staffs in turn have been much more sympathetic to vocational education programs in business education and distributive education (which enroll mainly females) than they have been to auto mechanics and to machine shop (which enroll mostly males).

Project TALENT reports that over 40 percent of high school senior females are involved in vocational curricula, compared to less than 25 percent of males. Moreover, the girls who enroll in vocational programs are considerably more intelligent than the males. The more intelligent males are likely to be enrolled in the college preparatory curriculum, due in part to a reverse type of discrimination in higher education. The proportion of females receiving doctorates has been declining for a long time, and many baccalaureate programs discriminate against women. It is reported that many universities have unofficial quota systems for females, and that many professional programs, e.g., veterinary medicine, have been almost entirely closed to females.

INFLUENCE OF FAMILY AND FRIENDS

The Horatio Alger literature recommended to youth a means by which they could increase their occupational level. The theory expressed repeatedly by the single plot of the many Horatio Alger stories was that if you worked diligently, your merits would be recognized by a benevolent upper class, and you would receive rapid occupational advancement. This theme is still repeated constantly in literature distributed by corporations as a part of their training programs. Many managers still believe it implicitly, which is not too surprising, since they generally are satisfied with their own occupational progression. Also it is psychologically satisfying to imagine that this state of affairs has been reached through diligence and personal effort rather than through chance or education. The fact remains, however, that without the aid of society, occupational mobility would be nearly impossible. And, even with the aid of public education, the Protestant ethic (and particularly the Horatio Alger version of the Protestant ethic) has not worked for a large proportion of the population.

Study after study shows that securing employment depends heavily on help from family and friends. Since friends and family tend to come from the same social class, and since social class is closely related to occupation, the availability of information about an occupation or about employment opportunities tends to be restricted to those occupations and to those types of employment which are represented in the limited circle of family and friends. The type of employment received depends heavily on the geographical setting, race, sex, and socioeconomic status. For a person in a rural area, only a very narrow range of occupational opportunities is available. There is a general belief that as transportation facilities improve, the influence of the geography of the home on occupational choice, will decrease. This seems questionable. For the last three hundred years people in this country have shown a willingness to move long distances in order to find employment, but the employment is usually similar to what they left. Improved transportation just seems to cause the worker to spend weekends in expensive and time consuming travel back to visit the area from which he migrated. While transportation facilities between cities have been improving (if one can afford an automobile or an airplane ticket), transportation within cities has not.

Entry to many occupations has been denied to persons of certain races, religions, and sexes. While these barriers seem gradually to be crumbling, they are breached most readily by individuals who possess either occupational experience or educational preparation or both.

OCCUPATIONAL STATUS AND CAREER COUNSELING

A number of studies have revealed that there is a definite hierarchy of occupations, and that this hierarchy is not only remarkably constant over time, but is also constant in the value structures of quite disparate groups of individuals. While no single factor determines whether an occupation is ranked high in status, such characteristics as high income and high educational requirements for entry are associated with "high level" occupations, while occupations which require manual effort tend to be ranked low. School counselors are quite responsive to the demands of parents and teachers and have learned that the safest course to pursue in occupational counseling is to encourage students to prepare for occupations which have parent/teacher approval. If a student is not interested in or capable of preparing for a high status occupation such as one of the professions, counseling which strongly suggests that he prepare for a profession may have the effect of decreasing rather than increasing his options. The schools should have a goal of providing adequate information about occupational opportunities, stressing the point that the status of an occupation is of little importance compared to job satisfaction. They should also encourage students to make occupational decisions which can be changed later if the student feels it would be desirable. Practice in decision making with regard to occupations is an essential part of the educational process.

Attitudes toward work are discussed in greater detail in the chapters on Philosophical Foundations and Sociological Foundations. It should be pointed out here, however, that if a student learns in the elementary school that manual work is not desirable, or if he learns that work in any form is to be avoided, he has already decreased his individual options. Attitudes toward work begin to be learned in early childhood and are often confirmed in the elementary school. Early education should emphasize the value of work to the individual and to the society, and in the elementary school each student should learn that any socially productive occupation is noble.

COGNITIVE STYLES

Individuals differ enormously in the ways that they learn. Yet the school often assumes that everyone should be able to learn and to think in verbal terms. Even in such obvious cases as the deaf or blind student, where an important channel of learning has been cut off entirely, the school is often unwilling to adjust its means of teaching and consequently drives the student from the school. Fortunately, specially trained teachers and new teaching methods are rapidly becoming available for those obviously disabled students.

Less obvious but more important, at least in terms of the numbers of students affected, is the plight of persons who simply do not operate well with verbal symbols. These students usually are substandard in reading ability, often because they are not interested in reading. Though most of them can read, they simply do not learn easily through reading. There is also a significant portion of the population which does not think well in terms of objects. Since the school has little to say about objects, this latter group is not handicapped greatly in school, though they may be markedly handicapped once they leave the school. We know very little about these two types of students.

The operation of these two cognitive styles can be observed in a setting where persons attempt to assemble an object which they purchased. Frequently, manufacturers, in order to save assembly and shipping costs, produce objects in an unassembled form and enclose instructions for assembly. The individual who does not think readily in verbal symbols or cannot read well or both is apt to discard the instructions and instead look at the parts to be assembled and at a photograph or sketch provided by the manufacturer. He then proceeds to put the object together. If his basic difficulty is poor reading skill, he may ask someone to read the directions to him, but this will be of little help if his cognitive style does not include facility with verbal symbols. The instructions which he hears will be of less value than the sight of the unassembled parts and the photograph of the assembled object.

Conversely, some highly educated persons who have no difficulty in reading the directions have difficulty in making the transition from the verbal directions to the actual objects to be assembled. In some cases, this may be due to inadequacies in their educational background (even if they have a Ph.D.). They may not know what a "flange" means or may not know what a "round-headed screw" is. Such educational inadequacies are to be regretted, of course, but they are easily corrected through a short course in industrial nomenclature, or through the process of continuing to assemble products of a similar nature. If, however, the difficulty is that they are unable to think in terms of objects and relationships among objects, their only course may be to employ someone to assemble the object for them or to be certain that in the future they do not purchase unassembled products.

The lessons from this example are obvious. First, all students who can do so should be taught to think in terms of symbols, objects, and the relationships between symbols and objects, instead of following the pattern of traditional education which emphasizes symbols. Secondly, if a student is having difficulty thinking in terms of symbols, he should not be shut off from education, but should be provided with educational experiences which increase his facility with symbols while they increase his individual options within the world of objects. Similar provisions should be made for the person who experiences difficulty thinking in terms of objects, even though the school typically is organized so that he can experience "success." Similar comments could be made about students who have trouble working with other people, or thinking in terms of other people's needs and interests, or learning in situations which involve individual study. If the school is to serve all people, it must provide programs which take into account the vastly different cognitive styles of its students.

Gagné points out that a lesson on the "reflection and refraction of light" could be presented in many different ways: (1) a demonstration could be used with accompanying oral communication; (2) a chapter of programmed instruction might be assigned; (3) an assessment exercise might be conducted by the teacher to see if the required principles have been learned; (4) a motion picture sequence might be used to show an unusual example of the principles being taught; (5) a discussion of how to go about investigating a problem shown in the film could be used; or (6) the teacher might assess ability to solve problems in reflection and refraction by means of a test on ability to transfer knowledge to a new situation (5, p. 294). This long list of media and methods of instruction is not complete; for example, a laboratory exercise in the discovery or testing of the principles to be learned could be added. He says "the real point to be made is that the use of variety of instructional modes is both feasible and potentially effective" (5, p. 294). Though correct, this statement overlooks the vital point that these methods and media of instruction are differentially effective for students. Cronbach points out that "many approaches have some success, and none works in all situations or on all students" (2, p. 352).

We know that students learn more rapidly those things which are interesting to them, and we know that student interests vary enormously from time to time and from one student to another. Moreover, there is increasing evidence that there are different "cognitive styles," that is, some individuals learn in considerably different ways from others. If a particular student does not learn well from a lecture, for example, we have four options:

A. We can choose another method of presenting the same material.
B. We can present material which is so interesting to him that he will learn even though the lecture method seldom teaches him much.
C. We can teach him how to profit from the lecture method.
D. We can allow him to sit through the lecture without learning anything.

All of these possibilities except the last seem to be defensible, yet that alternative is the one most frequently used.

The laboratory method which is so common in vocational education is much more effective with certain students than with others. If a student has goals which can best be met through vocational education, methods of teaching should be adapted which enable him to learn its content most effectively. Too often, vocational educators are as adamant in using laboratory methods as the history teacher is in using the lecture.

Some students will learn only if education appears to be relevant. If a subject appears relevant to the student, he will usually learn regardless of the method used, though he may learn less rapidly than he would with an optimum method. Because vocational education courses are elective, their teachers, administrators, and teacher educators too often rely on the strong interests of the student to substitute for inadequacies in educational planning.

INTERESTS

It is trite to say that individual interests differ. Yet the school rarely seems to capitalize upon these differences in interests. If the goal of the school is to teach the student to read, this goal is much more likely to be reached if the reading matter is of interest to the student. Great progress has been made in adapting reading materials to fit the interests of the majority of students, but the goal seems still to have all students read the same material. It is often found that students in vocational education are exposed for the first time, to reading materials which are interesting and important to them as individuals. The world of occupationally related literature, from the *Farm Journal* to the *Wall Street Journal* and from repair manuals for automobiles (often four inches thick for a single make and model of car) to instruction on a new surgical procedure, is probably as important to our society as the novels, essays, and poems which provide the bulk of instructional material for classroom reading programs. Yet the literature related to occupations is hardly touched in schools, even in vocational education. This is not to say that the school should avoid its responsibility to develop new interests on the part of its students. What it does say is that capitalizing on existing interests of students may be the best way of providing skills which can later lead to the development of additional interests.

APTITUDES

Individuals differ enormously in their aptitudes, but the school concentrates primarily on developing only a few of them. Athletic aptitudes are highly developed for those few students who are capable of performing on the varsity teams. Musical aptitudes for performance on band instruments and in certain types of choral groups are well developed if they are utilizable in performances which reflect credit on the school.

Similarly art aptitudes are fostered on the part of those students who have proved capable of producing works of art which can grace the school or its public displays. It seems that certain types of aptitudes are not developed by the school at all. Aptitudes in trouble-shooting, horticulture, child care, salesmanship, etc. are almost totally ignored. Yet, if individual options are to be increased, these aptitudes need nourishing as much as any others. A related problem is the discovery of aptitudes. A student who has an undiscovered aptitude certainly has had his individual options decreased, even if his school has a program for developing that capability.

INFLUENCE OF RESIDENTIAL SCHOOLS

For a small but significant fraction of our population a desirable educational program includes the provision of residential school facilities. Whether the educational program be a four-year college, a community college, a high school, or remedial education program, some students learn a great deal by being removed part-time from their home environment to one which provides more stimulus for learning. In some cases, this is necessary just to give the student an opportunity to make decisions without constant supervision. In other cases, it is necessary to provide an atmosphere which develops attitudes and values which are more acceptable to society than those which can be learned on the street or in certain homes. Examples of such schools include the Civilian Conservation Corps (CCC) of the late thirties which provided on-the-job training and useful employment in public works. More recently the Job Corps has provided an educational program of a more formal nature with heavy emphasis on occupational preparation. In all societies, the military has provided a similar type of residential training which removed the student from his previous environment. Residential colleges have a similar effect. Success of any of these undertakings seems to be closely related to whether or not their primary goal was the increasing of individual options. Where this has been the case, they have succeeded with a much larger proportion of their trainees than if the increasing of individual options had been a distinctly subordinate goal. These programs are invariably expensive, but the results achieved have often been quite economical when one considers that they have surely reduced the proportion of people who would otherwise be sent to penal institutions, exist on welfare, or become emotionally dependent upon parents. For quite different reasons, residential schools are needed in sparsely populated regions. It simply is not possible, using the techniques which are available today, to provide a comprehensive high school within commuting distance of students in some parts of our country. Between twelve hundred and three thousand students (estimates vary) is the minimum enrollment needed to establish a high school with adequate programs to serve all types of youth, and to do this economically. But economics is not the only concern. Many communities which now have high schools have no breadth of employment opportunities. Part-time cooperative employment for significant numbers of students in a variety of occupations is simply not possible. A residential high school in a larger and more diversified community offers education more economically, and more importantly, it can offer broader and better vocational education.

Education in Penal Institutions

It has been frequently pointed out that the proportion of inmates who return to penal institutions is extraordinarily high. One of the principal reasons for this is related to increasing individual options for former prison inmates. Employers carefully gather employment history information and view with suspicion any gaps which may indicate that the potential employee has been incarcerated. If the employer learns that a person has been imprisoned for any reason, he is most unlikely to employ the ex-convict in a position of trust. While this is sometimes an irrational decision which seeks to penalize the ex-convict further, it is in large part a rational reaction based upon an expectation that a person who has once been in prison is likely to return and hence does not warrant expenditures for training which would be justified for a potential long-term employee. Regardless of the cause, the fact that it is very difficult for an ex-convict to secure satisfactory employment is undoubtedly a major reason for recidivism.

A major factor in the realistic objections of employers to ex-convicts is found within penal educational systems. With the exception of those in some federal penitentiaries, there are few significant programs of vocational education in penal institutions. Almost all of the so called vocational educational programs which exist in these institutions are in fact "production" programs aimed at providing goods and services for consumption within the institution. Thus a person who is listed as a cook-trainee is likely to be ladling out soup in the cafeteria line. In a few cases this on-the-job training produces satisfactory results. Because it is important for prisoners to have their hair cut and because the quality of these haircuts is visible to visitors, instruction in barbering (or hair dressing) is probably the best vocational program in many penal institutions.

One of the main difficulties in vocational training in prisons is financial. There have been attempts to reduce the cost by establishing on-the-job training programs which produce goods which are sold to nonprofit institutions, but these are attacked by employer and employee groups as unfair competition provided by under-paid workers. One method of avoiding this problem is the work release program of such states as North Carolina, which involves more than two thousand prisoners who leave the prisons to work full-time, returning each evening or each weekend for incarceration. A second method has been proposed by Bernard Puchalski of the Iron Workers' Union. He suggests that prisoners be paid standard wages for goods and services produced, and that the state subsidize the difference between their productivity and those of trained workers, justifying these added expenditures as part of the cost of training. Both of these schemes would profit from a coordinated educational program designed along the lines of the very successful part-time cooperative programs which are employed in secondary schools and colleges. A major goal of an educational program in a penal institution as in any other educational institution should be to increase the individual options of the students.

Learning for Mastery

Schools which have accepted the obligation of allowing all students to attend have not assumed the parallel responsibility of seeing that these students learn all the types of knowledge they need. Benjamin Bloom (1) points out that it is more common for a school to accept responsibility for *presenting* material to all students than it is to assume responsibility for seeing that all students *master* certain specified skills, knowledges, and attitudes. As a result certain students who have been exposed to twelve years of instruction in the use of the English language are performing at a level typical of the average person who has received only half as much instruction. The goal is almost always specified in terms of the number of years of instruction rather than in terms of specified skills which are to be mastered. This phenomenon occurs at all levels of instruction from early childhood education through college.

If the school actually assumes responsibility for mastery of certain content by all students, it will find certain students who have not learned through the traditional approach which emphasizes the authority of the teacher as the source of educational relevance. If society does not permit the school to allow its failures to escape through dropping out or "social promotion," it will be forced to find techniques which meet the needs of each of these students. This in turn will lead to a recognition that for many students, learning will occur most efficiently when tied to the student's perception of relevance. Moreover, the school will realize that for many students, educational relevance is best perceived when the student sees that skills, knowledges, and attitudes are needed for occupational survival, and that these are taught in many different school subjects. This in turn suggests that the school should encourage identification of occupational goals at an early age, even though the goal of each student is likely to change several times during his school career. Moreover, it suggests that the high school or community college which denies vocational education to the half of its students who desire such instruction is limiting the options of those students. Proponents of the general curriculum say it is designed to increase options, but on every variable in every study it has been shown to be far less effective in this regard than the vocational curriculum or the college preparatory curriculum (which is occupationally oriented for most students).

REFERENCES

1. Bloom, Benjamin S., "Learning for Mastery," *Evaluation Comment,* I, No. 2 (May, 1968), 1-3.

2. Cronbach, Lee J., *Educational Psychology.* New York: Harcourt, Brace, & World, Inc., 1954.

3. Doeringer, Peter B. and Michael J. Piore, "Internal Labor Markets, and Technological, and Labor Force Adjustment," *Work Force Adjustments in Private Industry—Their Implications for Manpower Policy.* Manpower/Automation Research Monograph No. 7. Washington, D.C.: U.S. Department of Labor, 1968.

4. Drucker, Peter, "The Rise in Higher Education," in *The Revolutionary Theme in Contemporary America,* ed. Thomas R. Ford. Lexington: University Press of Kentucky, 1965.

5. Gagné, Robert M., *The Conditions of Learning.* New York: Holt, Rinehart & Winston, Inc., 1965.

6. Hall, Oswald and Bruce McFarlane, *Transition from School to Work.* Ottawa: The Queen's Printer, 1963.

7. Parnes, Herbert S., *et al. Career Thresholds,* Vol. I. Columbus: Ohio State University Center for Human Resources Research, 1969.

8. *Poverty Continues to Decline in 1969.* Consumer Income, Current Population Reports, No. 71. Washington, D.C.: U.S. Department of Commerce, Bureau of Census, 1970.

Chapter 4   LENDING INTELLIGIBILITY TO GENERAL EDUCATION

The least understood of the three major objectives of vocational education is that which suggests that vocational education can and should consciously interpret general education to vocational students. It has always been true that a high proportion of students in vocational education see little value in most of general education, and hence have little interest in it. Many of these students, as they progress through vocational education, suddenly see the need for (and hence the value of) many general education learnings which they had rejected earlier. This process occurs naturally, usually with no help from the vocational teacher. Unfortunately, after a vocational student has seen the need for learning material which he failed to grasp earlier, the school is often ill-prepared or even disinterested in helping him learn it later. In order to discuss this process further, we need to consider what general education and vocational education are, and what their relationships should be.

There are many definitions of the term "general education." Two contrasting versions are: (1) educating for leisure, usually through acquiring specific knowledges and attitudes, such as an understanding of the "great books" of the past, and (2) acquiring the ability (and confidence in that ability) to cope with one's environment in today's world. The definition used in this book is much closer to the latter than to the former of these, but in addition, general education as used here means that education which is needed by *every* student. It is assumed that the general education needed by every student will be supplemented by specialized education which is needed by some students but not by others, and that the totality of general education and specialized education received by each student will enable him to cope successfully with his environment and to feel confident that he can do so.

Vocational education is often thought to be antithetical to general education. Though in some types of vocational training programs, especially outside the public schools, there is indeed a separation between vocational and general education, it is assumed here that the two are complementary and necessary to each other.

In certain vocational training programs in private schools, no instruction is offered which is labeled as general education, though a considerable amount of general education does take place. Even in on-the-job training, the most specialized and nonintellectual part of vocational education, a considerable amount of general education occurs. The only conflicts which exist are personal ones among instructors, with a few general educators demanding more time for their material, and some vocational educators denying the relevance of some of the school instruction which is labeled as general education. Perhaps a consideration of what vocational education really is will help to dispel the notion that it and general education are incompatible.

Definitions of Vocational Education Content

The most inclusive view of vocational education content sees it as that content which is needed for occupational success. Under this definition, much if not most of general education would be included, because reading, for example, is needed for full success in every occupation. A very different definition states that vocational education content is what makes a person more competent in one occupation than in another. If vocational education is limited to this definition, it appears to be entirely specialized, since that content which enables a person to succeed in more than one occupation is relegated to general education. Because we defined general education as that education which is needed by every student, we cannot limit vocational education to training for a single occupation. This would eliminate a large part of education which is not needed by everyone, but which does help people become competent in more than one occupation. For example, typing and welding would be eliminated, because they are each important in more than one occupation, but they are not needed by everyone. A better view sees vocational education content as that which helps a person to succeed occupationally, but is not needed by everyone. Under this definition, vocational and general education together cover a much larger portion of education. All that is left out is that specialized education which is non-occupational in nature, e.g., education for a specific avocation.

No definition of vocational education is entirely satisfactory. In this book vocational education includes all education which makes a person more competent in one group of occupations than in another. (This part of vocational education is all specialized, since it is not the same for all people.) But the content of vocational education often includes also parts of general education which are needed for occupational success, but have been neglected by the general educator. Many educators, including some vocational teachers, see vocational education as being entirely specialized. Hence they reject the latter part of the definition used in this book. However, if essential parts of general education relating to occupational success are being neglected (e.g., development of psychomotor skills, ability to work in groups, an understanding of basic materials, processes and services, and the process of choosing an occupation) and if vocational teachers believe that this material is essential, then they must include it in their programs. When general educators assume the responsibility for teaching this general vocational education content effectively, vocational educators should be willing to surrender it. So long as it is no one's responsibility or everyone's responsibility, it is unlikely to be taught.

General and Generalizable Vocational Education

General vocational education is that education which is related to occupational life and is also needed by all students. Some examples include: (1) an understanding of the economics of the production of goods and services, (2) an understanding of the social security system, and (3) the ability to satisfactorily complete an application form for employment. According to the above definition, most of the content of industrial arts is general vocational education. However, because industrial arts is not concerned with certain major sectors of employment, it does not supply all of the general vocational education needed by students.

Generalizable vocational education, on the other hand, is specialized education about occupational life which is *not* needed by all students, but which has applicability beyond employment in a particular occupation in a particular establishment. Judged by this definition almost all vocational education except some orientation training and OJT is generalizable. Naturally, some types are more generalizable than others. Instruction on obsolete processes and products has much less generalizability than instruction on current products and processes. Some people think that since no one knows what the products and processes of the future will be, no vocational education should be offered. Actually, this is more an objection to occupational education in the professions than to preparation for other occupations, since the rate of technological change in the professions is much more rapid than it is in most other occupational fields. In any case, if we refused to educate people in a field because its future content was uncertain, we would be refusing to educate anyone on any subject.

Since products change much more rapidly than processes, education about processes is more generalizable than education about products. Work behavior, work group interactions, and work attitudes change even less rapidly than processes. Thus it is likely that instruction in attitudes is more generalizable than instruction in products or processes. However, no one has discovered a way to teach work attitudes without teaching them in a setting which involves products, processes, and services.

Vocational Education as a
Direct Method of Instruction

Until now, we have been considering the content of vocational education; however, vocational education is also a method of instruction. Even specialized vocational education provides a vehicle for teaching general education content, and for teaching it in a far more effective way than often can be accomplished in a standard classroom. Suppose a high school or community college has several different vocational programs. One part of each program is teaching students to work together effectively. This is a general education objective, since all students need to learn how to work together. Certain students can learn to work together on a science project, or on an athletic team, others in repairing an automobile, designing a sales campaign, or preparing a meal. While the science project might be labeled by the school as general education, the other examples indicate how general education goals can be achieved through specialized vehicles of instruction.

The effectiveness of vocational education as a method depends on such factors as: (1) teachers who are genuinely interested in the success of students, (2) goals which appear relevant to students, (3) an atmosphere of responsible freedom rather than regimentation, and (4) content that is viewed as a means to an end, not an end in itself. Vocational education has no monopoly on such factors. Other subjects, especially in the practical arts have some or all of them, but vocational education, more than most subjects, combines these factors in a way which appeals to students who are not motivated to learn content for its own sake. If a student does love learning for learning's sake, almost any method of instruction is effective. But if he does not, the method of instruction and the context of content become extremely important. The evidence suggests that vocational education as a method of instruction is highly effective with many students, and the evidence is clear that far more students want vocational education than can be accepted in a program of its current size.

Vocational Education as an Indirect Method of Instruction

Vocational educators are concerned that students learn more than is taught in vocational education classes. Occupational success depends on the student learning many things which are taught in general education classes. Reading, writing, and basic computational skills immediately come to mind, but concepts from science, economics, government, history, etc. are also essential. Too often these concepts are presented as though they had no occupational value, and the student who has not learned to value knowledge for its own sake may simply decide that this material is not worth learning. Later, often only when he has left school, he learns that these concepts are valuable, and wishes he had learned them. This leads to a common phenomenon: an adult, past the age when he learns most rapidly, enrolls in a basic literacy class as part of a manpower training program, and grows three years in reading achievement during one year of instruction. This usually occurs because for the first time in his life he sees a reason for learning to read. Such programs for adults will probably always be needed, because some schools will probably always fail to serve some students. But how much richer his life would have been if he could have been provided a reason for learning to read while he was still in school.

Vocational education provides a reason for learning basic academic skills. It lets the student know that these skills are important in life, and more particularly, are important in achieving his occupational goals. Too often, however, the knowledge of the importance of basic academic skills comes late in a student's school life. Most vocational education begins at age sixteen, and many schools do not offer remedial instruction in basic academic skills to students of this age. Many vocational teachers proceed to do the best they can, and teach basic academic skills in the vocational classroom. This is of some help, but most vocational teachers are not well prepared for this type of instruction. If the student could have learned earlier that basic academic skills *are* important, or if remedial classes could be offered concurrently with vocational education, more effective results could be achieved.

A second way vocational education achieves general education indirectly is by helping to keep students in school. Several studies show that half of high school freshmen want vocational education, and half want college preparatory education. The half that want college preparatory work get in, but of those who want vocational education, half are rejected and placed in the general curriculum. Project TALENT data show that two-thirds of all high school dropouts come from this general curriculum. Vocational education has a higher dropout rate that the college preparatory curriculum, and might have a still higher rate if it enrolled those students now assigned to the general curriculum. However, when student intelligence and socio-economic class are held constant, vocational education (except for programs conducted in socially segregated vocational high schools) appears to have the lowest dropout rate of any high school curriculum.

Historical Relationships Between Vocational and General Education

The history of education shows an uneasy relationship between general and vocational education. One of the best accounts of that history has been compiled by Vincent P. Lannie. He points out that early apprenticeship agreements in this country required the master to teach not only a useful employment, but also fundamental literacy and civic and moral responsibilities. But many masters were unable to provide adequate non-vocational instruction, and during the eighteenth century began to send their apprentices to evening schools for the three R's. This is the first example in this country of the separation of vocational and academic instruction.

The decline of apprenticeship in the early nineteenth century stopped vocational instruction (other than on-the-job training) for most American youth. Formal schools confined their occupational instruction to the professions, and generally were available only to children of the wealthy. Only a few visionaries like Robert Owen would call for education ". . . combining mechanical and agricultural with literary and scientific instruction . . ." and ". . . making every scholar a workman and every workman a scholar . . ." (7, p. 9). Gradually this idea of combining vocational and general education grew through lyceums and mechanics institutes until it culminated in the land-grant colleges.

Economic considerations as well as the opposition of academicians made the extension of vocational education into the common schools a far more difficult matter. But during the last half of the nineteenth century a method which appeared to provide a practical solution came from Russia. Della Vos, an engineer, had developed a system of "instruction shops" which taught students to use common tools as they completed a graded series of exercises. Although this system was adopted first at the college level, it quickly became the basis for the manual training program in the secondary school. This appeared to bring vocational and general education at this level together again. But manual training did not really meet vocational training needs. A single educational program based on faculty psychology could not meet the nation's needs for various types of skilled manpower. Thus the cry for "real" vocational education appeared, and resulted in state and federal legislation supporting more specific instruction in a limited number of occupational fields. The first step of the new vocational educators was to set up separate vocational schools. This not only had the unfortunate effect of separating general and vocational education, but it was clearly an attack upon the educational irrelevance of the literary instruction which was labeled general education. The response of leading American educators was the creation of the comprehensive high school, which was designed to serve all youth. The response of other educators, however, was to deny that vocational education had a place in the public school.

The comprehensive high school was implemented fully in very few communities, and most high schools drifted gradually in the direction of serving college-bound youth exclusively. In the late thirties this drift was reversed by the threat of the Civilian Conservation Corps and the National Youth Administration vocational schools. This awoke principals and teachers of "comprehensive" schools to the danger of a separate school system outside their control. They responded by developing vocational programs which were highly effective in the war effort. But following World War II, the drift away from vocational education began again, only to be reversed by the Vocational Education Acts of 1963 and 1968.

A cycle can be observed which is repeated approximately once every generation: (1) establishment of a reasonably comprehensive high school, (2) gradually decreased emphasis on vocational education, (3) establishment of separate vocational schools, and (4) the re-establishment of comprehensive high schools which emphasize vocational education. Elsewhere in this book it is pointed out that these cycles tend to coincide with the nation's needs for skilled manpower. But these cycles may also demonstrate two other things: (1) that many general educators think vocational education should somehow be improved in efficiency, and (2) the accuracy of the feeling many vocational educators have that general educators look down on them and try to minimize their influence.

Perhaps the basic difficulty is in implementing the concept of the comprehensive school. Too often, a school which bears this name tries to meet the needs of all students simply by putting programs for all students under the same roof. What we need is a community high school and a real community (junior) college which is not content to have competing programs under the same roof, but ". . . fuses academic and vocational education as every-day partners" (3, p. 23). One of the first ways to make vocational and general education every-day partners is to establish instructional programs which point out to students that instruction in every class is relevant to what they are now learning, and will be relevant in their lives ahead. Since we do not want to tell students an untruth, we need to make sure that all education really is relevant.

General Education and Relevance

Much of what is taught in our schools under the name of general education is not general education at all. Not all persons need trigonometry and calculus. Nor do all persons need the most advanced courses in foreign language, industrial arts, art, music, or most other subjects currently labeled "general education" in our high schools and community colleges. However, much of the material taught is general education and is needed by everyone. Many students, however, do not *see* that they need it, and hence, many of them lack motivation to learn some of the things they will need most. A lawyer, Mr. Hugh Calkins, Chairman of the National Advisory Council on Vocational Education, describes the situation very well.

Most of those who fail to learn to figure, read, and write in our schools, fail because schooling seems to them an exercise in futility. Books which are irrelevant to their interests, classes which are oriented toward further years of schooling after the 12th grade, mathematics which seems to serve no useful purpose, do not get the attention of boys and girls brought up to solve immediate problems. The elementary grades are where vocational and technical education must begin for all students. There is where the connection between reading and employment, arithmetic and income, writing and self respect, must be made clear. To the public, these connections are obvious. The public expects that school will make them obvious to the students also (4, p. 2).

The Calkins proposal of vocational education for all students in the elementary school has raised the hackles of many educators, both academic and vocational. Vocational educators do not like it, because they want to be sure that current programs in the secondary schools and community colleges are adequately financed before funds are "diverted" elsewhere. Academic educators are disturbed because they think vocational education is always specialized education, and they feel that there is no role for specialized education in the elementary school. But Calkins, a layman, is right, and the educators are wrong. Investments in vocational education, as in any other educational enterprise, should be directed toward activities which yield maximum effectiveness relative to the investment made. If education about occupations, work, and the economic enterprise can, in the elementary school, develop attitudes toward work which increase individual options, eventually help meet the manpower needs of the nation, and simultaneously lend relevance to the rest of general education, the Calkins proposal would lead to an extremely wise investment of vocational education funds. The academic educator objects that the Calkins plan neglects the fact that young students do not respond well to deferred rewards. It seems reasonable, however, to assume that the current emphasis (even in elementary school curricula) on preparation for graduate school delays rewards for most students far longer than would be required by the Calkins proposal.

Early Occupational Choice

One of the major restrictions on expansion of vocational education into the elementary school is the mistaken notion that early occupational education necessitates an early, irrevocable occupational choice. It is a generally accepted fact that the average age at which a person chooses his occupation has been increasing. This is almost universally viewed as a desirable trend. We rightly view with horror the days when students were forced to leave school even before the eighth grade to accept employment because the family needed added income. Traditions of other countries which require that a boy's occupation be identical to his father's are repugnant to most Americans, and yet we have gone to the opposite extreme. It has become an upper class ideal in the United States that a boy or girl should complete the baccalaureate degree before thinking about a possible occupation, and this "ideal" is being achieved.

Unfortunately, two completely different concepts have been mixed in this type of thinking. Early occupational education or even early occupational choice is very different from an early occupational decision which is unalterable. Many students do make occupational choices early. If they have made such a choice, the school and parents can and should capitalize on the fact by encouraging the student to read, write, and talk about it. Almost everything taught in the elementary school has an occupational application. Many of these applications should be pointed out to the student, and he should be encouraged to discover additional ways in which general education has value in the occupation he tentatively has chosen.

Of course it would be wrong for parents or the school to discourage the student from exploring other occupational opportunities by regarding the student's early occupational choice as immutable. Parents tend more to do this overtly than teachers. The student who has said for some time that he wants to be an engineer may have considerable problems with his parents if he later decides to be a plumber. The elementary school is much less directive. In most school texts there is no mention of occupations. Instead of writing about their hobbies or chores or occupational aspirations, students are required to write about what they did on their vacation, even if they did not take a vacation. Selections from literature emphasize adult upper class standards which, if they mention occupations at all, treat only the professions. In high school and beyond, however, the school becomes much more directive. If a student chooses a vocational curriculum, the school makes it extremely difficult for him to change from one occupational field to another, sometimes even requiring him to change schools. But the general attitude of the schools toward occupations is similar to the comment of a famous college president, that the best thing to do about vocational education would be to forget it. In "forgetting it" the school forfeits an enormous opportunity to capitalize on the student's interests of the moment and forces him into the strait jacket of constantly deferred gratification.

Practical Arts Instruction

Industrial arts and home economics are the only courses commonly offered below the high school level which have education about employability as a major objective. These programs are taken by a sizeable majority of boys and girls respectively. Until recently, home economics emphasized family life education for girls and completely neglected the dual role of homemaker and wage earner which is expected of a great majority of women. More curriculum materials and trained teachers are becoming available in home economics to enable junior high school programs to prepare students for this dual role and to emphasize its relationship to other general education courses.

Curriculum revision in industrial arts has in some respects gone further than home economics, but in other respects, not as far. A number of curriculum revision projects are well advanced, including the Industrial Arts Curriculum Program of The Ohio State University and the University of Illinois and the American Industry Program of Stout State University. Most of these programs emphasize the production of goods and overlook the fact that this type of production is becoming less important while services are rapidly gaining importance in our economy. Nevertheless, if instruction in "the world of construction" or the "world of industry" is taught to and perceived by the students as being illustrative of a much broader world of work, a great deal can be accomplished through these programs. Still missing, of course, is the entire world of service. Certainly the revised curricula are better than the material they replaced, which emphasized a world of leisure based on home workshops which in practice could be afforded only by the wealthy.

Another extremely desirable innovation is the program in "technology for the elementary school" which emphasizes the world of work throughout the elementary school. It has been employed mostly in the schools of New Jersey, but it suffers from a lack of adequately prepared elementary school teachers. Even more promising is the work of Bailey at Southern Illinois University. The biggest obstacle to these programs is the lack of generally available curriculum materials which can be employed by existing elementary school teachers. Most of these teachers have such intelligence, manipulative ability (at least in art areas), and teaching ability that it seems reasonable to assume that they would accept readily and employ quite successfully well prepared curriculum materials about the world of work.

Most industrial arts and home economics instruction occurs at the junior high school level and above. Through a process of segregation on the basis of sex, teachers of these two subjects artificially restrict the range of occupational activities with which a student may become acquainted. Most teachers in these fields deny that they practice sexual segregation, and attribute the segregation which does exist to student choice. Anyone who has ever attempted to enroll a boy in home economics or a girl in industrial arts, however, knows that with rare exceptions the segregation is imposed as much by the teachers as by the students. Although notable progress is being made toward restructuring home economics to include knowledge of wage earning occupations, most home economics education has been and will continue for many years to be centered on preparation for homemaking. Such preparation is desirable in and of itself, but it is insufficient in view of the fact that over two-thirds of women will be wage earners, and all women, as well as men, need to understand the process by which goods and services are produced.

Industrial arts suffers from an inadequate understanding of the nature of industry. In its broad sense, as when we speak of the "industrial revolution", industry includes agriculture, the distribution of goods and services, the provision of health services, and homemaking as well as the production and repair of manufactured articles. In part because John Dewey's school at the University of Chicago had certain craft instruction attached to it, and in part because certain leaders in the fields of manual training and manual arts felt rejected by vocational educators during the early part of the twentieth century, industrial arts has concentrated almost entirely upon *materials* employed by those who produce and repair manufactured goods, and has used the *methods* of a preindustrial society. This has maintained the traditions of the University of Chicago admirably, and it has asserted the independence of industrial arts from vocational education, but it has woefully short-changed the general education of boys and girls by omitting major portions of our industrial society. Moreover, by implicitly rejecting vocational education, it has by-passed an opportunity to be a major bridge between general and vocational education.

Business education, on the other hand, has provided such a link through its general education courses. Personal typing is open to boys and girls alike, as are personal note taking, commercial arithmetic, and general education offerings in bookkeeping, consumer law, etc. Business education with both general and vocational objectives was excluded from federal vocational education legislation until recently, so there has been no historical split within the field which sets one type of teacher against another.

The result has been that students in advanced vocational and business education courses are well aware of the importance of general education. And, general education teachers of many types are cognizant of the needs of business education. Another result has been that business education attracts far more capable students than other types of vocational education. It is true, of course, that as a program to prepare students for white-collar occupations, business education has been more acceptable to general education teachers than have other types of vocational programs. Nevertheless, the fact that general business education courses deliberately set out to serve as a bridge between general education seems to have been a major factor in its success. No other field of vocational education is as well accepted by employers and by general education teachers alike.

POLYTECHNICAL EDUCATION

There are two major difficulties in bridging the gap between general and vocational education. One is to make all teachers aware of the close relationships between these two aspects of education, and the second is to bring such awareness to students. It is to be hoped that improved pre-service and in-service teacher education can bridge the gap for teachers. For students, there is no systematic vehicle. Industrial arts and home economics are two types of instruction which could provide this bridge for students, but we have seen that both have chosen not to move substantially in this direction in the United States.

In eastern Europe, both the elementary and secondary schools have courses of instruction which are known as "polytechnical" education. The purpose of polytechnical education is to help the student ". . . to develop creative technical abilities and to inculcate a love and respect for physical labor and work" (7, p. 18). In his polytechnical education courses, the student learns how goods and services are produced and learns the scientific principles on which such production depends. He also learns to handle common tools and machines. Polytechnical education gives the student a broad general and technical background which helps him to select his future occupation and prepares him to take an active part in technical developments of the future. Polytechnical education is regarded as desirable in its own right, but it is recognized also as an absolute prerequisite for vocational education.

Polytechnical education in communist countries has an interesting history. Vocational education in the Russian schools had a long history before the revolution of 1917. These vocational schools were segregated by social class and were, of course, suspect by the revolutionaries. Lenin, drawing on the ideas of Marx, ordered in 1917 the substitution of the word "polytechnical" for "vocational" on the ground that the aim of schooling "is to train not specialists but people capable of doing any type of work" (8, p. 35). Despite this urging from the highest authority, Soviet educators were unable to develop a single educational program which would prepare people for any and all types of work. In many ways, early polytechnic education in the U.S.S.R. was similar to the manual training which educators in the U.S. imported from Czarist Russia. Wherever it has been tried, it has been found wanting as an effective means of vocational education.

It can be, however, a good system of pre-vocational education. This led to the current relationship in Russia between polytechnical and vocational education in which the former emphasizes activities and knowledge important to all work, while the latter enables students to achieve their own occupational goals and to meet the needs of society.

THE PHYSIOLOGICAL BASIS OF POLYTECHNICAL AND VOCATIONAL EDUCATION

Skatkin points out that a combination of classroom instruction with productive work is necessary for physiological reasons.

> When identical stimuli are acting on the cerebral cortex all the time, protective inhibition sets in, with the result that reflexes already developed become diminished, and the formation of new reflexes become difficult. This often happens when pupils are kept busy day after day only with mental work or with the same school subjects. They quickly tire, become inattentive, and start to lose the facility for understanding and assimilating the subject matter. This does not happen if different types of activity—mental work, gymnastics and sport and physical work—are intelligently alternated (8, p. 19).

In the elementary school polytechnical program, students ". . . plant and grow flowers, vegetables and trees, run a pet's corner and take care of rabbits and birds, look after the school yards, playing fields and the streets and squares adjacent to the schools; in the school workshops they make and repair school supplies, rebind library books, and make simple articles" (8, p. 21). In the high school, both in Russia and the United States, vocational education, physical education, and academic studies provide the alternation of types of activities which Skatkin feels is important. For some reason, few educational psychologists in the United States have felt this to be an important area of investigation.

Regional Accrediting Association Attitudes

The statement is sometimes made that regional accrediting associations require that all teachers have degrees and that vocational education be de-emphasized. These statements are quite incorrect. Regional accrediting associations insist that instructors be qualified in the subject they are teaching. They are much more critical of a vocational teacher who has a baccalaureate or more and yet does not know his field than they are of a vocational instructor who is only a high school graduate, has been prepared to teach, and is teaching capably. These associations do insist that general education courses be a part of any vocational curriculum, because they recognize that the interaction of vocational and general education is highly desirable. Accreditation teams are quite critical of schools, regardless of level, which offer only college preparatory curricula to their student body when a sizeable proportion of that student body will not graduate from college. It seems clear that in this as in many other aspects of education, the regional accrediting associations are used as excuses for not doing something that the school wishes to avoid.

Mechanisms for Eliminating Irrelevant Education

In schools, as in other bureaucracies, the bureaucrats seek to preserve their jobs. The high school teachers of Greek, Hebrew, manual training, and religion fought the introduction of English, science, and vocational education because they perceived correctly that the limited resources of the school would follow the choices of the students, and they saw that students would prefer these new subjects to the old. Many new subjects are needed in our schools today. Economics and sociology compete with history. Speech, journalism, and technical report writing compete with English composition and literature. Agribusiness competes with production agriculture, newer concepts of home economics compete with cooking and sewing, and part-time cooperative vocational education competes with in-school vocational programs.

One way of resolving these conflicts would be to let students choose, and adjust the size of programs accordingly. Teachers fear such a system, however, and have gone to great lengths to insure that certain programs are required for graduation. Often they have even enlisted the support of legislators who have written into law certain minimum educational requirements, and have thus protected the jobs of certain teachers. Vocational educators have followed this same route, and have been instrumental in securing support of legislators, governors, and state boards in protecting their field. For example, federal legislation up to 1963 specified that minimum amounts of money were to be spent on certain vocational education programs. State boards of education and of junior colleges have specified that vocational education should be allocated minimum amounts of money or staff time.

Whenever educators get outsiders to mandate minimum amounts of support for their course, they either confess that students do not want the programs they offer, or that certain educators are unwilling to support their programs. The best solution might be to let students choose the subjects which appear relevant to their goals. This would force reforms, and enlist the support of teachers for educational programs which point out to students the relevance of subjects which are being taught. Another alternative is to use cost-effectiveness ratios or other economic measures to decide what should be taught. Some of these economic tools are discussed in the chapter on economics. Here it should be noted that economic measures are not the only measures which should be applied. No one has a good solution to the problem of keeping education relevant. Until we find such a solution, we can help the situation by minimizing the number of required courses, maximizing the number of elective courses, and making special efforts to insure that instruction points out to students the relevancies (and irrelevancies) which exist.

Unlike the first two major objectives of vocational education, little attention has been paid to the third major objective of lending intelligibility to general education. If something is intelligible, we know its good points and its weaknesses. Knowing these, we can move to strengthen the good and eliminate the bad. General education and vocational education each have an obligation to make themselves intelligible. Just as certain disciplines such as economics are now in the process of making vocational education more intelligible to vocational and non-vocational educators and to citizens at large, so vocational education can shed light on the purposes and accomplishments of general education. Often we need interpreters to see the import of a message. Some of this interpretation happens by accident every day in vocational education classrooms and laboratories. More and better interpretation will occur as curriculum developers, teacher educators, and teachers in vocational education set out consciously to implement the goal of lending intelligibility to general education.

REFERENCES

1. Barlow, Melvin L., *History of Industrial Education in the United States.* Peoria, Ill.: Charles A. Bennett Co., Inc., 1967.

2. Bennett, Charles A., *History of Manual and Industrial Education 1870-1917*. Peoria, Ill.: Charles A. Bennett Co., Inc., 1937.

3. Brameld, Theodore, "Reaction," in *Vocational Education. A Prospectus for Change*, eds. Carl J. Schaefer and Jacob J. Kaufman. Boston: Massachusetts Advisory Council on Education, 1967.

4. Calkins, Hugh, "What the Public Expects of Vocational-Technical Education," Dedication speech. Columbus, Ohio Center for Vocational Education Research and Leadership Development, 1969.

5. Lannie, Vincent P., "The Development of Vocational Education in America: An Historical Overview," in *Vocational Education. A Prospectus for Change*, eds. Carl J. Schaefer and Jacob J. Kaufman. Boston: Massachusetts Advisory Council on Education, 1967.

6. Mays, Arthur B., *Principles and Practices of Vocational Education*. New York: McGraw-Hill Book Company, 1948.

7. Owen, Robert D., *Working Man's Advocate,* (April 24, 1830). Quoted in Lannie, Vincent P., "The Development of Vocational Education in America: An Historical Overview," in *Vocational Education. A Prospectus for Change*, eds. Carl J. Schaefer and Jacob J. Kaufman. Boston: Massachusetts Advisory Council on Education, 1967.

8. Shapovalenko, S. G., ed. *Polytechnic Education in the U.S.S.R.* Paris: USESCO, 1963.

9. Skatkin, M. N., "Marxist-Leninist Ideas of Polytechnical Education," in *Polytechnical Education in the U.S.S.R.*, ed. S. G. Shapovalenko. Paris: USESCO, 1963.

Part II DISCIPLINARY FOUNDATIONS OF VOCATIONAL EDUCATION

Chapter 5　INTRODUCTION

This section on the foundations of vocational education has no pretense of being exhaustive. Rather, it is designed to call the attention of the vocational educator to a few of the numerous ways in which four disciplines, philosophy, economics, sociology, and psychology, can contribute to an understanding of our tremendously complex field. The task of choosing the important contributions to be included has been extremely frustrating, since many topics of importance had to be omitted. Completely omitted, because of lack of space, are the important ideas and conclusions which disciplines other than these four have to contribute. Anthropology, political science and government, and even biology and the physical sciences have a potential contribution to make, but they have been omitted because their effect to date has been less direct. History has been omitted because it is relatively well covered elsewhere, e.g., by Barlow, Bennett, and Mays. It is hoped that this brief exposure will lead the student (and the practitioner who wants to continue to learn) to a more thorough study of at least these four disciplines. A bibliography which can provide a beginning of such study is attached to each chapter.

Relatively few practitioners of the academic disciplines believe that there is a need for formal occupational education for fields other than the professions. Some of them seem to believe in occupational education only for their own specialty. Their opposition to vocational education is often due to a lack of understanding of the depth of knowledge and skill required in fields other than their own. The vocational educator should not make a similar mistake and assume that a knowledge of the disciplines can be acquired easily on the job with no formal preparation.

A discipline is a way of thinking. It provides a conceptual framework for attacking problems. It describes, defines, and classifies information. Most importantly, it provides a means of predicting outcomes and of testing these predictions. By these standards, vocational education is not a discipline. At this state in our development, it is probably fortunate that we are not, since we need to try a wide variety of ways of viewing and attacking the problems which face us.

The disciplines have affected vocational education in two principal ways. They have produced researchers within each discipline who have explored their own interests, have accumulated knowledge and have disseminated it. After a long period of time, bits of this knowledge have become part of the education of most persons, and have affected decisions in vocational education. This is a very inefficient process, for not only is it slow, but vital bits of knowledge are not widely communicated.

Vocational education recently has begun to employ specialists from the academic disciplines to work on vocational education problems. This has been done directly in university vocational education departments, research centers, or in research coordinating units in state departments of education. More frequently it has been done indirectly through research contracts and grants. Fortunately the involvement of persons from the disciplines has been expanding rapidly, largely because these academicians are finding that the problems of vocational education are intrinsically interesting and challenging, and offer new insights within the disciplines.

Chapter 6 PHILOSOPHIC FOUNDATIONS

Occupational education programs may be provided to students at many different age levels, from early childhood to late adulthood, and in many different settings, from trial and error learning on the job, to highly structured graduate school education. When these programs are provided in formal schools, the educational philosopher has a great deal to say about their content, methods, and goals. Most educational philosophers have chosen (rightly or wrongly) to restrict their views to the elementary and secondary schools and to higher education, but they should have something to say about occupational education which is provided by employers, unions, philanthropic or governmental groups, or private trade schools, because these are also involved in the process of education.

What To Teach?

The most important question in educational philosophy is, "What should be taught?" Economists, sociologists, psychologists, and particularly educational philosophers are concerned with this question. Obviously it is impossible to teach and to learn everything.

The "explosion of knowledge" is real. So decisions have to be made and priorities established. Some material must be rejected; some must be taught to a fraction of the students, and some must be taught to all.

The key question is "What knowledge is of most value?" Today, when most philosophers pose this question, they are really asking, "What knowledge is of most value for *all* people?" (Though surely it is as important to ask "What knowledge is needed by each individual?") In Aristotle's day the question was, "What should a non-slave know?" In eighteenth century England, it was "What should a gentleman know?" But ever since John Dewey revolutionized our ideas of education, the prevailing view in this country has been that we should use education as a means of achieving the values of the American system. (Though occasionally individuals in our country who espouse extreme left-wing or right-wing views suggest that we accept Joseph Stalin's view of education as a weapon, "the effect of which depends . . . on who controls this weapon and at whom . . . it should strike" [15, p. 220].) The view of education as essential to democracy leads teachers to select course content which will enhance individual freedom and equal opportunity for educational development.

Since *all* students will live in a developing democracy, some educational philosophers believe that the school should present identical content to each student. The most persuasive case for identical content for all is presented by Broudy, *et al.*

> . . . some ideas are more general and consequently have a greater explanatory potential than others, and some cognitive operations are more pervasive and more strategic for understanding than others. . . . there are key ideas and criteria and . . . there are indispensable symbolic and logical operations without which interpretation cannot be adequate. A curriculum which includes these ideas can make a plausible claim to be 'needed' by all human beings and therefore to be studied by all of them (1, pp. 245-246 and p. 12).

Though Broudy, Smith, and Burnett were writing about the secondary school, they hold these same beliefs about the elementary school. So do many other educational philosophers.

However instead of the key ideas and indispensable operations called for by these philosophers, a common curriculum has developed which is based on success in further schooling. The key ideas have become those which glorify leisure, and the indispensable operations are those which lay the groundwork for success in graduate school. The net result is a common curriculum for kindergarten (or even early childhood education) through the junior high school with little regard for individual differences in talent or interest. Students who cannot carry a tune are expected to sing; those who are color blind are graded on their success in mixing colors; and those who enjoy manipulating objects spend as much time in their seats as those who enjoy manipulating ideas. Each student should have a right to try these activities, the right to fail in them, and the right to persist in that failure if he wishes it. But he should not be required to persist indefinitely in an activity which is not essential in his life.

A common curriculum based on success in further schooling was not what the philosophers wanted, but it is what has happened as a result of the mistaken belief that individual differences can be catered to by varying the teaching methods which are used, or by teaching at different levels of abstraction, depending on the intelligence of the pupil. The result is portrayed vividly in G. H. Reavis' biting satire, "The Animal School," where ". . . the duck was excellent in swimming, in fact better than his instructor; but he made only passing grades in flying and was very poor in running . . . he had to stay after school and also drop swimming in order to practice running . . . an abnormal eel who could swim exceedingly well and also run, climb, and fly a little had the highest average and was valedictorian." (11, p. 141).

In the high school (unlike the elementary school) the argument for identical content for all students has not been implemented. The pressures exerted by colleges and local employers who want certain content taught have been more persuasive. Only in the "general curriculum" have the views of educational philosophers had much weight, but those views have not had a fair trial in the general curriculum because the students who are enrolled are rejects from the college preparatory and vocational curricula. On every count, the results of the general curriculum have been very poor, but we do not know how much of this failure is due to an ineffective application of educational philosophy and how much must be charged to the segregation of students who are difficult to educate.

It is hard to quarrel with the Broudy, Smith, and Burnett curriculum theory as the basis for most of the content of the elementary school, and of at least the first two years of high school. Even for those students in the last two years of a secondary school vocational curriculum, they provide the rationale for a curriculum which should occupy at least half of the student's time. However, content based entirely on the demands of the next level of education, which results in "school for schooling's sake," cannot be justified. Nor can we justify content based entirely on the demands of employers.

WHICH KEY IDEAS AND SKILLS SHOULD BE TAUGHT?

The first criterion imposed by the educational philosopher is that nothing should be taught in the school that will be learned adequately and efficiently in another of society's institutions. The family, the church, the place of employment, and the communications media all have educative functions. The school has too much to do to allow it to spend its valuable time in unnecessary and inefficient duplication of functions. Unfortunately, however, some families are not as effective teachers as others. Some education by employers and by communications media is designed to benefit individuals other than the student. So the school has a responsibility to some individuals who would be short-changed by other institutions. For example, the school has a responsibility to teach consumer education because it is probably less biased than most other agencies who are also engaged in consumer education.

A second criterion for choosing content assumes that all students will have to live in a common culture, and that all instruction (at least through the twelfth grade) should be based on the demands of that common culture. Certainly all students will be expected to deal with certain common cultural views, but the lower-class culture is markedly different from that of the middle-class. Which culture should the school choose as its ideal? Since most teachers are products of the middle-class culture, that is the one which is most likely to be taught, though middle-class teachers faced with a group of lower-class students often decide not to teach certain topics on the grounds that "the poor little dears couldn't possibly be expected to learn because of the disadvantaged background from which they come."

A third criterion for content selection suggests that if we have a choice between teaching a concept which explains a broad aspect of the environment and one which explains only a narrow aspect, we should choose the former. The reason for this is based solely on efficiency of instruction. If a useful, broad concept can be learned in the same amount of time as a narrow concept, the general concept is obviously a better choice. Yet, a concept may be so general as to be inefficient for instructional purposes. A special problem arises in teaching a general concept which really will be useful, but does not appear so to the students. Students are usually asked to accept and learn such "cold storage" concepts because the teacher says they will be useful later. The younger the student the more likely he is to accept and learn on the basis of faith. If he is older, rebellious, and has had previous experiences which lead him to mistrust adults, he is more likely to demand evidence that the material is relevant for him. Too often, the teacher provides a justification which applies only to students planning to enter the professions.

A fourth criterion is based on the concept that each student should understand, be able to control, and be confident in his environment. Each of the organized disciplines is devoted to understanding and attempting to control a portion of the environment. Because they are well organized and have been subjected to continued refinement, they appear to be

efficient vehicles of instruction. However, practitioners of the disci-
pines are specialists, and tend to try to make specialists of their students.
It is impossible for an individual to become a specialist in each of the
disciplines (the typical large university has more than one hundred
departments, each representing one or more disciplines). Therefore, the
school must restrain this natural tendency of practitioners to recruit
disciples, and during the first years of schooling must devote its time to
instruction which is needed by non-specialists. This certainly includes
instruction about the importance of the world of work.

THE EDUCATION OF SPECIALISTS AND NON-SPECIALISTS

In a democracy, every student must have enough education to enable
him to understand the basic problems of society and to vote intelligently.
In addition, it is a basic tenet of democracy that the individual should
have the opportunity to develop fully his human talents. Every citizen
should be able to review his life and feel that he has had multiple chances
to explore his strengths and weaknesses, to try different paths of life,
and to choose life styles which fit his needs and talents. The school should
provide many of these opportunities, but above all, it should provide
the student with the skills, knowledges, and attitudes which will encourage
him to seek out opportunities, and take advantage of them when they
arise.

Citizenship demands general education (that education which is needed
by all). Vocational competence and personal development demand both
general education and specialized education (that education needed by
some, but not all). Most educational philosophers agree that the elementary school should concentrate on general education and the graduate school should concentrate on specialized education. The arguments
occur with regard to the role of the secondary school, the community
college, and the baccalaureate program. Those who believe that twelve
or sixteen years of general education are necessary for citizenship would
deny specialized schooling to anyone who drops out of the school before
high school or college graduation. Thus, Broudy, *et al.* feel free to say,

> Presumably . . . problem solving courses will come late in the school
> life of the pupil. This means, of course, that early dropouts may
> miss them altogether. This is regrettable, but then one regrets all
> dropouts if they occur before their learning potential is exploited
> to the full. There seems to be little point in giving problem solving
> instruction to those who have not been sufficiently motivated to
> master the other parts of the curriculum by which intelligent en-
> counters with problems are made possible (1, p. 272).

These authors do believe in specialized education, for they say,
". . . specialized training is so necessary for *everyone* that one layer of

our educational system should be devoted exclusively to it rather than treating it as a substitute for, or as an orphan of, common, general education" (1, p. 182). These philosophers would deny with passion that they are elitist, but it is difficult to otherwise classify those who would deny an essential part of education to those who choose not to continue in school beyond the compulsory age of attendance. The key to their position lies in the assumption that problem solving should be postponed because other things must be learned before intelligent problem solving is possible. This assumption is questionable, for psychologists and historians have demonstrated that complex problems have been solved by persons who had relatively little formal educational background.

More important, however, is the failure of many educational philosophers to recognize the value of specialized education as a motivating force for all education (perhaps because they, themselves, come from the group of students who see the pursuit of knowledge as intrinsically desirable for its own sake).

> Education is really not a series of separate little containers of knowledge, though we tend to act as if it were and thereby to establish further barriers to effective learning. A vocational objective . . . could be the vehicle to bring the containers together, to allow each student to see education in an action setting and to provide more flexible paths toward its attainment . . . The current tendency to give a student initial general education, then specialization, is inappropriate on pedagogical grounds, and is at the root of the major problems in curriculum development. Nor does it fit an educational philosophy which holds that culture and vocation cannot be separated . . . The intertwining of liberal and vocational elements in an educational program seeking to expand opportunity for a major proportion of our population is . . . a necessity (4, pp. 8, 10, 11).

Haskew and Tumlin are even more positive.

> Occupation-labeled courses frequently are prime vehicles for achieving such outcomes as ability to handle quantitative relationships, command of problem-solving processes, and many other 'prime essentials of schooling.' In fact, such achievements for some pupils have proved to be impossible in the absence of occupation-centered methodology. In the second place, occupation-centering is typically used as a magnet which holds pupils in contact with so-called general education. In the third place, some vocational education reinforces much abstract learning by affording opportunities for practical application; thus helping general education make sense (6, p. 68).

The student who chooses an occupational goal (even if that goal may later be changed) has an education "organizer" which serves as a unifying force and provides meaning to everything he studies. Some students can and do learn without this particular organizer, but for all students formal, specialized instruction lends further meaning to general education. Separation of general and specialized instruction into different institutions and non-concurrent blocks of time minimizes this interaction. At the same time, it maximizes educational segregation based on social class. In every educational institution, for at least part of the time, students from all backgrounds should learn together.

SOCIAL CLASS DISTINCTIONS IN OCCUPATIONAL EDUCATION

Most educational philosophers in the United States agree that occupational education should not be designed exclusively, or even primarily for potential dropouts, slum youth, minority youth, or for students who have lower than average academic ability. To do so would create class distinctions which are inimical to a democracy. There can be no serious quarrel with this concept. Project TALENT indicates that the full range of social class and academic ability is represented in vocational education. The fact that students of lower ability and from lower class homes are significantly over-represented in vocational education is not necessarily bad if the choice is made by the students and not by the school. It would be detrimental if the school, consciously or unconsciously, designed curricula which promoted segregation by social class. Every curriculum should be available, in fact as well as in theory, to the children of physicians and laborers, alike.

It is indefensible to accept a belief that ". . . only the hard core might well benefit in secondary school vocational education programs . . . he (the "hard core" student) belongs in vocational education programs, and . . . we must develop programs that get at understanding responsibility and all the rest that goes with the kind of positions hard core misfits can hope to fill" (14, p. 28). Yet it is true that failure to provide effective vocational education programs which serve all youth in the schools has led to the development of the federally-supported remedial programs operated outside the schools. Similarly, it is indefensible to hold that the school has an obligation to provide specialist training only for those students who plan to be professionals. Mays is correct in pointing out that "Neither the extent of education, expert knowledge, character of social service, or method of remuneration, nor any other factor appears that is common to (the professionals) but not found in other callings. One is therefore driven to the conclusion that the classification of *profession* is arbitrary, based solely upon custom or social dictum" (8, p. 9). It seems absurd to use this arbitrary classification as a basis for determining what should be taught in the schools.

It seems equally absurd to hold that specialized education is appropriate for "high-level" occupations but not for those at a lower level, or that specialized education is appropriate for middle and upper class students, but not for students from the lower class.

Most educational philosophers are middle-class professionals. In their desire for unity in education they often specify (probably unconsciously) a common curriculum based on the requirements for the professions. If these philosophers were from a lower socio-economic group, they might well (again unconsciously) base the contents of the common curriculum on the requirements of the skilled trades. The common curriculum based on the needs of professionals is supported whole-heartedly by most other academic professionals, and by many of the non-academic professionals who control school boards. Compelled by society to provide education for all, they keep control by insuring that the education offered meets their own needs. They deny the education needed by non-professionals, then (supreme irony) heap indignities on those who drop out of the educational system because of its lack of personal relevance.

DUALITY IN EDUCATION

Most contemporary American educational philosophers dislike dualism intensely. One group believes that there is an essential unity in everything, and searching for it is an important task. These educational philosophers apply this reasoning to the school. They feel that surely, if they will but look hard enough, they will find a common curriculum which will meet the needs of all students. They may well be right, but this curriculum has not as yet been found. The closest approach to it is the "general curriculum," a goal-less, non-vocational, non-college preparatory program, found in most high schools. Though students in the general curriculum are between the students in the college preparatory and the vocational curricula with regard to academic aptitude and socio-economic status, they are remarkably unsuccessful, both in and outside the school. Seventy percent of the high school dropouts come from the general curriculum, though it enrolls less than a fourth of the high school students. Of those who manage to graduate, fewer go on to post-secondary education than from any other high school curriculum (2, pp. 353, 359). And 88 percent of the enrollees in Manpower Development and Training Act (MDTA) programs come from the high school general curriculum, compared with 10 percent from college preparatory, and 2 percent from vocational curricula (9, p. 29). Since MDTA was established to serve high school dropouts and the hard-core unemployed, this preponderance of enrollment from the general curriculum is perhaps understandable. But obviously the general curriculum is not meeting the needs of the students enrolled in it.

Even if the general curriculum could be revised so that it did meet student needs, philosophers would not have solved the problem of dualism in education by setting up a common curriculum for the first twelve years of schooling, and specifying that the next two to ten years of education should be devoted to specialization. This would be more dualistic than the comprehensive high school ever has been, and it contains two defects. This plan forgets that when taught concurrently, specialized and general education reinforce each other. Secondly, it would deny the benefits of specialized education to those students who cannot (for economic reasons) or will not (from lack of motivation) attend school from age six to twenty-six.

Another major group of educational philosophers, the pluralists, also rejects dualism. They feel that the division of the real world into artificial dichotomies such as mind vs. body, theory vs. practice, academic vs. non-academic, and vocation vs. general is undesirable. As do most Americans, they tend to be pragmatists and value what "works well." What seems to work well in education is the provision of a variety of goals, content, and methods which can be matched with the variety of goals, abilities, and achievements which students bring to the school.

The great majority of educational administrators in the United States are pluralists, and are interested in meeting the needs of all of their students. What they need and want are positive suggestions of ways in which this can be accomplished.

The Uses of Knowledge

Broudy, Smith, and Burnett (1) identify four uses of knowledge: associative, replicative, interpretive, and applicative. Any bit of knowledge may be used in each of these ways, but some knowledge is more likely to be used in one way than another.

The *associative* use of knowledge occurs in such diverse fields as the appreciation of poetry and puns, scenery and scents. It is the calling to mind of knowledge by the association of one word or thought with another. The two do not have to be logically related. A product makes one think of the maker. A song makes one think of a place in which it was once sung. A single word, "die," makes one think of a dozen situations which have little relationship to each other. We could exist reasonably well without using knowledge associatively, but this use of knowledge gives an aesthetic richness to the use of words and other sensory images which they would not otherwise have. The more general or specialized education an individual has, the more likely he is to use this knowledge associatively, for one bit of knowledge calls to mind another.

Most formal schooling, both general and specialized, is concerned with the *replicative* use of knowledge. Recall of facts and use of skills in exactly the way they were taught in school is very common. "What is two plus two?" calls forth the answer, "Four," in or out of school. If a particular bit of knowledge has only replicative use within the school, it is worthless. The more that material learned in school relates to life, the more it can be used replicatively. However, since the school can never foresee all the requirements of life, it must teach students more than just the replicative uses of knowledge.

The highest levels of education lead to the *interpretive* and *applicative* uses of knowledge, through which we view new situations, interpret their meaning, and choose appropriate courses of action. Problem solving, family life, trouble shooting, invention, and adaptation all require interpretation and application. Some philosophers hold that application can be done only by specialists, and that it should not be a part of general education. These men would stop with interpretation. To say that general education should stop short of problem solving seems quite unrealistic, for we all need to solve problems which are unrelated to our field of specialization.

Most of vocational education (and most of general education) is devoted to the replicative uses of knowledge. Many critics of vocational education believe that it consists of nothing else. If this were true, vocational education would have little long-range utility, for the replicative use of knowledge cannot cope with changes in job content unless the worker is re-trained. Actually, the only types of vocational education that stop at this level are certain on-the-job (OJT) training programs and elementary technical programs in the armed forces. In such programs, nomenclature is memorized, and rigid step by step procedures are mandatory. Better quality OJT and advanced level military technical education, like all of the rest of vocational education, place strong emphasis on the interpretive and applicative uses of knowledge.

Both general and vocational education need to stress the applicative and interpretive uses of knowledge more. If this is done, the associative uses of knowledge will take care of themselves. All three uses are markedly facilitated by the interaction of general and vocational education. Replicative uses of knowledge are most subject to obsolescence caused by developing technology. Fortunately, this very technology is quite efficient in retrieving knowledge for replicative use. This lessens the need to teach masses of facts, recipes, and set procedures in school.

Types of Knowledge

A classification scheme which overlaps the four uses of knowledge, has been proposed by Elizabeth Macia and adapted by D. G. Lux and other staff members of the Industrial Arts Curriculum Project (7, p. 7).

1. Event or descriptive knowledge describes phenomena and the interrelationships among phenomena. The sciences are largely made up of this type of knowledge.
2. Valuational or prescriptive knowledge is concerned with whether or not something is worthwhile, good, true, or beautiful. The fine arts and humanities concern themselves principally with this area of knowledge.
3. Formal or structural knowledge is an attempt to find a structure or form for all knowledge. Formal mathematics and logic are attempts at such structures.
4. The knowledge of practice, or praxiological knowledge, covers man's ways of acting efficiently to reach the goals that he values. Instruction in all the professions and vocations must include such knowledge, an internship, plus previous or concurrent instruction in related aspects of the other basic types of knowledge.

PRAXIOLOGY

The term "praxiology" comes from the Greek "praxis" meaning "a doing" or "an action." The common suffix "ology" indicates a systematic study. Praxiology is the key to occupational education and to most other purposeful education at all levels. It must be differentiated from practice itself ("practice" is used here as a noun, not as a verb). Imitation, which is the sole content of much on-the-job training, is practice, not praxiology. Practice without praxiology will usually have adverse effects, since it is not based on theory. When the job content changes, that part of practice immediately become obsolete. If an inadvertent change in process or material occurs, the change is not self-correcting, so practice alone leads to changes which are often in an undesirable direction.

Praxiology must be based on descriptive and valuational knowledge, but it goes beyond them to search for efficiency and rationality in practice. It provides an answer to the question, "Why should we follow this particular procedure?" Practice without praxiology says, "This is the procedure to follow. Don't inquire why." But praxiology goes further. It provides at least tentative answers to questions such as: "What procedure should be followed if conditions of practice are changed?" "What is a rational way of deciding which of two procedures is more efficient?" "Is this procedure necessary at all?" Practice combined with praxiology leads to real skill, or as Hegel put it, to consciousness without self-consciousness.

The elementary and secondary schools have almost completely ignored praxiology, and have stressed descriptive knowledge. Minor emphasis has been placed on valuational and structural knowledge. Praxiology has flowered in the university, with graduate programs being almost solely devoted to it. Even at the undergraduate level, engineering, education, chemistry, marketing, agriculture, nursing and many other professional programs devote considerable time to praxiology.

Both praxiology and practice (the noun, not the verb) are examples of knowledge which is use applicatively. According to Broudy, Smith, and Burnett the applicative uses of knowledge are valuable only to specialists and should be taught outside the common school. Unfortunately, they do not distinguish between practice and praxiology, and do not recognize that general education, praxiology, and practice are mutually supportive for all students. Moreover, for many students, all three must be present for effective learning to occur.

With the possible exception of a few brain-damaged students, no one in the common school should ever be taught a practice without concurrently learning the theory behind that practice. Except in time of national emergency, no student should be taught the practice and praxiology of an occupational field without being taught at nearly the same time a substantial amount of the descriptive and valuational knowledge which is part of general education. Teaching these types of knowledge concurrently leads the student to see relationships and relevances which could not otherwise be learned. Even better would be a program which was taught concurrently by teachers who *planned* their general and specialized instruction to be mutually supportive.

The comprehensive high school and the community college regularly design their vocational curricula to make sure that general education, praxiology, and practice all are taught during the school year, though they rarely make certain that their presentations are mutually supportive. Attempts to design separate schools devoted only to practice or to practice plus praxiology are educationally and socially unwise, yet many armed forces schools and industry operated schools do just this. Segregation by educational goals is justified by the operators of these schools on the basis of efficiency, but the efficiency, if it exists at all, is short-term and often benefits the proprietor more than the student. This can be illustrated by an example from training in the armed forces. During World War II, vocational educators in the armed forces designed programs for electronics technicians which were some two years in length. They included theory of the use of electronics (praxiology); skill in design, construction, and troubleshooting (practice); plus basic science (descriptive knowledge) and communication skills (descriptive plus valuational knowledge). These programs produced excellent electronics technicians, yet the armed forces were dissatisfied because instead of re-enlisting, most of the graduates were employed by private industry when their enlistments expired. This well-rounded vocational curriculum was replaced by a short instructional program which emphasized only practice, and enabled the graduates to repair only one piece of equipment, using a rigidly prescribed procedure. These graduates were not desired by industry, so they were more likely to re-enlist. After the soldier was thoroughly acclimated to military life, he was offered the opportunity to attend a broad electronics education program if he would agree to enlist for a period of time which would make it financially desirable for him to stay on to retirement at about age forty. Clearly the revised system was more advantageous in the short run to the armed forces, but it was less desirable for most students. The armed forces leadership is now coming to believe that in the long run, this decision has had adverse effects on our national defense. Much, if not most, of the vocational education offered by small employers is dominated by similar considerations, for they, too, cannot afford to lose trained workers to competitors. Large corporations are more likely to offer broad vocational education, since their workers have better opportunities for promotion within the company, and are therefore less likely to leave. However, few American companies can count on a life-time commitment from all their employees to the extent that Japanese companies once could. This leads American companies to provide broad vocational education only to those employees who seem most promotable.

The Concept of Vocation in Philosophy

Aristotle believed that there were two types of work: bread-labor, work for the purpose of subsistence; and leisure-work, or labor which was interesting in and of itself. Slaves and serfs engaged in bread-work, because if they did not they would starve. Freemen pursued careers in government, religion, and in the arts and sciences, not to earn a living, but for the satisfaction which came from doing something interesting. Since these were the same reasons used to choose a leisure-time activity, the term leisure-work seemed appropriate. Bread-labor might by chance be interesting. Slaves who were artisans and teachers often enjoyed their work. But this was purely fortuitous and of little importance. The key question was, could you stop work without economic penalty? If the answer was "no," the work was clearly undesirable for the free citizen, even though it might be necessary for the state.

Though Paul states that if a man will not work he shall not eat (II Thessalonians, 3, 10) the medieval church interpreted this to mean that while the natural law imposed this obligation on the human race, it did not apply to certain individuals. Thus those who engaged in religious contemplation or those who begged for the church (mendicant friars) were exempt. There was a ranking of occupation from the servile tasks of the peasant to the highest duties of the clergy. But all vocations were assigned by God, and it was futile and blasphemous to attempt to change vocations. The Reformation produced a considerable change in attitude. Partly because of the Plague, there was no longer an adequate supply of slaves or serfs to do the unpalatable but necessary tasks required by society. In this setting we find Luther stating that every legitimate calling has exactly the same worth in the sight of God, though each vocation was still assigned by heaven.

The modern view of philosophy and economics toward work began with Adam Smith, who recognized that "It is not from the benevolence of the butcher, the brewer, or the baker that we expect our dinner, but from their regard to their own interest. We address ourselves, not to their humanity, but to their self-love; and never talk to them of our own necessities, but of their advantages" (13, p. 14). This was a bit too crass, however, and we find Ruskin and Tolstoy, among others, recognizing that man does not work only for economic self-interest, but because work is psychologically necessary. If you do not work, you die spiritually. Perhaps the most extreme expression of this point of view comes from K. D. Ushinsky, the great Russian educator: "The tangible fruits of work constitute human property; but the only source of human dignity, and at the same time of morality and happiness, is the inner spiritual, life-giving power of work itself" (16, p. 26). Most people would not accept a concept of work as the ". . . *only* source of . . . morality." Yet in his book, *Round the Bend*, Nevil Shute, a supporter of capitalism and individualism, expounds a religion based on work, with the highest morality based on work performed accurately and conscientiously (12).

Now if work is important to human dignity, how do we find this dignity in modern life? It was relatively easy in Benjamin Franklin's day. He said, accurately, "He who hath a trade hath an estate." Back then the skilled worker performed a variety of interesting tasks and could expect to perform them for the remainder of his life, using, essentially unchanged, the knowledge he had learned as an apprentice.

The growth of modern industry and business has been based on two factors which often are inimical to the dignity of work: (1) specialization of work, and (2) constant changes of work content to promote efficiency. Specialization of work decreases the variety of each workman's tasks, sometimes to the point that a single bodily movement is repeated rapidly all day long. The constant search for greater efficiency means that at least part of a worker's knowledges and skills will become obsolete. "Specialization . . . makes the development of skill possible . . ." (17, p. 161) for every worker; changes in work content make it necessary to re-train every worker periodically. Marx and Engels were wrong in their belief that specialization would chain each worker for life to a particular repetitive job and a particular tool. Change is so rapid now that many people do not spend even a year on the same task. Also, Engels did not foresee the rapid introduction of automation which is taking over the menial tasks of the past.

The dignity of work lends dignity to the worker. Conversely, "Labor acquires a character of irksomeness by virtue of the indignity imputed to it" (17, p. 30). Unfortunately our schools now teach that labor, other than academic labor, is not dignified. Let us examine why this is so.

Elements Missing in General Education

The major group determining the school curriculum is made up of academics, many of whom have had little or no experience outside the school. They have gone through each level of schooling, and have had no employment outside the school. Their social contacts are limited too often to people in the professions who share a similar school background. These academics write textbooks, sit on curriculum committees, and, as teachers, decide what will be emphasized in classrooms. As administrators and faculty members, they control the reward structure in the schools. Advisory committees which attempt to suggest major changes are not reconvened. School boards are told to stick to "policy" decisions while the academics determine what will be taught and how. The primary influence of the student is the negative one of dropping out. The primary influence of the general public is the negative one of refusing to approve tax increases for school operation, and the general public is influenced greatly by academics who insist that the prime measure of a school's success is the proportion of graduates who enter college. As a result of this "academic incest," the school tends to value school for its own sake, to design each level of schooling to prepare for the next, and to regard anyone who drops out of school prior to completion of a doctorate as a failure. This has resulted in the elimination of a major portion of our heritage, called by Max Weber the "protestant ethic," and the substitution of a meritocracy based on school achievement.

THE UNTAUGHT CURRICULUM

In spite of its name, the protestant ethic has little to do with religion. The name comes from the fact that during the later phases of the Reformation, most Western peoples substantially changed their views of occupations. Christians from Paul through Luther saw a "calling" or occupation as something sent from heaven. In practice, a man's occupation was almost invariably the occupation of his father. But because it was felt to be heaven-sent, it would have been impious to choose a different occupation, for this would be rebellion against God. "Let every man abide in the same calling wherein he was called" (I Corinthians vii, 20, King James version). Calvin's followers had a very different view. For them, an occupation was to be chosen by the individual and to be pursued strenuously and exactingly with a sense of religious purpose. This produced capitalists and workman who were frugal and diligent, and resulted in industries and businesses which were efficient beyond any level previously attained. Prior to the acceptance of the protestant ethic the proverb was "Either eat well or sleep well." After its acceptance, a man could do both. The major factor in allowing him to sleep well was a contented feeling which Weber calls ". . . the irrational sense of having done his job well" (18, p. 71). Rational or not, it was a major factor in the industrial development of the West, because it produced skilled and conscientious labor and management. The traditional cycle of sin, repentance, atonement and release which incorporated the freedom to sin again, was incompatible with the undeviating promptness, sobriety, and attention to duty which made the industrial revolution possible.

The concept of leisure also changed radically. Up to Calvin's time, leisure occupied all of the day which was not required for earning subsistence. For lower class workers, the working hours were long, but were broken by feast days and by enforced leisure due to unemployment. For managers, "The number of business hours was very moderate, perhaps five to six a day, sometimes considerably less" (18 p. 66). After Calvin's time, leisure was seen as a voluntary absence of work which had been earned, and which refreshed the worker so that when he returned to work he would perform more effectively. The goal of leisure was work, rather than the goal of work being leisure. "The old leisurely and comfortable attitude toward life gave way to a hard frugality in which some participated and came to the top" (18, p. 68). Both managers and workers were affected. The former greatly increased the rigor of their supervision, setting new quantity and quality standards, and the workers had to be trained to meet these standards.

Benjamin Franklin was the prophet of this new concept in America, and his proverbs were a major component of American education during the eighteenth and nineteenth centuries. Partly due to his influence, the protestant ethic was accepted by nearly everyone in the northern United States. After the destruction of the plantation system following the Civil War, it was accepted by majority groups everywhere in the country. In this case, our lack of European traditions was a tremendous benefit to our expanding industrial economy. Franklin may also be regarded as the prophet of vocational education in America. Although the colleges and the public schools lagged by fifty to one hundred years, respectively, in accepting the responsibility of producing well qualified non-professional workers through formal vocational education, they accepted Franklin's statements of the values of the protestant ethic early and taught them assiduously throughout the nineteenth century. Private trade schools, business, and industry taught these values and the specific skills and knowledges needed for workers and managers to put the values into practice.

During the twentieth century, schools began to doubt the efficacy of the ideals of the protestant ethic. Some people interpreted these ideals to mean that personal success could and should be achieved at the expense of others. Anti-trust laws, income taxes, and other restraints were imposed in an attempt to retard the dominance of certain groups who had justified their acts in terms of the protestant ethic. More importantly, it became clear that the protestant ethic was not bringing success to a sizeable portion of the population. Though some were getting rich, others were starving. Some minority groups which were quickly assimilated had no long-term difficulty. Others, such as the Indians, Mexican-Americans, and Negroes, who were visually different, did not profit at all from acceptance of the protestant ethic. They could work as hard and conform as closely as possible to the ethic and still not succeed because they were stereotyped with those of their group who did not conform because they preferred their own ethic. Orientals who accepted the protestant ethic even more fully than the white majority were rejected on the ground that they worked too hard.

At the same time a series of moves was made to take religion out of the public schools. In the first half of the twentieth century most public schools were clearly Protestant. They forced students of other faiths to observe Protestant religious holidays, used Protestant religious literature, and hired Protestant teachers. (In those communities where Catholics were a strong majority, Catholic holidays, literature, and teachers were the norm.) Something needed to be done, and most schools, to avoid controversy, simply stopped teaching all values except academic ones: don't cheat on examinations, don't plagiarize, and honor thy teacher and thy principal. The protestant ethic was a casualty, not because it was religious (for American Catholics, Jews, and Protestants alike accepted it), but because it was a value, and all out-of-school values had to go. It was not an important in-school value because it had been replaced by the academic meritocracy which held that those who were low in academic aptitude were doomed to failure regardless of how hard they tried. Conscientious work and other protestant ethic virtues were a necessary but not sufficient condition for school success. Yet, if you had a sufficient measure of academic aptitude, it was not even necessary to work conscientiously to obtain success in school.

The net effect is that today the values of work simply are not taught as a part of general education. Nor are they taught in the home. The child no longer sees his parents at work, for the place of employment excludes visitors except on the annual visiting day when no work is done. No longer does the child have work of his own to do, for he is likely to do as much harm as good in the mechanized home. In school he is exposed to those "jolly community helpers," the policeman, the fireman, and the postman, but they are not workers, for in the school version of their lives, they need no training, perform only delightful functions, need no supervision, and receive no pay. Even in vocational education laboratories the values of the protestant ethic are usually absent. Unless the student is enrolled in a cooperative education program, carries newspapers, lives on a farm, or is involved in that interesting simulation of employment, Junior Achievement, he has absolutely no contact with employment or with the ethics of work. Clearly, the protestant ethic and related vocational values form the major untaught curriculum of the school.

The preceding discussion has identified two major difficulties with the traditional protestant ethic: (1) it has not worked well for those minority groups which are easily stereotyped, and (2) it has been used by certain individuals to justify personal advancement at the expense of others. The latter can be disposed of by identifying it as a perversion of the ideal, but education must teach that such perversions exist and should be dealt with firmly by society.

The problem of the "visible" minority groups, however, is more difficult. There are those who say that if a portion of a minority group does not value work, it would be morally wrong for the schools to impose such a value on them. But the schools do not impose the value. It is society which values work, and it is one of the major tasks of the school to prepare students to survive and achieve in society. It is the most blatant hypocrisy to teach a student that he can hold any values he pleases, and then to throw that student into a competitive world which gives him a choice beween accepting its work values, or leading a life of squalor. It is perfectly acceptable for the school to work to change society's values, but it is not acceptable for the school to lie to its students by telling them that as long as they conform to the academic values, they may hold any values they like outside of school.

In spite of the fact that schools do not teach it, the vast majority of people in our society believe in the ideal man of the protestant ethic: a man who works diligently, enjoys his work and does not let unrelated activities distract him from it, and saves his money and goods for tomorrow, even if it means self-denial today.

During the depression of the thirties, when 25 percent of the labor force was unemployed, it was apparent that this ideal was not working. But today most people have forgotten the depression, or regard it as temporary aberration due to the greed of stock market speculators who were not following the ideals of the ethic. The only real modification in this ideal since Weber stated it in 1904 has been the acceptance of the view that for a few (but very few) persons, chance can cause disadvantage; and the addition of the portion of the Hippocratic oath which enjoins one from doing harm. The major group which does not accept this revised protestant ethic is the lower-lower class, for whom the protestant ethic has not worked. But the lower-lower class is decreasing rapidly in size. The other classes in society accept the protestant ethic as readily as did the merchant aristocracy of one hundred years ago, and for the same reason—it makes one feel good to be able to attribute one's success to his own merits, rather than to chance or to other factors over which he has no control. This suggests that, contrary to the views of alienated youth, the protestant ethic is not disappearing, but is stronger than ever, outside the schools.

Work and Leisure

Thomas Green draws a sharp distinction between "work" and "labor." He feels that labor is futile, because we labor in order to use up what has been produced and thus add nothing of consequence to society. Work, on the other hand, is a "quest for potency" which allows us to express our individuality. To find the place where our actions can have real consequences is the only means for discovering who we really are, and only in a leisure society can we maximize the opportunities for every man to find work. Schools do not prepare the student for work and leisure but rather prepare him for labor. Recognition of the futility of such preparation is a major cause of alienation between students and schools (5).

Until recently, most people felt we were well on the road to the leisure society valued so highly by Green. The popular literature assured us that every year man worked less and had more time for leisure. Thus work was seen as becoming less important, and education to enable people to enjoy this new leisure appeared to be more and more essential. Automation was seen as a force which would immediately decrease the work week, and eventually would result in only a small proportion of people needing to work at all.

One of the foremost authorities on leisure, De Grazia, agrees that the time actually spent at work is decreasing, but after adding up all of man's non-leisure activities, concludes: "Never before have so many Americans had so little time to call their own" (3, p. 64). More recently, data from the United States Bureau of Labor Statistics show clearly that for the last twenty years, even the time actually spent at work has been increasing (from forty to forty-three hours per week on the average). It is also very probable that automation is increasing the amount of time spent in work and work-related activities. Automation and other changes in work structure are decreasing the proportion of unskilled workers (in part because these jobs are most easily automated), and increasing the proportion of technicians and professionals. Unskilled workers have always had the greatest amount of leisure time, and professionals have had the least. These changes do not eliminate the need for education for effective use of leisure time, but it is clear that this need is not increasing as rapidly as the need for education to cope with increased work demands.

Summary

General education is that education needed by all students. (In practice, the education *given* to all students includes much which is not general education.) In addition to being valuable for citizenship, it provides the *basis* for personal and occupational development of the individual. Thus, some general education should precede specialized education (which is not the same for all individuals). General education and specialized education reinforce each other. Hence they should be taught concurrently during the latter part of an individual's schooling. Most of the content of specialized occupational education should focus on knowledge of the practice and the theory of practice (praxiology) required by one or more occupations.

Unfortunately, specialized occupational education is offered so late in the formal school that few dropouts from high school receive any of it. Yet many educational philosophers favor further postponement of all specialized education until post-secondary education. This would ensure that the majority of students would not get specialized occupational education in school. This postponement must not be allowed to occur until the vast majority of students are able to avail themselves of post-secondary education. Nor can the postponement be justified if a vital part of a student's education is delayed to be used as bait to force him to stay in school and to keep him off the labor market.

In addition to specialized occupational education, the school has an obligation to provide general occupational education for all students. This education should begin early and should emphasize the importance of vocations in life and the values of work to man and to society.

The major untaught curriculum of the school has to do with values, especially the values of work as they affect life. The protestant ethic, which formed a major portion of the content of elementary and secondary school education in the United States during the eighteenth and nineteenth centuries, has been discarded by the school along with most other values. All that remain are the academic values which deal with relationships between students and teachers. Though the protestant ethic has not worked well for "visible" minority groups, it is accepted in slightly revised form by the vast majority of our society and is likely to continue to be accepted as we work to make society better. The worst possible course for schools to take would be to teach students that the values held by society are unimportant and can be discarded with impunity.

Youth who have been taught that work is unimportant and that the protestant ethic is passé are in for a rude shock when they leave the sheltered world of the school and enter the real world of work. Education which differentiates between labor and work, and which prepares the student for work is desirable as a way of reducing alienation. In the final analysis, however, education which leads to effective work is necessary simply because work is essential to the survival of society. A society without labor (in Green's sense) is conceivable, but a society without work is not.

REFERENCES

1. Broudy, Harry S., B.O. Smith, and Joe R. Burnett, *Democracy and Excellence in American Secondary Education.* Chicago: Rand McNally & Company, 1964.

2. Combs, Janet, and W.W. Cooley, "Dropouts in High School and After School," *American Educational Research Journal*, V, No. 3, 343-363.

3. DeGrazia, Sebastian, *Of Time, Work, and Leisure*. New York: Anchor Books, Doubleday & Company, Inc., 1964.

4. Feldman, Marvin J., *Making Education Relevant*. New York: Ford Foundation, 1966.

5. Green, Thomas F., *Work, Leisure and the American Schools*. New York: Random House, Inc., 1968.

6. Haskew, L.D. and Inez Tumlin, "Vocational Education in the Common School," in *Vocational Education*, ed. M.L. Barlow. Chicago: University of Chicago Press, 1965.

7. Lux, Donald G., *et al. A Rationale and Structure for Industrial Arts Subject Matter*. Industrial Arts Curriculum Project Series C-002. Columbus: The Ohio State University, 1966.

8. Mays, Arthur B., *Principles and Practices of Vocational Education*. New York: McGraw-Hill Book Company, Inc., 1948.

9. Pucel, David J., *Variables Related to MTDA Trainee Employment Success in Minnesota*. Minneapolis: Department of Industrial Education, University of Minnesota, 1968.

10. Ray, Elizabeth M., "Social and Philosophical Framework in Vocational, Technical, and Practical Arts Education," *Review of Educational Research*, ed. J. Moss, Jr. XXXVIII, No. 4, 309-325.

11. Reavis, George H., "The Animal School," *Educational Forum*, XVII (January, 1953).

12. Shute, Nevil, *Round the Bend*. New York: Ballantine Books, Inc., 1951.

13. Smith, Adam, *Wealth of Nations*. Book I. New York: Modern Library, Inc. (A Division of Random House, Inc.), 1958.

14. Stadt, Ronald, "Man and Technology in Secondary School Curriculum," *Journal of Industrial Teacher Education*, VI, No. 2, 21-30.

15. Stalin, Joseph, *Nochal'naya Shkola*, 1946. Translated by Maurice J. Shore in *Soviet Education*. New York: Philosophical Library, Inc., 1947.

16. Ushinski, K.D., *Collected Works*, Vol. II. Moscow R.S.F.S.R.: Academy of Pedagogical Sciences, 1948. Translated by S.G. Shapovalenko, ed. in *Polytechnic Education in the U.S.S.R.* Paris: UNESCO, 1963.

17. Veblen, Thorstein, *The Theory of the Leisure Class*. New York: The New American Library of World Literature, Mentor Edition, 1953.

18. Weber, Max, *The Protestant Ethic and the Spirit of Capitalism*. Translated by Talcott Parsons. New York: Charles Scribner's Sons, 1958.

Chapter 7 ECONOMIC
FOUNDATIONS

Economics helps to identify "... the most efficient ways of utilizing available human, natural, and capital resources to fill the needs and achieve the objectives of society" (14, p. 5). All of these resources are scarce, and often they could be used in alternative ways. Occupational education is that program designed to develop people (our human resources) to use natural and capital resources wisely, and to participate fully and efficiently as productive members of society. Obviously economics and occupational education are related in important ways.

The Economic Revolution
and Vocational Education

There have been three great stages of economic history: (1) the agrarian stage in which natural resources were the critical determinant of wealth, (2) the industrial era when the accumulation and use of capital were the keys to economic growth, and (3) an emerging post-industrial economy in which human resources are rising to prime importance (14, p. 5). Vocational education began during the second of these three phases, so it was natural that it concentrated on meeting the needs of employers who had to have trained people in order to utilize their capital efficiently. In this type of economy, human resources development was clearly subordinate to the short-term needs of the labor market. When employers had an immediate need for skilled workers, vocational education flourished. When their needs were temporarily met, vocational education was expected to lie dormant, regardless of the people who needed vocational education to develop to their fullest potential.

This short-term approach neglected the need for long-range forecasting of labor market demands. It neglected the role of vocational education in motivating general education learnings. And, worst of all, it neglected the fact that human resources are perishable. Minerals, if undeveloped, wait indefinitely without deterioration. Machines may obsolesce, but if protected from the elements do not physically deteriorate from disuse. On the other hand, human beings, if undeveloped, neglected or underutilized, continue to get older, and less able to learn rapidly. Moreover, the attitudes of humans change as they become accustomed to the welfare check instead of to meaningful work.

In 1963, Congress recognized that vocational education needed to shift its goals to fit the needs of phase three of the economic revolution. These new goals emphasize development of human potential and the employment needs of people, regardless of short-term labor market needs. (Long-term shifts in labor market needs still have to be considered, however, for no one wants to prepare people for occupations in which additional workers will not be needed.) The net effect has been a sizeable expansion in occupational education — in numbers of people served, in types of people served, and in breadth of programs offered.

The smallest change has occurred in the proportion of people served. For the past forty years, approximately 25 percent of secondary school students have taken vocational education courses, with the percentage by states ranging from 10 to over 50 percent. High school enrollments in vocational education are likely to increase markedly only as the general curriculum is discontinued school by school. In post-secondary education, however, enrollments have increased significantly, with most of the increase occurring in technical education programs.

The most pronounced shift has been in types of people to be served. The Smith-Hughes Act of 1917 specified that vocational education students must be able to profit from the instruction offered. The instruction offered was designed to meet the needs of local employers who needed skilled workers. Students who were not able to meet employer's standards were excluded, regardless of the students' personal needs. Blacks, Indians, Mexican-Americans, the handicapped, and students who scored low on employment screening tests, have all been excluded at times from certain vocational education courses on the grounds that they could not profit from the instruction offered.

The new occupational education views the world differently. It would not exclude any students but would design courses and curricula to make sure that each student could profit from the instruction offered. It would be inclusive, rather than exclusive. Coincident with this change is a new flexibility in hiring standards and worker utilization by employers, with new opportunities for the disadvantaged appearing every day. Discrimination still exists, and barriers still remain, but the vocational educator has even less justification now for saying that certain individuals should not receive vocational education because they would be unemployable.

Equally important as we move from the second to the third stage of economic history is the increase in breadth of vocational education. Originally designed to meet the short-term needs of the local employer, the early occupational education programs were narrow, specific, and sometimes non-transferable. With the shift in goals to human resource development, vocational education emphasizes transferability of skill and knowledge, and strives to provide opportunities for geographic and occupational mobility. While vocational education was shifting its goals, economists were developing methods of stabilizing the economy and minimizing the rapid changes in general employment levels which had been common. With a relatively stable economy, the differences between short-term and long-term labor market needs have decreased. This allows the economist and the vocational educator to concentrate on long-range forecasting and preparation of people for long-range needs.

Economists' Contributions to Vocational Education

Vocational education frequently has been criticized for training people for occupations that no longer exist. This is not an accurate statement, since we know of no occupation which has disappeared entirely. The criticism really implies one or both of these questions:

1. Is vocational education preparing more people than can be absorbed into a given occupational field?
2. Would vocational education be more efficient if it decreased certain of its expenditures or increased other types of expenditures?

These are economic questions, and the vocational educator needs to have the help of economists to answer them. In order to be of help, economists need pertinent data. Decisions as to what data are pertinent must be made jointly by vocational educators and economists. Then the data must be collected and analyzed on a continuing basis. This process is in its infancy in vocational education. One of the first requirements is for vocational educators to acquire economic literacy and for economists to acquire literacy in vocational education. Only then can they talk to each other.

The first question asked previously concerns the number of people that should be prepared to enter a particular occupational field. To decide whether or not vocational education is preparing more people than can be absorbed into a given occupational field, four basic types of data are needed:

   A. How many new entrants to the occupation will be needed to meet expected expansions or contractions in the labor market, how many new entrants will be needed to replace workers who die, retire, or shift to a different occupational field, and what training will they need to compete successfully?
   B. What proportion of the people trained to enter an occupation actually do enter it, either immediately, or later in life?
   C. What are the types and amounts of re-training needed if we are to use our capital and natural resources wisely?
   D. How many persons are completing all types of vocational education programs in this occupational field?

Let us consider each of these questions more fully.

   A. How many new entrants to the occupation are needed to meet expected expansions or contractions in the labor market and how many new entrants will be needed to replace workers who will die, retire, or shift to a different occupational field? The latter part of this question looks at the *replacement* part of the manpower demand picture, but the two parts of the question are interrelated. The replacement workers can come from two different sources. If the demand in an occupational field is expanding, they must come principally from new entrants to the occupational field. These new entrants may be youth who enter the occupation or older workers who are re-trained to allow them to change occupations. But if the total demand for workers in the occupation is decreasing, replacements can come, in part at least, from people presently in the occupation. For example, suppose that in an occupational field which employs ten thousand workers, one thousand persons are needed annually as replacements for those who die, retire, or shift to other occupations. If total demand is unchanged, vocational education (of all types) needs to supply one thousand workers per year. But if the total demand expands 5 percent to 10,500 workers, vocational education needs to supply one thousand workers as replacements plus five hundred workers to meet expansion needs. Thus a 5 percent increase in total demand results in a 50 percent increase in the supply needed from vocational education.

If fifty vocational teachers can prepare the one thousand workers needed for normal replacement demand, and if five of these teachers usually resign, retire, or die each year, only five new teachers are needed annually. But a 5 percent increase in total demand calls for these five teachers, plus twenty-five new teachers to prepare five hundred additional workers. Thus a 5 percent increase in the demand for workers results in a 500 percent increase in the demand for vocational teachers. Because many vocational teachers are drawn from the ranks of workers, the situation is even worse. When we most need teachers, we also most need workers, so wages go up, and it is impossible to recruit teachers. Moreover, some teachers will return to their former, non-teaching occupation because of its higher wages.

If total demand for workers *decreases*, the situation is reversed dramatically. Using the same example of ten thousand workers, with one thousand needed annually for replacements, a 5 percent decrease in total demand drops the need for vocational graduates to five hundred each year. This cuts the total number of teachers needed to twenty-five. But we have fifty teachers who have been supplying the normal replacement demand of one thousand workers. Five of these teachers leave the field, and five are trained to replace them, but we have a 50 percent surplus of teachers as a result of a 5 percent decrease in demand for workers. The economist calls this phenomenon acceleration. This simple example illustrates graphically why vocational education historically has followed a "boom or bust" cycle of expansion or contraction. Only the fact that most in-school vocational programs have trained 20 percent or less of the new entrants to the labor market, has saved us from grave difficulty. Obviously, the nearer vocational education comes to providing the entire supply of new workers in a given occupational field, the greater the importance of the acceleration principle in vocational education planning.

The new philosophy of vocational education which calls for the best possible development of people, rather than meeting short-term labor market demands, should aid greatly in reducing the effects of acceleration. Programs which meet the needs of people must take long-term labor market demands into account. The labor economist must be responsible for determining long-term labor market needs, and the vocational educator must use this information in decision-making at the national, state, and local level. The only attempt at the national level to do this forecasting systematically and regularly has been published by the United States Department of Labor as the *Occupational Outlook Handbook*. It covers some seven hundred occupational fields and attempts to forecast moderate or sharp increases or decreases in demand for workers (both for replacements and for expansions in total demand). While these forecasts have been criticized sharply by economists, they seem sufficiently accurate for most vocational education planning. In any case, the *Handbook* summarizes the best available information. A new edition of the *Handbook* is prepared every two years. Between editions, the *Occupational Outlook Quarterly* provides current information. The *Handbook* has a good record of success in forecasting general magnitudes and directions of occupational change, though it has been conservative in estimating needs in new fields. It is, of course, of little value in determining the needs of a particular locality. Attempts to forecast the amounts of training which will be needed by each type of worker are less satisfactory than projections of quantitative demand.

B. What proportion of the people trained to enter an occupational field actually do enter it, either immediately, or later in life? It is very rare for all trainees to enter employment in the occupational field for which they were trained. This is as true of the education of lawyers and engineers as it is of barbers and stenographers. As a greater proportion of trainees enter their field of specialization, the more closely the number of trainees will approach the number of new entrants who are needed. This proportion varies widely by occupational field, from 67 percent for agriculture, to 92 percent for health occupations (24, p. 31). If 80 percent of the ten thousand students who are prepared to be automobile mechanics actually work in this field, it is the eight thousand rather than ten thousand students who must be considered when we make a decision as to whether or not we are educating too many people to be automobile mechanics. Women are more likely to delay entry into an occupation than are men. We need to know how many women are prepared to be typists but do not begin work as typists until ten years after they have left school.

C. What are the types and amounts of re-training needed if we are to use capital and natural resources wisely? This is the question asked most frequently by training directors of large corporations. They need to plan training programs within the company, and purchase educational services outside the company (both for their present employees and new recruits who are inadequately trained). They must consider not only the needs of their own firm, but also of competing firms. Small competitors usually do little formal training, and, therefore, will try to recruit employees from the large firm. However, the small firm may have a much better OJT program than the large firm, where jobs are often far more specialized. This may cause the large firm to recruit from the small one.

The planning of re-training programs is in its infancy. Most such training is in response to an immediate need, when a new product, process, or service has been introduced, and management suddenly discovers that it has an insufficient number of trained employees to cope with the change. This leads to a crash program of re-training. For example, the armed forces periodically install new weapons systems. It takes several years to develop such a new system, but it also takes time to design a training program, install it, and produce re-trained personnel. Ideally, the trained personnel ought to be available at the same time the new product or process is introduced. In practice, however, the new product or process is introduced, and by trial and error we determine what sorts of personnel are required to handle it. Only then is a training program planned. This traditional method works reasonably well when the product or process is introduced gradually, but it proves difficult when it is desirable to introduce the new procedures simultaneously throughout the organization.

As we gain experience in planning re-training programs on the basis of prototype products (rather than on the basis of experience in the field), we can shorten the lag between the introduction of new products, processes, and services and the availability of trained personnel to deal with them. The necessity for simulation in the training of personnel for space exploration requires the development of procedures for reducing this lag to near zero.

A second type of re-training is designed to cope with recurring problems which have not been solved by earlier training efforts. A typical example is the almost continuous re-training of first-line supervision. The tasks of the first-line supervisor change, but not rapidly. Much of their re-training is an effort to solve a long-term problem, for example in human relations, which earlier training programs tried and failed to solve. Whether the supervisor failed to learn the first time, or whether he no longer uses what he learned, re-training seems to be constantly necessary.

Still a third type of re-training is designed, not by the employer, but in response to demands from potential trainees. Schill, in his study of technicians in Illinois, found that a large majority of the technicians had acquired some post-secondary education (20, p. 35). His subsequent analysis revealed that most of these technicians had sought out courses which they thought would be useful to them in their careers, and had avoided courses which did not appear to be immediately useful. The majority was not interested in degrees or formal curricula. Many adult education students in secondary schools and community colleges have a similar orientation. This would suggest that educational programs should allow the consumers of education to make choices of courses they feel they need in a free market place, without tie-in sales which require them to take undesired courses as pre-requisites. More likely, as Associate in Arts degrees acquire more currency in the market place, A.A. students, like B.S. students, will accept undesired courses in order to get the valuable degree. We need to employ the methods of the economist to learn more about the role of the educational consumer in a free market place.

D. How many persons are completing vocational education programs in an occupational field? No data are available on the number of vocational graduates in the country as a whole, though some states are beginning to collect such information. This information is of course readily available at the local level, but unfortunately it has a limited value for local program planning because of actual and potential worker mobility. Assuming that this information will be more widely available at the state or national level in the future, we must recognize that our knowledge will still not be perfect since graduates of poor programs will be listed along with graduates of excellent programs. Moreover, especially in adult programs, students often leave to take excellent jobs without bothering to graduate. A third problem with data on graduates is that adult vocational education programs are often not designed to enable a person to enter employment in a particular field, but rather to be a more efficient worker in his present occupation. This results in a more effective manpower pool, but the trainee cannot be counted as an addition to the labor supply. Another problem is that some vocational graduates do not intend to enter the occupational field for which they were prepared. For example, some students take a vocational auto-mechanics course simply because they like cars as a hobby.

Vocational educators do need: (1) to know how many people are completing vocational education programs, at each competency level, (2) to be able to differentiate between new entrants and those who have been upgraded in skills and knowledge, and (3) to identify those who have no intention of accepting employment in the field for which they were trained. Obviously, these data must cover *all* vocational education, not just that which is federally reimbursed. The entire supply of trained manpower must be counted, evaluated, and considered in planning. The state director of vocational education in Pennsylvania has in operation a continuing census of this type, and finds that the private sector of vocational education is very willing to supply this information in return for a copy of the results. The private sector, as well as public vocational education, needs these data for planning. Most vocational educators assume that someone else will collect the information. To date this assumption has proved to be unfounded.

The evidence provided in the above answers suggests that no field of vocational education is preparing too many people for today's labor market, though we probably come close to it in production agriculture. This does not mean, however, that we are spending our funds in vocational education most wisely, or that vastly increased investment might yield equal returns, or that our priorities are correct.

The second question posed at the beginning of this chapter asked, would vocational education be more efficient if it decreased certain of its expenditures or increased other types of expenditures? The obvious answer to this question is "yes." But before we can know *how* to increase efficiency in education, we need answers to at least some of the following questions:

A. In what types of education do society and individual students get the best return on their investment of time and money?

B. What is the interaction between student ability, social class, and motivation, as they affect the costs and the effectiveness of various types of educational programs?

C. How much time is required for the graduates of a vocational program to adapt to the techniques of the contemporary productive enterprise?

Let us consider each of these questions in detail.

A. The economist believes that each individual and society should review each major expenditure they make, to decide if the money could better be spent elsewhere. Assuming that the individual has full information and is free to act, he almost always will make the best choice. In many cases, these are untenable assumptions, so the economist is interested in increasing freedom to act, and in providing information which enables better choices to be made. The economist's usual operational definition of "better" is in terms of earnings per additional dollar invested. The present crude estimates indicate that one dollar invested by society in elementary education yields over 20 percent per year (mostly in increased earnings by the former student). Probably an additional million dollars invested would have a yield nearly as great. But additional dollars spent in the same way are unlikely to yield at the same rate as the original investment.

A dollar invested in high school education does not pay as large a return as a dollar invested in elementary school education. Part of the reason is that students who attend high school are assumed to be losing money which they could be earning if they were not in school. But the return on money invested in high school education is still far higher than is obtained by investments in many fields presently supported by government or individuals (25, pp. 4-9).

Calculations of rates of return on high school education have assumed that one high school curriculum is as valuable as another. This is certainly not true. So economists have decided to concentrate on studies of rates of return to vocational education because its monetary goals seem clearer than those for either the general or the college preparatory curriculum. Even within vocational education, it is likely that some courses of study yield greater rates of return than others. Failure to take this into account tends to cause the results of studies on vocational education to be inconclusive. Most studies have shown that vocational graduates get jobs faster, earn more money per hour, and are employed more hours per year than comparable graduates of other curricula. (Possibly they take jobs away from graduates of other curricula, rather than reducing total unemployment, though we are not sure of this.) But vocational education generally costs more than other curricula. The ratio of costs to benefits (both expressed in dollars) is a key economic measure, and inevitably will be used more and more in decision-making in vocational education. A newer and more promising technique, cost-effectiveness analysis, compares costs with measures of effectiveness which do not necessarily have to be stated in terms of dollars, and asks which of several alternatives would produce the best results.

Warmbrod lists a number of cost-benefit and cost-effectiveness studies. The more recent and more refined studies generally show more favorable results for vocational education than did the earlier exploratory studies. It may be accidental, but the studies which show the lowest rates of returns for vocational education are concentrated in the highly industrialized northeast portion of the United States. Highest rates of return (both in absolute terms, and relative to other types of educational investment) seem to be found in studies conducted in industrially developing portions of the country (25, pp. 10-34).

Fortunately we are past the time when economists seriously asked, "How do graduates and dropouts from various educational programs differ in lifetime earnings?" By consulting census data they found the number of years of education and the amount of income possessed by different individuals and concluded that 'X' years of education produced 'Y' income. This led to statements such as: "A high school diploma is worth 'Z' dollars." They neglected to take into account the effect of socio-economic level which leads a millionaire's son to go to college, and to also have a high income after college graduation, while the child of an unskilled laborer will probably quit school early and have a low income. Such analyses also overlook the influence of ability and motivation, yet "long education causes high income" has been adopted into the conventional wisdom along with the belief that while vocational education may give a student a head start, the general curriculum or college preparatory student will soon pass him in earnings. As nearly as can be determined, this belief is not supported by a single study in which the effects of socio-economic level were controlled.

B. We have very little information on the interaction of ability, social class, and motivation, as they affect the cost and the effectiveness of various types of educational programs. We know that the higher a student's ability, social class, and motivation, the higher his success in school will be. Since success in school is closely related to lifetime earnings, these three variables are probably also related to earnings. We also know that through the country (1) the college preparatory program attracts students with the highest verbal ability, (2) the general curriculum attracts the second most able, and (3) the vocational curriculum gets students with the lowest verbal ability. These curricula are in exactly the same order with regard to the average social class of their students. (See Chapter 10 for further data.) We do not know their order with regard to the various types of motivations.

Based on this information, it is predictable that of those students who do not go on to college, high school graduates of the vocational curriculum would earn less than graduates of the other curricula. We do not have data on life-time earnings, but several studies agree that for the one to nine years on which we do have information, vocational graduates earn more. It seems likely, however, that over a lifetime, as a person acquires additional vocational education on the job, or through evening schools, the effect of his high school or college education (vocational or general) will become less a factor in earnings, and verbal ability and social class will become more important in determining earnings.

Obviously it is difficult to decide which of the three educational programs is most effective when they have very different types of students. Instead, what we need are studies which tell us what types of education are needed for each type of student. The economist would ask, which program provides the desired outcome for a particular type of student, at the lowest cost. Or he would ask, which program provides the greatest amount of the desired outcome, for a particular type of student, holding cost constant.

Sometimes question "B" is phrased: "Given a choice among graduates or dropouts from different educational programs (e.g. vocational, general, college preparatory, public, private, etc.) which will employers choose?" It is obvious that this question cannot be answered without taking into account the background of the students being compared. The sociologist is interested in noting that corporation presidents answer this question very differently from personnel interviewers and foremen, but the economist is more interested in who is actually employed.

We have almost no data on the relative effectiveness of public and private schools, and our data on effectiveness by level of education (high school, college, and adult) and by types of educational environment (in-school, cooperative, or in-plant) are hopelessly muddled by differences in student characteristics. It does little good to note that placement rates (in the occupation for which trained) run about 20 percent higher for cooperative education graduates than for in-school vocational graduates, when we are reasonably sure that cooperative education students are more carefully screened for admission and retention than are the in-school students.

C. How much time is required for the graduate of a vocational program to adapt to the techniques of a contemporary industrial enterprise? The charge is frequently made that vocational education provides instruction on obsolete processes, using outmoded equipment. Obviously this charge is incorrect with regard to cooperative education, where a major part of the instruction is provided in employment. It may be true, however, in many in-school vocational programs. The principal reason for this is that up-dating equipment costs a great deal of money. Obsolescence may be more apparent than real, however. The vocational instructor is an economic man, and if allowed to do so, he uses his scarce resources to purchase items which will most improve the instruction he is providing. Often he chooses to introduce a new process, rather than to replace an old piece of equipment. He knows, for example, that the basic design of the lathe has been unchanged since about 1850. Newer lathes look better and are more convenient to operate, but they are so sleek that the student would have to dismantle one to see how it worked. When an old piece of equipment is used for *basic* instruction and and as a simulator for more complicated equipment, it may be a better instructional device, and a better investment, than a newer, more expensive tool.

Economics can help to make such investment decisions if we can determine the costs of instructional equipment and their effect on institutional outcomes. The economist will have to decide whether or not this would be a wise investment of his time, however, in view of Eninger's findings. He showed that less than 10 percent of the trade and industrial education high school graduates found that the tools and equipment at work were "very much different" from those in school. (Trade and industrial education is more frequently criticized than other vocational programs for the obsolescence of its equipment.) More than three times as many graduates, however, found that the work *methods* were "very much different" (8, pp. 25).

The economist is not very impressed by this sort of evidence. He wants to know the economic effect of various types of educational obsolescence (planned or not), and we do not have these data. If we had them, it is likely that they would show that the most damaging type is that of obsolescence of the instructor. It is he who makes the majority of the educational decisions which affect the economic future of his students.

ECONOMIES OF SCALE

There is an optimum size for any organization which produces goods or services. Below or above this optimum size, the price or quality of the services rendered will be less satisfactory. The small school cannot afford to offer a large variety of curricula or services because there would be too few students to attend the classes or use the services, causing the cost per student to be very high.

Similarly, the small employer cannot afford to employ a training director or a supervisor of apprentices because the cost per trainee would be too high.

Within limits, the way we organize to provide goods or services can change the optimum size of the organization. A small school which is in a diversified community can provide a broad range of vocational education by using cooperative education programs instead of laboratory based programs. Or it may join with other nearby schools to establish an area vocational education program. The small employer can reduce the training cost of each apprentice by cooperating with other employers and employee groups in a joint-apprenticeship program. However, when the size is so low that it is impossible to provide needed services, the only solution is to increase the size of the organization.

"There is a great deal of evidence to indicate that school districts need at least two thousand high school pupils (not necessarily in one school) to organize effective and economical programs of education in all fields, including vocational education" (16, p. 10). In the United States, only some two thousand of the thirteen thousand school districts which operate high schools have two thousand or more high school students. McLure's estimate seems conservative, for few high school units with less than three thousand students actually operate broadly comprehensive schools. But even if he is correct, three actions would appear to be necessary to achieve necessary economies of scale: (1) a great deal of secondary school consolidation, (2) establishment of residential schools where students are widely dispersed geographically, and (3) changes in the organization of schools to allow diversified curricula to be offered in medium-sized schools. The formation of intermediate school districts to provide services which cannot be offered by small schools is an example of such an organizational change.

The Internal Labor Market

Every institution makes a distinction between the employment rights and opportunities of those people who are employed in its various units and the rights of those who are outsiders. This distinction is recognized by both the employer and the employee in an attempt to separate sharply the jobs contained within the employing unit (the internal labor market) and those jobs and job-holders which are outside.

Classical economic theory recognizes only the external labor market and assumes that workers are free to move from one company to another if there is a job vacancy and if they are qualified to fill the vacancy. Doeringer and Piore point out that this is not correct. "There are hiring jobs or entry ports into these internal labor markets. These are the job classifications that employers list with the employment services and in help-wanted ads, or fill through informal recruitment. They are the points at which employers reach out into the labor market to bring workers into the plant" (7, p. 9).

These "entry ports" are more numerous in some industries than in others. ". . . in industries such as steel, petroleum, and chemicals, well-defined promotion sequences and tall promotion ladders are found; a worker is hired as a yard laborer or other unskilled worker, and, through a series of promotions over a period of time, works up into the semi-skilled, and often skilled, production and maintenance jobs in the plant" (7, p. 9). This type of closed internal labor market, with almost all re-cruitment of blue-collar workers occurring in the unskilled jobs at the bottom of the employment ladder, is most characteristic of large employ-ment units which have a heavy capital investment per worker. Thus, they are large enough and rich enough to provide the large amount of training which is required as workers move from one job to another. Western Electric reports that 95 percent of their blue-collar workers are employed at the first two grade levels and that within any one-year period, half of the employees will have changed job classifications once (7, p. 29).

In sharp contrast, ". . . in men's apparel and in many shoe and textile plants, there is an open structure, so that practically every production job is a hiring classification" (7, p. 9). Most seasonal industries have similar open internal labor markets. The open labor market is most often asso-ciated with industries which have a low capital investment per worker, small unit size, seasonal operations, or weak employee organizations.

When there is a tight labor market for skilled workers (too few skilled workers in relationship to the number of employment opportunities for skilled workers), the number of entry ports in closed internal labor markets tends to increase. Very little is known about the mechanisms of or reasons for this change. Possibly the employer fears that his turn-over rate of skilled employees will increase, so he protects himself by hiring and stockpiling skilled employees from outside the closed labor market. At the same time, during a tight labor market, the employees may be more willing to allow additional entrants from outside, because they know that the existence of a tight external labor market increases their own options for employment outside the closed internal market.

In theory, the closed internal labor market should protect the employer from skill shortages caused by tight labor markets, since all recruitment is at the unskilled level. In practice, however, the most highly skilled employees can leave a firm which has a closed internal labor market to accept employment with a firm which has an open internal labor market. Since the closed internal labor market restricts recruitment of skilled workers from vocational education or other firms, the employer is faced with greatly expanded training costs as he attempts to upgrade his present employees.

The closing of entry ports invariably increases the value of the internal labor market to existing employees. Hence, the closing of entry ports tends to be irreversible and to lead to major labor conflicts if management attempts to fill job vacancies from outside the firm which previously had been filled from the ranks of current employees. At various points during a tightening labor market, standards for employment are reduced: (1) acceptable test scores are lowered, (2) educational requirements are reduced, and (3) unfavorable job history elements are accepted more freely. Reduced hiring standards, unlike changes in recruiting and screening procedures, are usually accompanied by increased training costs and higher production costs which are occasioned by decreased aptitude for learning, increased cost of supervision and decreased product quality.

The Closed Internal Labor Market

In a closed internal labor market, all jobs are filled by employees who enter the company through a single (usually unskilled) job classification. Through a process of transfer or upgrading, they fill all blue-collar jobs. The primary factor in deciding whether or not a person is eligible for upgrading is seniority. A variation of the closed internal labor market exists where a variety of low-skill hiring classifications exist with titles such as assembler, sweeper, cleaner, hand-trucker. From these entry level jobs workers are promoted on the basis of seniority to semi-skilled and even highly skilled production jobs. On the other hand, they may not be eligible for the highly skilled maintenance and repair jobs which are filled either by promotion of apprentices or by hiring fully skilled workers. Clerical jobs often have a variety of entry ports, depending upon the skills which newly hired employees bring to the establishment.

The key to the existence of an open internal labor market seems to lie in the availability of personnel who have transferable skills. If skilled employees cannot be recruited from other companies, or from vocational schools, a closed internal labor market seems to be inevitable. If adequate vocational training is available, it tends to promote the existence of an open internal labor market. However, the existence of relatively high unemployment rates in a particular occupational field can lead employee groups to insist on a closed internal labor market.

The efficiency of a closed internal labor market depends substantially upon the degree to which each job in a promotional ladder requires skills which are dependent upon experience and training received in lower level jobs. Where jobs require skills which are essentially independent of jobs lower in the hierarchy, the closed internal labor market is quite inefficient, for the full costs of training must be incurred by the employer each time the worker is promoted or reassigned. If a company is expanding rapidly, has high rates of turnover, or has sharp seasonal changes in labor force, the inefficiencies of the closed internal labor market make a competitive situation difficult to maintain because of the high training costs involved.

EFFECTS ON RECRUITMENT

If an employer hires almost all of his blue-collar workers at the unskilled job level, he expects that seniority will give these workers a right to fill from ten to thirty successively higher-skilled and higher-paid jobs during their working life. Consequently he will attempt to employ workers who have high intelligence, good human relations skills, and who will have a loyalty to the employer rather than to an occupational field. Persons who have these characteristics can be trained and re-trained rapidly and will not be interested in the short-term advantages which might be gained by shifting employment from one company to another. In short, the employer looks for an employee who will spend a lifetime working for one institution. The parallels with traditional Japanese recruitment and training are striking (see references 1 and 13).

Recruitment into closed internal labor markets tends to penalize persons from low income and racial minority groups. The employer is concerned not only with whether the new employee can perform satisfactorily at the entry port job, but also whether he will be able to perform satisfactorily the higher level jobs to which he will be entitled by increasing seniority. Low measured intelligence or a stereotype of instability in employment is a serious barrier to employability in a firm which has a closed internal labor market.

The Internal Labor Market
and Vocational Education

Where there is a closed internal labor market, relationships between the employer and vocational education are substantially altered. Since the employer assumes full responsibility for the vocational training which is necessary to upgrade his present employees to fill better positions in the company, he is faced with a "make or buy" decision. That is, he may decide to conduct the training himself or to purchase it from an outside vendor. The outside vendor may be a public vocational educational system, a private trade school, the manufacturer of certain equipment which is installed in the employer's plant, or any other group which can provide adequate training. The employees will usually be paid for the time they spend in training, and the organization which provides the training will have no control over who is admitted to the program. Whether the employer purchases training or provides it himself, the content of the training will be designed to make the employee competent to perform a job to which he is already entitled by seniority.

In an open internal labor market, however, vocational training, whether public or private, will attempt to provide saleable skills and knowledges in various levels of occupations. The trainees will forego earnings (though they may receive stipends from public sources as a means of encouraging them to take training in order to reduce welfare costs). Those persons who complete training satisfactorily will seek employment at whatever skill level they have achieved. Adult workers will enroll in part-time classes designed to upgrade their skills in the expectation that these additional skills will enable them to obtain higher level jobs. (In a closed market few adults attend such classes since the possession of additional skills does not provide the seniority necessary for higher level jobs.)

Specificity of Skills

Gary Becker identifies a range of training from the very specific ". . . that has no effect on the productivity of trainees that would be useful in other firms" (3, p. 18) to the very general, which increases productivity by the same amount in all firms. He feels that specific training should be provided by the employer, while it would be appropriate for society to provide general training. An example of general training would be instruction in how to read.

While the content of a particular hour or day of training may be quite specific, no training program for an individual is "completely specific." Even training for a job which is performed in only one firm by one individual, would teach a person certain knowledges and attitudes with regard to punctuality, quality control, etc., which would be of value in many firms. Of course different types of training vary tremendously in their general usefulness across firms. It should be pointed out, however, that Becker's use of the terms "specific" and "general" is markedly different from their typical use in education. Training in typing, which would be considered quite specific by most educators, would be regarded as "general" by Becker, since typing skills are useful in many firms.

As a guide to deciding whether or not a public agency should provide a given type of training, Becker's definition is far more useful than the one commonly used by educators. If training is useful in only one or two firms, it is more difficult to justify public expenditures of funds than if the trainees were able to use their skills in many firms. The educator's definition of "general" suggests that education should be reserved for non-occupational activities such as citizenship, leisure, physical well-being, etc., which are common to all citizens, and should exclude activities related to employment, since there is no common type of employment.

It is a basic technological principle that the greater the number of tasks a machine can perform, the less efficient it is in the performance of any one of these tasks. Industrial engineers tend to assume that this same principle applies to people: the greater the number of tasks a person is trained to perform, the less efficient he will be in the performance of any one of them. The application of this concept to machines and people results in the designing of machines and jobs to make them more enterprise-specific, since each enterprise is interested in reducing its costs through increased efficiency. However, standardized equipment is generally cheaper because (1) it can be produced in larger quantities than specialized equipment; (2) it has standardized parts available which reduce repair and maintenance costs, and (3) its general utility makes it more adaptable to changes in product specifications. Similarly, broadly trained people can: (1) be produced effectively through courses designed to meet the needs of a group rather than an individual, (2) be recruited from one type of employment to another, and (3) adapt more readily to changes in product demand.

Therefore educators must try to strike a balance between programs which are so general as to have little or no occupational value, and programs which are so specific as to decrease the options available to the graduate. Job designers must also strive for this balance between job content which is almost entirely specific to a particular business enterprise and job content which is so broad as to be inefficient.

Jacob Stern has suggested that the more "volatile" the technology, the more general the training for that technology should be (21, p 60ff). This is justified on the grounds that a volatile technology is changing rapidly, hence training should be general in order to avoid rapid obsolescence. In a relatively stable occupation, however, more specific training could be justified because its utility would continue longer. This analysis assumes that in a rapidly changing technology, specific concepts change more rapidly than general ones. While this assumption sounds reasonable, it is possible that the most rapid changes occur at a level somewhere between the most general and the most specific. If one looks at instructional programs in new occupational areas (which often are changing rapidly), Stern's principle is regularly violated. Because no instructional materials are available, the instructor of a new course uses catalogs, operating manuals, and his personal experience to teach a mass of specific skills which are not bound together by generalizations. At the same time, because few courses are available for the new occupational field, the remainder of the student's program is made up of standard courses which appear to be most relevant. Thus the student is exposed to extremes of specificity and generality with no intermediate subject matter to serve as a bridge between the two. When instruction for an occupation has become widespread, a market exists for instructional material which bridges this gap. The combination of a market and adequate writing time results in publications designed to fill this need.

Planning to Meet Manpower Needs

The most serious manpower problems arise when there is a serious discrepancy between supply of and demand for trained workers. Most of this book is concerned with factors which affect the supply side of this equation, but variables which affect demand are also important and need to be understood by the vocational teacher and student. Economists have worked much more intensively on problems of demand than on problems of supply. Indeed, many economists have held that supply automatically adjusts to demand. There is some truth in this statement, for humans are adaptable. It is also true that demand adapts to supply as employers change their hiring requirements in loose or in tight labor markets, and as machine designers and industrial engineers adapt tools and processes to the labor available. The long continued increase in youth unemployment would indicate that neither supply nor demand has succeeded well in adapting to the other.

The government attempts to alleviate the manpower problems caused by the action or inaction of other parts of society. But the government has other demands which it must meet.

> Governments need a basis of comparison for allocating among competing demands. One kind of comparison . . . is between broad categories — the manpower program as against all other government activities. The result of that comparison presumably influences the size of the entire manpower program in the total of government budgets. A second type of comparison is between different elements within the manpower program. That comparison should influence the allocation of manpower funds among the various functions and activities, such as forecasting, information analysis and distribution, testing, counseling, employer contacts, the matching of applicants and job vacancies, different types of training, sheltered workshops, and job creation efforts (12, p. 172).

Some of the factors which must be taken into account in reaching these decisions are outlined below.

GEOGRAPHIC MOBILITY OF EMPLOYERS

If the demand for skilled workers in a given location greatly exceeds the expected future supply, the employer may decide to move or select a new location for expansion. In choosing a new site, he will be concerned about the availability of productive employees. The governors of several states have wooed employers with promises of vocational training programs to meet their needs. This has been assailed by certain economists as counter-productive from a national point of view (though they admit it may be good from the state's point of view). If a state decides to increase the demand for workers to counter wide-spread unemployment or under-employment in that state, and if the employer moves from a locality where demand for workers greatly exceeds supply, the use of federal vocational education funds will probably be justified. What cannot be justified, on a national basis, is for one under-developed state to steal employers from another under-developed state (22, p. 138ff).

GEOGRAPHIC MOBILITY OF EMPLOYEES

As in the case of employer mobility, geographic mobility of employees affects both supply and demand in the sending and receiving localities. Social, racial, age, and sex discrimination reduce worker mobility. Increased general education and vocational education promote mobility of the individual who has the education. Increases in hiring standards (whether justified or not) usually call for increased general or vocational education, and thus decrease the mobility of that part of the labor force which cannot meet these demands. Adjustments to hiring standards are certainly not automatic. A study of unfilled job orders of the Federal-State Employment Service has shown that most of these opportunities are in occupations which have been in short supply for a long time. Clearly, the national trend is toward expansion of opportunities in occupations which require long periods of education or training (professions and skilled work) and relative declines in demand for most occupations which can be learned in a short time (unskilled labor). Without a corresponding increase in training opportunities, these increased hiring standards will reduce worker mobility.

DESIRABLE AND UNDESIRABLE GEOGRAPHIC MOBILITY

Economists usually think of increased geographic mobility as being desirable, since many of their analyses assume that workers are free to move to accept improved working conditions. At some point, however, worker mobility becomes wasteful. Employee turnover is expensive to the employer. This expense increases if the new employee has come from a different occupation and thus must be completely retrained. A capable employee is often destined for increased responsibilities, so if he leaves, the employer loses not only his value in the present job, but also his potential value in the new one.

Mobility may be costly to the sending and receiving community. Persons leaving non-depressed areas are likely to be the most able inhabitants, thus bleeding the sending community of needed talent. Persons leaving depressed areas may be the most able of the unskilled, depriving that group of leadership, and may still be a liability to the receiving community because of their inability to cope with urban problems.

Mobility can be very costly for the employee. He may lose pension rights, seniority rights, and vacation rights. Certain costs are incurred in selling and buying a home. But sometimes the worker has no choice. If he is laid off, fired, or forced out by job dissatisfaction, he must look elsewhere. (It is odd that if the worker's income is high enough, society pays some of these costs through income tax exemptions. But if the worker pays no income tax, an exemption from a portion of the tax is of no value. It seems clear that the lower the worker's income, the less help society will provide.)

Vocational education graduates are regularly reported to have higher job satisfaction, higher earnings, and less change of occupation than comparable graduates of other school curricula. Yet, if their training is in demand, they have greater opportunities to move. Therefore, vocational education graduates are in a position to avoid forced mobility, and to accept mobility based on informed choice. Usually forced mobility is undesirable, and mobility based on informed choice is desirable.

Increased general and vocational education provides the *option* for increased geographic mobility. But if adequate employment possibilities exist in the community where the student finished his vocational training, he will have lower geographic mobility than less well trained individuals who must move in order to find suitable employment. This seems to be self-evident, but it is contrary to the conventional wisdom which states that the more specialized training an individual has received, the more likely he is to move to find employment. It is still true, of course, that the more specialized a trainee is, the harder it is for him to find exactly what he wants at home.

FIRM-SPECIFIC SKILLS AND KNOWLEDGES

Almost every job contains certain *elements* which are unique to the company in which the job is performed, e.g., a special form which must be used for reports, a word which has a special meaning in that company, or even a secret process. A few jobs have a high proportion of *content* which is specific to one firm. If an employee had only skills and knowledges which were firm-specific, his mobility outside that firm (and perhaps even within the firm) would be quite low, for he would not have skills which are saleable on a broad market. Firm-specific skills and knowledges should seldom be taught outside the firm in which they will be used. By definition they are useful only to persons who plan to continue working for a particular company, so they are not suitable for vocational instruction for a group of individuals, some of whom will seek employment elsewhere.

We know very little about the proportion of either firm-specific or general skills and knowledges which are present in various occupations. Presumably the professions have a high amount of general skills and knowledges and a low amount of firm-specific content. The same is probably true of the carpenter foreman's job. In contrast, semi-skilled workers and the foremen who supervise them probably have a low amount of general knowledge and a high amount of firm-specific knowledge.

There are three major costs incurred by an employer when he replaces any worker: (1) the cost of persuading applicants to apply for a job, (2) the cost of determining whether or not to employ a particular candidate, and (3) the cost of training to bring the new or promoted worker up to the performance level of the person he replaced. A major factor in determining these costs is the degree of firm-specificity in the job.

As firm-specificity increases, the possibility decreases that workers who have the needed skills will be available. This lack of availability increases all three types of costs, particularly the cost of training.

People who think vocational education is the sole responsibility of the employer assume that job success is due almost entirely to firm-specific content. Vocational educators, however, assume that firm-specific content is relatively unimportant, and can best be learned after mastery of generalizable content from both general and vocational education. Both ideas are probably correct, depending upon the occupation. Where job success depends almost entirely on firm-specific content, the employer should have the responsibility for specific vocational education. It is to his advantage to provide it, since he can employ workers who will have low mobility, which will lower his turnover rate. This is not to say that the employer will want to provide firm-specific training if he can persuade the schools to provide it to his satisfaction.

A common problem occurs when a large employer in a small community serves on an advisory committee to a vocational education program. If a decision needs to be made as to what type of computer (or typewriter, or milling machine) should be purchased for instruction, the employer will probably recommend a product or process which is used in his firm. That product or process may be used by other firms as well, but to the extent that its use is not universal, students trained to use it will have their mobility restricted. The decision should be based on the cost-effectiveness of each possible choice, rather than on whether or not the product or process is used by a local employer.

If economists were interested in costs and effectiveness *within* vocational education, they could provide information which would help to make such decisions. To date, however, they have been more concerned with *external* efficiency; that is, the returns to society and to the individual on completion of a particular program.

UNREALISTIC HIRING STANDARDS

When there is an over-supply of workers, employers frequently increase hiring standards beyond those actually required by the job. During the depression of the thirties, people with college degrees were hired to drive buses, and high school graduates were willing to accept employment as un-skilled workers. When the depression ended, there was a mass exodus from such jobs, and companies vowed never again to make the mistake of setting unrealistic hiring standards. But during the fifties it happened again. High school graduation, no record of arrests, and an unbroken record of employment came to be required for many jobs which did not really need these qualifications. Part of the problem of increased hiring standards, however, has been created by agreements to promote workers on the basis of seniority. For example, the typical bargaining agreement in the steel industry calls for all new workers to be employed in unskilled jobs. As the workers acquire seniority, they have the opportunity for promotion to more and more responsible positions. This causes management to seek new employees who are promotable, and to demand qualifications which fit the jobs to which the worker might eventually be promoted, rather than standards which fit the jobs for which the workers are being employed initially (18).

Unrealistic hiring standards are often a not too subtle means of discrimination based on race, sex, age, or social class. Unemployed blacks often have police records and score low on paper and pencil tests. If you do not want to hire blacks, you can design hiring standards which will make it impossible for more than a few to be accepted. Employers are more blatant about discrimination on the basis of sex, though one relatively subtle way of refusing to hire women is to require that all new employees be able to lift eighty pounds, but not allowing women to lift more than twenty-five.

SPECIALIZATION OF WORKERS

Since the start of the industrial revolution, the classic way of meeting increased demands for workers has been to redesign the job or occupation, usually by splitting it into fragments which can be learned quickly and can be performed routinely. This allows lowered hiring standards and less training, and also decreases pay per worker and increases output per worker. Assuming that these changes result in decreased cost per unit produced, they are all desirable in the eyes of the traditional economist. Decreasing the content of the job still works well for some workers, especially for those who are not too intelligent, for they do not find such jobs boring. It works reasonably well for workers who have no saleable skills, for they have no other options, and usually are willing to accept boring jobs during a period of emergency. Naturally this traditional method does not work well in the long run for workers who are bored by repetition, and who have enough skills to allow them to seek better paying or more satisfying employment.

There is an interesting and vitally important relationship between the school curriculum and employer's efforts to design jobs to utilize the available manpower. Some graduates of the high school general curriculum and those graduates of the college preparatory curriculum who do not go to college may actually be sought for certain types of employment because they have higher verbal intelligence than drop-outs or graduates of the vocational curricula. But because they rarely have saleable skills, they are placed on routine jobs which do not demand expensive training from the employer. Because they are relatively intelligent they find these jobs boring. It is a complete anomaly that two curricula which purport to be liberating insure that certain of their graduates are enslaved by the lack of relevance of their preparation. In contrast, the graduates of the high school voca-tional curriculum and those graduates of the college preparatory cur-riculum who do go on to college (and thus acquire saleable skills) have markedly higher job satisfaction.

Probably, as the average level of education increases, workers will be less content with specialization which results in boring jobs which require little training. This suggests that jobs should be designed to have content which offers more variety. But this would force the employer to (1) recruit workers who have adequate vocational edu-cation or (2) increase the amount of training he offers to his workers. Since small employers do not benefit from the economies of scale which are available to large employers, they find training programs to be extraordinarily expensive. Increased demands for employer-sponsored training either force small employers out of business, or cause them to recruit trained workers from large companies. Large companies, of course, frequently lure trained workers from small companies because small companies are less mechanized and their workers are less special-ized. Stealing a worker often costs a company less than training one. The costs to society incurred when a small company fails because it has lost trained workers may be quite high, however. In the United States, vocational education often acts as a subsidy to the small employer, unlike England, where the Industrial Training Act forces all employers, regardless of size, to share most of the costs of training for their industry.

SUBSTITUTION OF WORKERS

Another method of changing the demand for employees is to sub-stitute one kind of worker for another. Technicians may be used in place of engineers, licensed practical nurses in place of registered nurses, and typists may replace stenographers. This inter-changeability is not complete, of course. Technicians know how to do things that engineers do not, and vice versa. Moreover, because of legal and tradi-tional restrictions, engineers are permitted to do things that technicians are not permitted to do (even though they are perfectly capable of doing them), and some engineers refuse to do things which they feel are beneath them.

A very common method of substituting one kind of worker for another is to lure certain types of workers from a declining industry to an expanding industry. The workers most sought are those who have skills which are directly transferable, e.g., pipe welders in a shipyard can got to work with very little re-training as pipe welders in the construction industry. The more re-training required, the less likely the employee will be sought.

WHO SHOULD RECEIVE VOCATIONAL EDUCATION?

One of the principal arguments for vocational education and man-power training is that for many years there have been shortages of workers (especially at the technician, white collar, and professional levels) when there has also been a large group of unemployed and under-employed individuals (especially among the unskilled). The assumption is that if we had adequate vocational education, the surplus of unemployed and under-employed persons could be trained to eliminate the shortage of high-level employees. But most of the unemployed and under-employed unskilled workers would need from four to ten years of general and vocational education to qualify for the majority of the chronically vacant high-level jobs. This indicates that it would be impractical to solve the problem of manpower shortages by simply re-training the unskilled and the unemployed for the vacant high-level jobs. It simply is not economically feasible to provide the complete re-education which is needed.

Two courses of action are possible, and both are being used. First, unskilled workers could easily be converted to semi-skilled workers, and semi-skilled workers could be re-trained as skilled workers, etc., through each level of the occupational ladder. This necessitates re-training a high proportion of the labor force. The second course of action is to train a high proportion of youth for high-level jobs, sending only the dropouts to lower-level employment. If employed exclusively, this method would make the plight of the older worker even worse, by preempting employment opportunities to which he might be promoted. Labor unions and large companies concentrate on the first of these methods. In-school vocational, technical, and professional education concentrate on the latter.

Many Manpower Development and Training Act programs have the fatal defect of preparing minority group members for entry-level employment, but making no provisions for upgrading the workers (most of whom are whites) who currently hold those jobs. This leads to a pileup at the bottom rungs of the occupational ladder. Some large companies will themselves do this upgrading job in order to protect their relationships with their present workers, but small companies lack the means to do this upgrading. The availability of two socially antagonistic competitors for one semi-skilled job can only lead to racial conflict. This conflict is almost certain to be sharp during periods of economic recession. MDTA programs cannot be criticized severely for creating this problem, for they have been placed in the same position that other parts of vocational education were in for fifty years. They are limited, in practice, to training for skills which are needed immediately in the geographic area in which the training is given. Unlike vocational education, they have been restricted to short-term training, both by a typical institutional training period of less than a year (which is far too short for trainees who need basic, as well as vocational training), and by heavy pressure for immediate results (always measured in terms of short-term removal from the unemployment rolls, rather than in terms of continued employment and personal growth). The heavy concentration on MDTA training for entry-level jobs is the result.

The Roles of the Economist and the Manager in Decision Making

A few educators hold a belief that all education is good regardless of its costs, but this view is not held by most people who control the purse strings. There are many more "good" ways to spend money than there is money to be spent, so decisions have to be made about allocation of our scarce resources. In educational decision making, "failure to take . . . cost-benefit factors into account *explicitly* means that they are considered *implicitly* on a set of assumptions unknown to the decision maker" (11, p. 17).

Outside the field of economics, economists usually do not make decisions. Rather, they provide information which allows others to make better decisions. Managers have to make decisions. Some are easy; others are difficult. In some cases, the type of decision which is made is relatively unimportant; what is important is that *some* decision be made. In other cases, the nature of the decision is crucially important; the life or death of an organization or the occupational liberation or enslavement of an individual may depend on the quality of the decision which is made. Most decisions fall between these two extremes.

To aid managers in better decision making, a variety of management information systems has been developed. All operate on the general principle of providing needed data in a form and at a time which helps decision making become more simple and more rational. Many of them allow the manager to divide important and difficult decisions into a series of less difficult steps. Most of them provide for corrective information (feedback) to inform the manager when decisions are wrong and need to be changed.

The need for management information systems in vocational education became obvious in 1963 and critical in 1968. Prior to 1963, the federal and state governments acted as conduits for the distribution of funds under relatively rigid rules and in non-interchangeable categories. Line-item budgeting was the rule. The vocational education act of 1963 loosened these restrictions, however, and the amendments of 1968 removed all subject-matter categories and mandated local and state planning for allocation of the still scarce resources of vocational education. This necessitates decision making which is far more difficult and important than any we have made in the past.

Since management information systems are developing so rapidly, it is impossible to make long-term recommendations about which systems will be most useful. At the present time, the most useful techniques appear to be those called Program Planning, and Budgeting Systems (PPBS). They are a group of closely related systems which emphasize management information, theoretical models, analyses of possible economic and non-economic results of different tentative decisions, and cost-effectiveness analysis of the actual results of the decisions made. Every vocational education administrator should be able to understand and use these systems or the improved systems which inevitably will replace them.

Economic Knowledge Needed by Vocational Education Students and Teachers

Quite aside from the question of whether or not a government should make an investment in a vocational education program, or an individual should make an investment of time (foregone earnings) and money in taking such a program, is the question of what economic content should be presented in a vocational education curriculum. This question is particularly pertinent since most high schools offer no economics instruction to the non-college-bound. Until high schools recognize that economics is a vital part of general education, and until sufficient numbers of economic teachers can be trained, some other action must be taken.

> To be adequately prepared for employment, the vocational student must come to the labor market armed with a general understanding of the workings, values, and institutions of the American economy, the information and wisdom for occupational choice, a motivation to produce, and the ability to do so. All of these need not be provided by vocational teachers, but it is the responsibility of vocational leadership to see that the requisite knowledge is obtained (14, p. 6).

Home economics and business teachers are now developing instructional programs in consumer education, which necessarily involves considerable economic education. If they could collaborate with the few social studies teachers who are trained in economics to prepare instructional materials, if vocational education made instruction in economics a requirement for completion of the curriculum, and if vocational teachers emphasized the application of economics in their regular courses, perhaps we could meet Mangum's challenge. The only other way of providing economic knowledge in high school is to ask the vocational teacher to provide it himself. This alternative is not attractive, for once we decide what economic content should be taught, we need to find ways for the vocational teachers to learn it. Most vocational teachers have had little contact with the study of economics, and except for a few in business education, none are prepared to teach it. Fortunately, this difficult situation need not exist in vocational and technical curricula in community colleges, since economics teachers are usually available, and presumably can offer the economic instruction needed.

REFERENCES

1. Abegglen, James, *The Japanese Factory*. Glencoe, Illinois: The Free Press, 1958.

2. *Acquisition of Skills*. Research Program on the Training of Skilled Manpower, Report No. 4. Ottawa: The Queen's Printer, 1960.

3. Becker, Gary S., *Human Capital*. New York: Columbia University Press, 1964.

4. Combs, Janet and W.W. Cooley, "Dropouts: In High School and After School," *American Educational Research Journal*, V, No. 3, 343-363.

5. Corazinni, A.V., "The Decision to Invest in Vocational Education: An Analysis of Costs and Benefits," *Vocational Education* (Supplement to *Journal of Human Resources*), III (1968), 88-120.

6. Doeringer, Peter B., "The Internal Labor Market and Internal Training," in *Work Force Adjustments in Private Industry*, J.T. Dunlop. Man-power/Automation Research Monograph No. 7. Washington, D.C.: U.S. Department of Labor, 1968.

7. Doeringer, Peter B. and Michael J. Piore, "The Internal Labor Market and Internal Changes," *Work Force Adjustments in Private Industry —Their Implications for Manpower Policy*. Manpower/Automation Research Monograph No. 7. Washington, D.C.: U.S. Department of Labor, 1968.

8. Eninger, Max W., *The Process and Product of T. & I. High School Level Vocational Education in the United States*. Pittsburgh: American Institute of Research, 1965.

9. *Formal Occupational Training of Adult Workers*. Manpower/Automation Research Monograph No. 2. Washington, D.C.: U.S. Department of Labor, 1964.

10. Hovey, Harold A., *Techniques for Evaluating Government Programs*. New York: Frederick A. Praeger, Inc., 1968.

11. Kaufman, Jacob, "The Role of Economics in the Training of Leaders in the Field of Vocational and Technical Education," in *The Advanced Degree and Vocational-Technical Education*, ed. J.L. O'Brien. New Brunswick, New Jersey: Rutgers University Press, 1966.

12. Lester, Richard A., *Manpower Planning in a Free Society*. Princeton, New Jersey: Princeton University Press, 1966.

13. Levine, Solomon B., *Industrial Relations in Post-War Japan*. Urbana: University of Illinois Press, 1958.

14. Mangum, Garth L., *The Economic Education of Vocational Educators*. Columbus, Ohio: The Center for Research in Vocational and Technical Education, 1969.

15. McGivney, Joseph H. and William C. Nelson, *Programming, Planning, Budgeting Systems for Educators*, Vol. I. Columbus, Ohio: The Center for Research in Vocational and Technical Education, 1969.

16. McLure, William, "The Future of Vocational and Technical Education," *Bulletin of the National Association of Secondary School Principals*, XXXV, No. 262 (1961), pp. 7-12.

17. *Occupational Outlook Handbook*. Washington , D.C.,: U.S. Department of Labor, 1968.

18. Piore, Michael J., "Management Reactions to Changed Conditions," in *Work Force Adjustments in Private Industry*, J. T. Dunlop. Man-

power/Automation Research Monograph No. 7. Washington, D.C.: U.S. Department of Labor, 1968.

19. Piore, Michael J., "On-The-Job Training and Adjustment to Technological Change," *Journal of Human Resources*, III, No. 4 (Fall, 1968), pp. 435-449.

20. Schill, William, *Curricula Content for Six Technologies*. Urbana: University of Illinois Press, 1965.

21. Stern, Jacob, "Conceptual Models to Analyze Occupations for Educational Purposes," in *Guidelines and Supportive Papers for Planning and Conducting Short-term Teacher Education Activities*, ed. Lewis D. Holloway. Iowa City: University of Iowa, 1970.

22. Stromsdorfer, Ernest W., "Aspects of Geographic and Occupational Mobility," in *Manpower Information for Vocational Planning,* ed. Robert C. Young. Columbus: The Center for Vocational and Technical Education, Ohio State University, 1969.

23. Veblen, Thorstein, *The Theory of the Leisure Class*. New York: The New American Library of World Literature, Mentor Edition, 1953.

24. *Vocational Education, The Bridge Between Man and his Work*. Washinton, D.C.: General report of the Advisory Council on Vocational Education, Superintendent of Documents No. FS 5.280:80052, 1968.

25. Warmbrod, J. Robert, *Review and Synthesis of Research in the Economics of Vocational-Technical Education*. Columbus, Ohio: ERIC Clearinghouse, The Center for Vocational and Technical Education, 1968.

Chapter 8 SOCIOLOGICAL FOUNDATIONS

Industrial sociology is an important area within the discipline of sociology which provides new ways of thinking about work behavior. Industrial sociologists feel that ". . . work behavior is social behavior and, as such, may be one of the most fulfilling and enriching experiences of life" (11, p. xii). Sociologists who study industry do not restrict themselves to factories or manufacturing, but are concerned with all types of work and the social context in which work is performed. Thus, "An office, a sales organization, a hospital, a school, a day nursery, a window-washing company, and a farm which sells its products are all industries" (11, p. xii) because they are all organized to assist in the performance of work. Industrial sociologists are also interested in the effect of social forces and social activities on work, the worker, and work organizations. They feel that these are so interdependent that a change in one is certain to affect the others. Obviously they have much the same breadth of interest as have occupational educators. The following coverage of a few of the concerns of industrial sociology indicates some of the ways in which the sociologist can help the vocational educator.

The Roles of Work and
Work Groups in Society

According to the sociologist, work is a goal-directed group activity. Even the solitary writer, or the childless housewife must interact with other workers with related goals. For the group to function effectively, there must be a division of labor, with technically competent individuals and a set of rules which governs the relationship of each worker to the group. This organization may be set up by the group itself or imposed by a bureaucracy. Since the work group is relatively cohesive and often resents direction from outside, most changes come from within the group. In addition to meeting the needs of society for its products or services, a work group provides an opportunity for the worker to get rewards from association with others. It protects the worker-member from outsiders; it provides a channel of communication (through the "grapevine") that prevents surprise; it reassures the worker of his personal worth, and it controls the worker's behavior to protect him from injury by outside forces. The work group defines work in all its dimensions, provides status for the worker, and determines the values and merits of his work.

To a large extent, work determines how much money a worker receives, where he will live, what kind of recreation he will enjoy, who he will meet socially, and those whom he will avoid meeting. Eighty percent of the labor force say they would work even if they did not need the income, because it keeps them occupied and healthy. Without it they would feel lost, useless, and bored. This does not mean that work is alway pleasurable. In order to meet the goals of the work group, the individual must subordinate some of his own goals either willingly or because he finds it necessary in order to receive subsistence. Major conflicts arise when an individual worker is torn between loyalties to two different groups, for example, between his work group and a group based on race, sex, or the union. Professionals find similar conflicts between loyalties to their colleagues and to their clients or students. (6, pp. 1-30; 11, pp. 1-4, and 10, pp. 1-14).

Less than 15 percent of workers in the United States are self-employed. Over 85 percent work in some type of organization. Organizations are more or less bureaucratic, with small businesses being least so, and government and the military being highly bureaucratized. The dominant characteristic of an industrial society is the pervasive role of the large, bureaucratic work unit. While 90 percent of the business firms have less than twenty employees, these firms employ only 25 percent of the labor force. Well over a third of workers are employed by firms which have one thousand or more employees. Since these proportions have changed little during the last fifty years, it seems that we should continue to provide vocational education for employment in both large and small organizations. Because few firms with less than a thousand employees have the necessary economy of scale to permit them to provide formal training to their employees, we should be particularly concerned about vocational education for the majority of workers who are and will be employed by such companies.

The Effect of Industrialization on the Labor Force

As a country becomes more highly developed (that is, as it develops more effective work organizations), it passes through a sequence of steps which affects its occupational structure, its types of work organizations, its communities, and its entire cultural value structure. This sequence applies also to those portions of a country (such as Appalachia) which have been late in moving toward industrialization.

The best description of the social process of industrialization comes not from industrial sociology, but from four labor economists. One of the questions they asked was: "How is an industrial work force recruited and settled into industrial life?" (7, p. 7). This is obviously a key question in vocational education. Though they were not able to answer the question fully, they answered it in part by identifying four stages of commitment on the part of the labor force (7, p. 145).

A. The uncommitted worker takes employment for a specific, temporary purpose. He needs to raise money for taxes, to tide his family over a period of famine or low agricultural prices, or to buy alcohol or drugs. Since he plans to stay in industrial employment only for the time necessary to get money for his particular purpose, he is not interested in vocational training and usually is employed in unskilled work. If he had skills prior to acquiring a drug or alcohol addiction, he uses these skills, but as they gradually become obsolete, he is not interested in upgrading or replacing them with other skills. This type of worker has a high turnover rate which is costly, and his employment can only be justified if no other workers can be found, or if very low wage rates can be paid.

B. The semi-committed worker is torn between two ways of life. He expects to spend a sizeable portion of his life in industrial employment, but really prefers life in his home community, where he would be engaged in subsistence agriculture (farming which provides money only for bare necessities). In the United States, if he lives in a city, he often drives long distances on weekends to maintain his ties with the home community, or (if he works close to home) he farms and holds industrial employment simultaneously. The economist usually interprets part-time farming as a desire for more income, but the sociologist sees it as a lack of full commitment to industrial employment, and as an attempt to keep a foot in both industrial employment and in his traditional social environment. If the worker can make enough money to support his family through non-industrial employment, he often will leave industry, returning only when economic conditions force him to do so. Since he does not thoroughly enjoy industrial employment, he often takes full advantage of "sick leaves," and takes holidays on every possible occasion.

C. The generally committed worker no longer has strong ties with non-industrial life. He sees himself as a permanent member of an industrial work force, usually in an urban area. Since he must sell his labor to survive, and since he has relatively few skills to sell, he is dependent on a changing job market. He tends to seek security through a labor organization, and expects it to persuade the employer to provide re-training if his skills become obsolete.

D. There are two types of specifically committed workers: the enterprise-committed and the occupation-committed. Both are permanent members of the industrial work force.

1. In Germany and Japan (and, some sociologists feel, increasingly in the United States), large numbers of workers are tied to a particular work organization. Their turnover rate is low, for they expect to spend their entire life with one employer. When asked, "What do you do?" they tend to say, "I work at Monsanto," or "I am in the office at Caterpillar Tractor." Large corporations and industrial-type labor unions encourage such company affiliation through pension plans and seniority rights which guarantee a career ladder of varying length to the enterprise-committed employees. A major difference, however, between America and Japan is that in the former the worker tends to identify with the employing organization only when his own work denies him significant status.

2. A quite different type of committed employee is tied to a particular occupation. A large proportion of the work force in Great Britain and the United States is made up of these occupation-committed workers. A high proportion of professionals, semi-professionals and skilled workers feel no compunction about leaving a particular employer if opportunities in their occupation appear to be better with another employer. If they are represented by a labor union, it tends to be of the

craft type, rather than an industrial union. The turnover rate for this type of committed worker may be high if one looks at employment by company, but it tends to be low in terms of the occupation because the worker keeps the same occupation as he moves from employer to employer.

The more highly developed the economy in a particular geographic area, the higher the proportion of committed workers. Companies with sophisticated and expensive equipment cannot afford the high turnover and high rates of absenteeism which are characteristic of the less committed worker. Because committed workers are more frequently found in cities and rich agricultural areas, companies tend to expand in such areas, rather than in poorer areas. At the same time, in industrialized areas, employers, unions, schools, and families all exert pressure to convert uncommitted workers into committed workers. This pressure from homes and schools is likely to be much lower in less industrialized localities. Indeed, the local value structure may be such that full work commitment is discouraged. These factors hasten the industrialization process in the already industrialized areas, and retard it in less industrialized sections.

The evidence is not clear as to whether the enterprise-committed worker or the occupation-committed worker will predominate in mature industrial cultures. Large employers are more frequently found in mature industrial economies. The formation of large enterprises seems to favor the enterprise-committed worker, since a large corporation provides greater stability of employment and a wider range of career opportunities within the corporation than does a small company. On the other hand, the requirement of a high degree of worker skill and specialized education seems to lead to occupational commitment. Increasing demands for education and skill are also characteristic of mature industrial economies. In Japan the evidence indicates that the result is a gradually decreasing enterprise commitment and an increasing occupational commitment.

Judged by these standards, it would appear that the plumber has an enterprise commitment rather than an occupational commitment. However the enterprise to which he is committed is the United Association of Journeymen and Apprentices of the Plumbing and Pipefitting Industry of the United States and Canada (his union), rather than to the plumbing contractor for whom he happens to be working at the moment. If the union insists on apprenticeship as the major path to employment in the occupation (most unions do not), and determines which men will be available for employment on a particular type of job, that union assumes many of the characteristics of an "enterprise."

Vocational education in American schools has been primarily concerned with developing occupation-committed workers. In-plant training has been primarily concerned with developing enterprise-committed workers. Manpower Development and Training Act programs are aimed at less fully committed workers, but the planners of these programs have not been consistent in deciding whether their goal is to persuade workers to adopt an occupational or an enterprise commitment.

The future of vocational education in the schools is certain to be influenced by the type of "commitment" which becomes predominant. If occupational commitment becomes the norm, vocational education in the school is likely to expand rapidly, and training offered by employers is likely to be restricted to the training needed to help the employee adjust to the *unique* problems of his work situation (plus training to compensate for the inadeqacies of the vocational education that the employee received in the schools). On the other hand, if enterprise commitment becomes the norm, there is need for much less vocational education in the schools, for workers are likely to enter employment at the unskilled level, and be trained and re-trained by the employer each time the worker's seniority allows him to enter a higher level job.

TABLE 8–1

Effects of Full Industrialization
Which are of Importance to Vocational Education

Increases	Decreases
Proportion of the population which is working for pay	Amount of sickness
Proportion of women working for pay	Proportion of workers in agriculture and manufacturing
Average size of the work organization	Proportion of young and old workers
Proportion of workers who provide services	Proportion of unskilled workers
Amount produced per worker in agriculture and manufacturing	Proportion of education devoted to the classics
Amount of general and vocational education	
Geographical and occupational mobility	
Proportion of people in cities	
Expenditures for transportation	
Length of life	
Amount of leisure for young and old persons	

In the meantime, vocational education is likely to continue to concentrate on these occupations for which occupational commitment is the norm, (such as machinist, nurse, and typist) and to avoid involvement in educational programs for types of employment where enterprise commitment is common (such as the steel industry, the automotive industry, and the meat packing industry). Though there are many individual exceptions, it appears that persons with low occupational competency are likely to be loyal to the enterprise, while those with high occupational competency have first loyalty to their occupation. The latter will exhibit loyalty to the enterprise only if it gives them greater opportunities within their occupation than does a competing enterprise (6, p. 105). Therefore if vocational education succeeds in raising occupational competency, it will also raise the level of occupational commitment.

Table 8-1 indicates demographic factors which are increased or decreased by full industrialization. It suggests a number of changes in the subject matter, clientele, and geographic site for reallocation of vocational education resources.

Social Class and Work

Social class is most often characterized as "upper," "middle," and "lower" or "working." These three categories are sometimes further sub-divided unto upper-upper, lower-upper, upper-middle, lower-middle, etc. The divisions between classes are not sharp, but persons in each class tend to have different values and behavior. Social class is closely related to occupation. Indeed, "Most students of social class behavior agree that . . . (as) a single measure of the overall complex of class behavior, . . . a scale of occupations is clearly the most efficient instrument to use" (11, p. 96).

Managers and professionals tend to be upper-class or upper-middle class. Skilled workers, semi-professionals, small proprietors, and white collar workers most frequently are lower-middle class. Semi-skilled workers are frequently upper-lower class, and those people who work only when they choose to do so are usually lower-lower class. The higher the social class, the higher the income, education, material possessions, status and responsibilities. In some countries, movement from one social class to another is an extremely slow and difficult process. It is not easy even in the United States. Upward movement usually occurs as a result of increased education, though seniority in large firms is becoming more and more important as a route to higher level occupations. Downward movement can occur because of technological change, economic failure of the employer, or continued failure of the worker to perform job duties satisfactorily.

Vocational education is most concerned with occupations which lead people to lower-middle class status. Upper and upper-middle class occupations are usually associated with college degrees, and while a relatively high proportion of vocational graduates go on to college, vocational educators tend to ignore the demonstrated value of their programs to motivate people to want increased education. Vocational education for youth is most frequently designed to provide *entry* to lower-middle class occupations. Vocational education for adults is most concerned with combatting technological change and other factors which tend to reduce the occupational level of the worker, and with providing this education before substantial dislocation has occurred. Manpower Development and Training Act (MDTA) programs, on the other hand, have concentrated on lower and lower-middle class entry occupations for people over age eighteen, and with providing help to the dislocated or underemployed adult only after he is in serious straits.

Since lower class occupations (unskilled and semi-skilled work and domestic service) are likely to be in decreasing demand or to have relatively low wage scales, it is understandable that vocational education prepares few people to enter them. There is an obvious distinction between preparing people (from any class) to enter lower class occupations, and preparing lower class youth and adults for middle class occupations. Yet vocational education does little of either. Vocational educators are middle class, and given a choice between a lower class student and a middle class student, they usually give preference to the latter. But the lower class student needs vocational education much more than does the middle class student, for family status and community resources tend to assure the middle class student entry into a middle class job. The success of Skills Centers (MDTA) and Opportunities Industrialization Centers (private) proves clearly that significant numbers of lower class persons are interested in and can profit from vocational education.

Income, Class and Occupation

Since most middle class parents desire their children to move to white collar or professional occupations, and since little is done to prepare lower class youth for high level manual occupations, there is a shortage of skilled manual workers. This shortage is compounded by the high costs of apprenticeship, which has led employers (often with the assistance of unions) to keep apprenticeship opportunities so scarce that they do not begin to meet replacement demands in skilled occupations.

TABLE 8–2

Factors Associated With Low Occupational Status

Not Directly Modifiable by Schools	Modifiable to a Certain Extent by Schools	Readily Modifiable by Schools
Female Sex	Low Geographic Mobility	Low Educational Attainment
Minority Race	No Union	Low Occupational Skill and Knowledge
Youth or Old Age	Low Intelligence	Low Awareness of Occupational Opportunities
High Unemployment	Low Independence	Little Understanding of Effects of Absenteeism, Productivity, Promptness, etc.
Low Wages	Low Optimism about the Future	
Low Fringe Benefits		
Decreasing Employment Opportunities	Low Aspirations for their Children	
Low Governmental Regulation	Low Loyalty to Occupation	
Low Education of Parents	Low Loyalty to Employer	
Low Occupational Status of Parents	Low Loyalty to Fellow-Workers	
Low Social Status of Parents	Poor Health	
Low Seniority	Poor Diet	
Low Savings		
High Physical Exertion		

A shortage of workers in any field leads in the long run to increased wages. Wages for many skilled manual occupations are now higher than for occupations which traditionally have paid more and have had higher status. The 1970 contract for plumbers in California yields a wage of twenty-three thousand dollars for a normal work year. Moreover, working conditions in high status occupations often are not good. Pressures are severe, with mental health difficulties being highly correlated with occupational level (the correlation is .85 according to Clark, [2]). Heart attacks and ulcers are more frequent. Hours are longer. Though farmers work the most, with fifty-two hours per week, managers, proprietors, and professional and technical workers are close behind. Laborers and private household workers have the most leisure (or under-employment).

In spite of the free time they provide, working conditions in lower class occupations are not good either. Unemployment is highest in lower class occupations, and decreases sharply as status of the occupation increases. Freedom from unemployment seems to be nearly as important as income in determining the status of an occupation. All in all, medium status occupations seem to offer the best working conditions.

Table 8-2 lists factors associated with low occupational status which have been identified by industrial sociologists. These factors are classified according to the extent to which it appears the schools can modify them directly. Obviously the schools can have substantial *indirect* effects on the items in the two left-hand columns, for example, by persuading the community that sex and race are not desirable as determinants of occupational status. If the school fails to act in the areas where it can make a sizeable difference, direct or indirect, it is clearly delinquent.

Careers and Unemployment

Economists traditionally have excluded students and housewives from their analyses, on the ground that they were not productively employed. Industrial sociologists, however, have included them on the ground that their work is productive even though it does not result in monetary income. Until recently, neither discipline has been particularly concerned about people who are neither working nor looking for work. Illustrative of their lack of concern is the fact that even today an unemployed person is defined as one who is looking for work but cannot find it. A person who is not looking for work is not unemployed; he is just not counted.

Sociologists and psychologists identify five phases in work life: (1) preparatory (usually in school), (2) initial (first employment), (3) trial (a period of job changing as the worker tries to find work which is attractive), (4) stable (usually the longest period, when there are relatively few changes in occupation), and (5) retirement. Most unemployment occurs during the initial and trial stages. It is also relatively high among people who have been forced into retirement but have not accepted this retirement either because they cannot afford to do so or because they want to work for other reasons. Both types of unemployment have been increasing in the United States, but we know considerably more about youth unemployment than about unemployment of older people.

YOUTH UNEMPLOYMENT

Youth unemployment in the United States has been increasing steadily for at least forty years, if it is measured in relationship to general unemployment. In late 1970, youth unemployment (ages fourteen to nineteen) was about three times as high as general unemployment (18 percent versus 6 percent). No other industrialized country has such a high rate of youth unemployment. Both sex and race strongly effect youth unemployment. Female, black youths of ages eighteen to twenty have an unemployment rate of over 30 percent. Graduates of high school vocational programs have markedly lower unemployment rates (currently 5 percent) than graduates of the general curriculum or the college preparatory curriculum (currently over 15 percent for those who do not go to college). Even high school dropouts have greater earnings and the same amount of unemployment at age eighteen than do high school graduates from non-vocational curricula who do not go to college (3). For some unknown reason, however, almost all of the youth who were unemployed secure regular employment by age twenty-five. This is true whether or not they have received vocational training after leaving high school.

The high rate of youth unemployment has been blamed on many factors, including the federal minimum wage, the draft, and laws governing work in hazardous occupations. None of these, however, adequately explains the long-term rise in youth unemployment, for it has continued to go up regardless of changes in any of these factors. Vocational education, (including apprenticeships) and college attendance are the only readily modifiable factors which seem to prevent youth unemployment effectively.

CYCLICAL AND SEASONAL UNEMPLOYMENT

"The greatest menace to stable career patterns is cyclical and seasonal unemployment" (11, p. 601). We have seen that unskilled and semi-skilled workers are hardest hit by unemployment. Not only is the total need for unskilled and semi-skilled workers decreasing, but because the learning period for such jobs is very short (often a matter of hours or weeks) almost anyone can replace such a worker on short notice. Since persons who have higher level skills are difficult to replace, they are usually kept in employment for short periods of time when they are not really needed. The unskilled or semi-skilled, however, frequently are dismissed immediately when there is a cyclical or seasonal decrease in demand.

TECHNOLOGICAL UNEMPLOYMENT

This type of unemployment results from changes in occupational content or in the numbers of people needed in an occupation as a result of the introduction of new products or processes. If the employer's business continues to be economically strong, he often assumes responsibility for re-training some of the displaced workers (sometimes because he is forced to do so by a labor union). But if the employer goes out of business, the workers have no recourse. In any case, a marked change due to technological innovation creates severe problems of adjustment for the worker. Society can help people make these adjustments by providing re-training programs, which are a vital part of vocational education.

PHYSICAL AND EMOTIONAL DISABILITY

By inheritance, or more frequently through accidents of the environment, people acquire physical and emotional disabilities which can disrupt a career Vocational rehabilitation programs are very effective remedies for such disabilities. These programs include diagnosis of the problem, treatment (including provision of artificial limbs, psychiatric help, and counseling), vocational training or re-training, placement, and follow-up.

RETIREMENT

One test of the importance of work in our lives is found in the activities of retired persons. Less than 20 percent of males drawing social security retired to enjoy leisure. Almost three-fourths of the retirements are involuntary: either the employer retires the worker, or he is forced to retire by poor health. "Most . . . returned to work whenever their health permitted it, and they could obtain employment" (13, p. 3). With increasing social security benefits, retirement is slightly more palatable. Studies during the forties and fifties found less than

6 percent retiring to enjoy leisure, and almost 90 percent being retired involuntarily.

RESTRICTION ON JOB ENTRY

Formal or informal restrictions of many types keep certain people from entering most prestigious occupations. Some restrictions are imposed by the teaching-learning process itself: the length of training time required to enter many professions discourages some potential entrants. The four or more years required to complete most apprenticeships also keeps people out. Other people are eliminated by requirements of good high school grades, high test scores, or absence of criminial records. If these restrictions help to insure successful completion of the training program or success on the job, they may be justified. If they do not have a relationship to occupational success, they should be removed. Other restrictions clearly have no relationship to job success in most occupations: race, sex, religion, accent, friendship or blood relationship to a worker who is employed in the occupation, etc. These are unjustifiable restrictions. For youth, the most exasperating requirement is that they must have had previous experience in the work to be performed. One cannot get experience without working, and one is not allowed to work without experience. It is this barrier that vocational education most successfully removes.

WOMEN AND WORK

Of every ten women, nine work for pay at some time during their lives, and the average length of time they work is twenty-five years. Over half of the working women are married, and over half are in white collar jobs. All of these figures have increased very rapidly, many of them threefold in the last fifty years. Employment of women in clerical jobs has increased sevenfold during this same period. In contrast, the proportion of women who work in domestic service has dropped from one-fourth to well under a tenth (11, pp. xiii, 61, 64). These changes have come about in part because of cultural changes which make it permissible for women to work (though it still is more permissible for them to work during periods of labor shortage or national emergency). Another important factor is the increased vocational competence of female high school graduates. According to Project TALENT, more than 40 percent of females in high school are enrolled in a vocational curriculum (compared with less than 25 percent for males). By far the majority of these girls are in business and commercial programs. This undoubtedly is related to the fact that 70 percent of the female high school graduates who do not go to college are working in clerical occupations. Nevertheless, women still do not have nearly as many opportunities for occupational choice as do men. Half of all women workers are in eight occupations, and 75 percent are in only twenty occupations. Half of the women workers are in occupations where 75 percent of the workers are women, and there seems to be a tendency for men to leave an occupation once women are solidly entrenched in it.

The high proportion of women who work outside the home causes problems in the home. While the culture permits women to work for pay, it also expects them to continue most of their responsibilities for work in the home. When their children are young, most women stop work outside the home. This is due in part to the increased work load imposed by the young children, and in part to pressure from society, which feels that the woman should give children her full attention at least until they begin school. But additional children also bring additional financial burdens, and a second paycheck is usually needed by the family. This leads many women to endure a period of combined work for pay and child care for which they are not at all prepared. Even without young children in the home, the task of the married female worker is enormous. She is expected to carry two jobs simultaneously, and to subordinate her career ambitions to those of her husband. For example, if he must move to accept a promotion, she is expected to quit her job and accept whatever is available in the new locality. This suggests that women need schooling in vocational education not only for wage earning, but for the dual role of wage earner and homemaker. This requires substantial changes in traditional homemaking courses, and these changes are occurring, but very slowly, since many such courses assume that the woman will not be employed outside the home. Until our culture changes further, vocational education for most women should be for wage-earning occupations which are available in almost every community. Otherwise, when the woman moves with her husband, she may be forced to accept employment in unskilled work which will contribute little to the family purse or to her own personal satisfaction.

LEARNING ON THE JOB

Sociologists are very interested in how outsiders become members of existing groups. Before a person can become a member of a work group, he must acquire both technical and social skills. Effective vocational education will provide part of each, but those skills which are unique to a particular work group can only be learned on the job.

Obsolete vocational instruction may actually hamper a graduate as he seeks to be accepted by the group. Vocational educators are well aware of the need for up-to-date technical skills, including knowledge of time-saving shortcuts and methods of working safely. But they often overlook the need to provide instruction in social skills.

The most common method of teaching these social skills on-the-job is through "horse-play." The new worker is told to perform an impossible task, is sent for a non-existent tool, or made to look foolish in some other way, which convinces him that acceptance by the group is highly desirable. He is taught what constitutes a good day's work and is expected to do neither more nor less. He learns which persons have views which are acceptable to the group, which must be listened to politely, but then ignored, and which must be pointedly ignored. He learns those to whom he can speak frankly and those who he must mislead. Very often there are only subtle clues to indentify a correct action, but the penalties of an incorrect action are swift and often severe. All of this instruction is informal, unplanned, and very time-consuming. This explains in large part why learning an occupation on-the-job frequently takes many years. It also helps to explain why so many studies show that "getting along with others" is at least as important as having technical skills. And it helps to explain why high scores on "personality" tests have little relationship to job success. If the new worker is lucky, he will be taken in hand by an older worker who plays the part of parent and teacher, and accelerates the learning of social skills necessary for group acceptance. This is done through direct instruction, rather than through the more common method of trial, error, and punishment.

The vocational teacher, like the all too rare fatherly fellow-employee, can smooth the path of the new graduate by providing him with direct instruction in the social skills of work in a particular occupational field. Since the vocational graduate may go to work in any one of a variety of groups, he will have to learn on-the-job the characteristics of a particular group. But a very large part of the social skills of work are common throughout an occupational field, and can be learned in advance.

As was pointed out earlier, most vocational course content concentrates almost exclusively on technical skills and pays little attention to the social skills of work. Even if the course outline includes provision for teaching social skills, it is almost essential that the teacher have recent, direct, personal contact with the occupation if he is to provide effective instruction in these skills. Many clues to correct social action in the work group are so subtle that a person who does not know them intimately may teach incorrectly. Fortunately, work social groups are quite similar to student social groups in the vocational education laboratory, and students can and do learn from each other. Many of these learnings cannot take place, however, in the standard classroom. It is very likely that much of the effectiveness of preparatory vocational education is due to the setting which is provided for learning group social skills. This setting is rarely provided in non-vocational curricula.

Job Satisfaction

The extent to which workers are satisfied with their jobs varies strikingly by occupation. The higher the prestige of the job, the greater the satisfaction usually reported by the workers. But most workers are satisfied in even the least prestigious jobs. For example, the typical semi-skilled worker finds a rhythm to his work which is very satisfying. It is fortunate that people like different types of jobs, or the work of the world would never get done. There is a tendency for professional workers (who do most of the writing about jobs) either to romanticize less glamorous work, or, more frequently, to assume that because the writer would not like repetitive work, no one else would like it either. Such writers frequently make the mistake of comparing the typical worker of today with the artist-craftsman of medieval times. It would be more accurate to compare the job satisfactions of today's employee with the 90 percent of medieval workers who were serfs and worked as animals.

Most people like jobs best if they have little direct supervision and have contact both on and off the job with other people in the same line of work. The least satisfied workers are those in service occupations and those managers who work for others. The dissatisfaction of managers is so great (31 percent) that it results in job satisfaction for all white collar workers being lower than that for blue collar workers. This is in marked contrast to the high job satisfaction for professionals, sales personnel, and skilled and semi-skilled workers (12, p. 191-198). The best explanation of this comes from Crozier (4), who found that managers had low job satisfaction because they were not in a position to control their own destiny, or to affect the direction of their work group. This contradicts the conventional wisdom, which sees managers as having great power and considerable satisfaction from the use of this power.

Job satisfaction is related to school curriculum. All studies report graduates of the high school vocational curricula to have higher job satisfaction than graduates of other curricula who do not go on to college. The most likely reason for this is also found in Crozier (4, p. 100-111). He found, in a highly bureaucratic work organization, that the maintenance workers had high job satisfaction, with production worker being less satisfied, and supervisors being most dissatisfied. He attributes this to the fact that bureaucracy sharply limits the decision-making opportunities of all except the technically trained. In a factory where the chief value is to keep the product flow moving, the technically trained personnel are the only ones who have options. While they are under heavy pressure to restore production from a broken down production line, they know they are needed, and all other employees recognize their importance. Bureaucrats are not the only persons who defer to technically trained workers. Housewives and deans treat plumbers and professors with kid gloves. Vocational education provides technical competence. It seems likely that as the world of work becomes increasingly complex, technical competence is going to be increasingly valued, and this will lead to continued high job satisfaction.

Alienation

It has often been noted that vocational and professional students are less likely than other students to be alienated from their families, schools, and government. This may be due to selection factors which emphasize conservatism and stability of purpose. More likely, it is due to vocational education providing a clearcut route to upward mobility and to the satisfaction of personal needs. If your education seems to you to be personally relevant, you are unlikely to go on strike to demand relevance in education. We badly need studies to determine whether or not it is true that vocational students are less alienated than other students. If this is true, we need to know why.

REFERENCES

1. Bendix, Rinehard, *Work and Authority In Industry*. New York: John Wiley & Sons, Inc., 1956.

2. Clark, Robert E., "Psychosis, Income and Occupational Prestige," *American Journal of Sociology*, LIV (March, 1949), 433-440.

3. Combs, Janet and William W. Cooley, "Dropouts: In High School and After School," *American Educational Research Journal,* V, No. 3, 343-363.

4. Crozier, Michael, *The Bureaucratic Phenomenon.* Chicago: The University of Chicago Press, 1964.

5. DeGrazia, Sebastian, *Of Time, Work and Leisure.* New York: Anchor Books, Doubleday & Company, Inc., 1964.

6. Gross, Edward, *Industry and Social Life.* Dubuque, Iowa: William C. Brown Company, Publishers, 1965.

7. Kerr, Clark, *et al. Industrialism and Industrial Man.* New York: Oxford University Press, Galaxy Edition, 1964.

8. Lipset, Seymour M., *et al.* "Job Plans and Entry into the Labor Market," *Social Forces,* XXXIII (1955), 224-232.

9. Lipset, Seymour M. and Reinhard Bendix, "Social Mobility and Occupational Career Plans," *American Journal of Sociology,* LVII (1952), 366-374 and 494-504.

10. Mays, Arthur B., *Principles and Practices of Vocational Education.* New York: McGraw-Hill Book Company, 1948.

11. Miller, Delbert and William Form, *Industrial Sociology.* New York: Harper & Row, Publishers, 1964.

12. Morse, Nancy C. and R.S. Weiss, "The Function and Meaning of Work and the Job," *American Sociological Review,* XX (1955), 191-198.

13. Wentworth, Edna C., *Employment After Retirement.* Washington, D.C.: Government Printing Office, HEW 68-5, 1968.

Chapter 9 PSYCHOLOGICAL FOUNDATIONS

The educational philosopher is most concerned about what should be taught, but the psychologist is concerned with *how* it should be taught if everyone is to learn and how to determine what has and has not been learned. Knowledge is seldom acquired by presenting the student with a great mass of information, even if it is important information. And if the knowledge is not learned and retained, education has not taken place. These statements sound trite, but a large proportion of high school and college teachers act as if all that they need to do is to lecture, and learning will automatically take place. Vocational educators seldom make this mistake, though they may err in the opposite direction and over-teach by insisting on repetition which goes on well after the concept or skill has been thoroughly learned. Either type of error leads to educational inefficiency. The psychologist offers help in improving the efficiency of both teaching and learning by pointing out the importance of the process of instruction and the need for adaptation according to the learner's individual characteristics. Through the process of vocational counseling he provides a method of encouraging students to make important decisions which will lead to continued learning after the student has left his teacher and the formal school.

The Process of Learning

Perhaps the best statement of the relationship of psychology to teaching and learning is provided by Cronbach (4, pp. 3-28). Psychology gives the teacher new viewpoints which help him to (1) design instruction which is most likely to aid each student's learning, (2) determine whether learning has occurred and (3) re-design instruction to ensure that learning occurs. Gagné defines learning as "... a change in human disposition or capability, which can be retained, and which is not simply ascribable to the process of growth" (6, p. 5). We decide whether or not learning has occurred by observing changes in behavior before and after the student has been taught (by a teacher or by a situation likely to promote learning). Teachers often think of learning only in terms of improved performance, but poor performance can also be learned, and much of learning affects interests and values, which in turn can affect performance. Interests, values, and performance are closely related, with changes in any one of these having sharp effects on the others. We are more interested in, and value more highly, those areas in which we perform well. This seems to be a prime reason why students who regularly fail in academic subjects often take a completely different attitude toward school after success in vocational education.

We learn through our senses (including our muscular or kinesthetic senses), and thus modify the chains of nerve activity in our central nervous system. This leads to a changed pattern of muscle action in response to future stimuli. This pattern of action is called "behavior," and the effects of behavior are called "performance." Most experimental study of the learning process has been done on animals, especially the rat. This has led to great emphasis on trial and error learning and conditioned response learning. Both are very important for rats, but relatively unimportant in human learning. The first serious work on human learning was the study of how we learn "nonsense syllables." These are syllables such as RIV or GEX which have little or no meaning either to the teacher or the student. They were used because they were not known before the experiment began, while syllables like JIG or NAN probably would have been known by some, but not all students. If some students had had this prior knowledge, it would have been difficult to determine how much had been learned during the experiment.

A great deal is now known about how we learn nonsense syllables. Unfortunately, this type of learning is relatively unimportant in real life, and we now know that the way we learn *meaningful* material is very different from the way we learn nonsense material. Regardless of the learning conditions, meaningful material is always learned faster and retained longer than nonsense material. It is often overlooked that material which appears meaningful to the teacher, may seem to the student to be nonsense. In this case, it is learned slowly and retained for only a short time, just as is material which appears to be nonsense to both teacher and learner. One of the chief values of vocational education is the fact that it can change material which some students consider nonsense, into relevant and meaningful material.

The generalization that meaningful material is more easily learned than nonsense material is about the only generalization that can be made about all types of learning, though psychologists, like educational philosophers, have been searching for a single pattern to explain a wide variety of events. (It has been stated that learning requires "readiness," motivation, and that one type of learning affects another, but it appears that these are only different ways of expressing the desirability of meaningfulness.)

It is the job of the teacher to provide the external conditions which facilitate learning. This sounds simple, but it is not, for these conditions are different for each learner, and must be modified, even for a single student, with each new learning acquired by that student. The conditions are also different for each type of learning. The discovery of this fact by Gagné (6) made a major contribution to the psychology of learning. He identified eight types of learning, ranging from responses to signals to complex problem solving, and he specified the conditions of learning for each type. If a person attempts to teach concepts, principles, and problem solving in the same way he teaches signal learning, stimulus-response learning, chaining, and other simple types of learning, the results will not be good. The student will probably learn the *words* which state the concept, but will not learn the real meaning of the concept. "Words facilitate the development of concepts only when the ideas they represent are understood. Verbalization without understanding is likely to hinder the learning of concepts . . . The ability to verbalize a concept is not a guarantee that the learner can apply or relate the concept and language" (11, p. 10). Too often teachers accept the words instead of being certain that the concept itself has been learned.

It has long been known that people forget certain simple types of learning quickly, but remember quite well the more complex types of learning. The reason is that those people who really learn the more complex types of content do this because that content is meaningful. On the other hand, the simple types of learning can be acquired by almost everyone, but unless they are meaningful or used often, they are forgotten.

Gagné (6, p. 96) points out that "chains" (sequences) of motor behavior are not forgotten easily, and can be re-learned very rapidly. He cites examples of swimming, bicycle riding, and playing a musical instrument. Similar motor "chains" form a major portion of the content of many vocational courses, e.g., typing, welding torch manipulation, making biscuits or a buttonhole. Many educational philosophers advocate postponing specific vocational education until just prior to the time it will be used, on the ground that much of its content is apt to be forgotten. But the evidence from psychology suggests that it would be even more appropriate to postpone instruction on the voting laws until just before the student was allowed to vote.

ACTIVE PARTICIPATION

Occasionally a person can learn a complex sequence of responses such as typing by trial and error. More often he learns imperfectly, after a long period of time, and the bad habits he learns can interfere with later learning of more efficient methods. The learning of skills usually occurs more efficiently if the learner sees a demonstration of the skill from a teacher or from a film first, then tries to perform the action himself. The more complex the skill to be learned, the more important it is to have competent instruction to accompany practice.

KNOWLEDGE OF RESULTS

If the student knows how well he is doing, and what are the strong and weak points of his performance, two beneficial results occur: he spends his time learning those things that really count, and his motivation for learning is increased because he knows he is not wasting time. Knowledge of results works best when it is immediate rather than delayed, and it is most important when the student sets goals for himself which are difficult to achieve (9).

Vocational education laboratories and cooperative education training stations offer a variety of opportunities for feedback (knowledge of results which leads to corrective action). But the typical vocational education lecture or discussion provides as little immediate feedback as the typical academic class, often because the instructor is unaware of its importance.

Vocational education has an advantage over many subject matter fields, however, because its goals are clear to the student and are related to the real world outside academia. It seems reasonable that knowledge of results would likely be of little benefit unless the subject matter appears important to the student, or unless he is one of those people who find feedback useful because they see learning as a game which is important for its own sake.

Individual Differences

Perhaps the greatest contribution of psychology has been its study of individual differences — the ways in which individuals differ from each other. Other disciplines accept the fact of individual differences, but often proceed to treat all members of a group as if they were the same. Even educators do this, though they ought to know better. Individuals differ in a large variety of ways: in social class, intelligence, motivation, maturation physical characteristics, etc. Since the ability to learn is noticeably affected by most of these factors, one would expect that educators would be experts in identifying these differences and in providing a learning environment which makes the most of them. Unfortunately, however, we know surprisingly little about how individual differences and learning affect each other. Until psychology can tell us more about this process, the safest course of action seems to be to provide a wide variety of teaching-learning opportunities in the hope that one or more of them will be effective for each individual.

The "academic" subjects have in common a very high emphasis on verbal ability. They are usually taught in ways which emphasize memorization, verbal fluency (including reading skill), interest in knowledge for its own sake, and postponement of rewards. The classroom setting, in which they are most often taught, rewards those who sit still, pay attention to symbols (rather than to objects), and have a long span of attention. Some students do very well with these tasks in these settings. But other students do not.

Laboratory courses are effective with some students who do not learn well in a classroom. "Non-academic" courses such as art, music, physical education, industrial arts, and vocational education emphasize environments for learning which are markedly different from the academic classroom or laboratory. Equally important is the fact that they emphasize learning tasks which are attractive to some students who are not at all successful in their academic courses.

Some students, of course, enjoy and excel in almost any learning task in any school setting, for great abilities in one area tend to be accompanied by great abilities in many other areas. We are all familiar with the athlete who is an "A" student in music, the practical arts, and academic studies. Poor nutrition and some types of brain damage hamper performance in most types of learning. But a large proportion of students fall between these two extremes. They learn some things well, but not others. They may have physical problems (color blindness, slow maturation, low metabolic rates, etc.) which interfere with some types of learning, but not with others, or have special interests and motivations which cause them to succeed in some fields but fail in others. The school which tries to make all pupils excel in all fields is portrayed in that excellent satire, *The Animal School,* by G. H. Reavis. Even worse is a school which offers a narrow program which rewards only those students who excel in verbal learning, who enjoy working with symbols instead of with people or things, and who work well in the classroom setting. The fully comprehensive school provides a variety of paths to school success and capitalizes on individual differences rather than trying to force all individuals into a common mold.

SOCIAL CLASS AND LEARNING IN THE SCHOOL

We have discovered recently that social class is one of the most important individual differences affecting school learning. "In the United States, [during the nineteenth century,] . . . the public schools quickly became the common school, attended by representatives of all classes . . . excluding only those upper-class children in private schools, those poor who went to no schools, and Indians and Southern Negroes, who were without schools" (3, p. 9). In most other countries, however, there have been two parallel systems of education, one designed for lower class students, and the other attended by upper-class and middle class children. This situation continues to the present day though reformers of education in most countries recognize that it is undesirable, and often view the American comprehensive school as an ideal.

One of the goals for a dual school system is ". . . that of maintaining the existing social order — a system . . . designed to prevent a wholesale challenge by the children of the working class to the positions held for children of the middle [and upper] classes (3, p. 10). The truly comprehensive high school rejects this goal, and substitutes for it a goal of opportunity for vertical social mobility. It attempts to achieve this goal by two means: first, exposure to and choice from a variety of school curricula which have different social class outcomes; and second, contact with students from a variety of social classes, with the expectation that students will learn from each other that social classes exist and that upward social mobility is usually desirable. Obviously, a school which offers a narrow range of curricula cannot use the first of these methods. And, a school which is segregated by social class cannot use the second.

The desirability of giving students a choice from a broad range of curricula has long been recognized in this country, but the undesirability of segregation on the basis of social class has only recently been recognized. The most complete documentation of the effects of segregation by social class came about by accident. Coleman set out to discover the

effects of low levels of school expenditures and high proportions of inexperienced teachers on the achievement of black students. He found that
these had much smaller effects than he had thought, but he found that
schools which had a heavy majority of students from low socio-economic
levels almost invariably had low achievement levels, even when other
variables were held equal. Project TALENT data showed that while students of every social class are enrolled in vocational education, lower
class students predominate. The establishment of separate schools for
vocational education therefore tends to mean establishment of schools
which segregate students by social class. This, in turn, is almost certain
to result in lowered achievement.

INTELLIGENCE

... the word "intelligence" has *two* valuable meanings. One is (A) an
innate potential, the capacity for development, a fully innate property that amounts to the possession of a good brain and a good
neural metabolism. The second is (B) the functioning of a brain in
which development has gone on ... There are then two determinants of intellectual growth: a *completely necessary* innate potential
(intelligence A), and a *completely necessary* stimulating environment. It is not to the point to ask which is most important ... given
a perfect environment, the inherited constitution will set the pace;
given the heredity of a genius, the environment will do so (7, pp. 294
and 302).

Intelligence tests measure A and B combined, and are not able to separate the two factors which determine test results. Moreover, the intelligence test "only purports to measure verbal ability and to predict school
performance — not ability or performance in the mechanical and social
areas" (1, p. 59). Indeed, the only reason such tests are successful in
predicting school performance is that almost all school activities emphasize verbal ability.

For many years, psychologists felt that the hereditary aspects of intelligence were all important. They noted that intelligence test scores were
relatively constant throughout school careers, and attributed this to the
influence of innate potential. They neglected to note that each child's
environment changed little during his school career. Recently, it has
been found that the intelligence test scores of children of immigrants were
much higher than the test scores of their mothers and fathers. Assuming
adequate nutrition, the scores should have been about the same. And it
has been found that very young children from poor homes gain considerably in measured intelligence when they are placed in a stimulating
school environment at an early age. This leads to the conclusion that

The IQ can be trusted as an index of intelligence A only when the social background of the (people) compared are identical; and this adds up to the proposition that we cannot in any rigorous sense measure a (person's) innate endowment, for no two social backgrounds are identical . . . Intelligence in sense B is a different matter. We know, beyond dispute, that the adolescent with generally low intelligence-test scores, whether Negro, poor white American, or foreigner, is a poor prospect for college training, or training as a mechanic, or Army officer, or dress designer . . . To be a bank manager, an airplane pilot, a mathematician, a secretary, or a surgeon requires a certain common conceptual development that must occur in this or a closely related culture, and in childhood mainly; and intelligence tests on the whole can provide a rather good index of the extent to which that development has occurred (7, pp. 300-301).

Vocational education is, of course, much less interested in intelligence A than in B, for it can have no effect on the former. Its effects on the latter are probably minimal. Early childhood education offers promise of modifying B, but vocational education comes too late in life to change intelligence appreciably. Because intelligence is measured by tests which are largely verbal, it has even less chance of changing *measured* intelligence. This leaves vocational education with the necessity of living with the intelligence which its clients bring to it. But this acceptance of intelligence can be done in one of two ways. The first way is to screen potential students out on the basis of intelligence test scores. There are three methods of accomplishing this screening:

A. If there are more applicants for a vocational education program than can be accommodated, intelligence test scores are sometimes used, together with other factors such as previous grades, to screen out the "less able." This results in a reputation for a program with high standards of admission and increases the proportion of graduates who are eagerly sought by employers.

B. A slightly more sophisticated use of intelligence tests is commonly employed in training within business and industry. On the basis of past experience, it is often found that trainees who score above a certain level on intelligence tests have relatively high turnover and accident rates (possibly due to boredom). On the other hand, trainees who score below a certain level are less likely to complete the training program successfully. This leads to selecting trainees whose test scores fall in a band between high and low scores.

C. A related use of intelligence test scores is found in an organization such as the army which must accept trainees having a broad range of intelligence, and must supply specified numbers of vocational graduates in each of a variety of occupations. On the basis of past experience, we determine which programs require very high scores for successful completion, (e.g., electronics) and which can be completed successfully by trainees with low intelligence test scores (e.g. fabric repair and production welding). Test scores are then used to distribute the available trainees among the vocational programs, with each program being geared to turn out the required number of graduates. Similar techniques are followed in communist and fascist countries with more or less fully planned economies.

These uses of intelligence test scores can be justified if the goal of the vocational program is to produce trained workers to meet labor market needs. They are not justified if the goal is to enhance individual options. Instead, potential trainees should be counseled on the basis of the probability of their success in the occupation chosen. If the trainee decides that he wants to pursue a vocational program even though he has only a 20 percent chance of success in the occupational field, he should be permitted to do so, for he might be one of the twenty in a hundred who would succeed.

The screening of potential vocational education students on the basis of intelligence test scores should be approached with care, for there is little relationship between intelligence and occupational success. Twenty percent of sales clerks have IQ's below 80; the correlation between intelligence and success as an executive is $-.10$, and there is a wide variety of unskilled occupations which can be performed successfully by people with a mental age of 8 or less (IQ 50 or less) (13, pp. 95-98). This is not to say that intelligence is not important in vocational success. Three ways in which it is important are: (1) for an occupation there is certain minimum intelligence below which success is unlikely (but above which intelligence has little effect on success), (2) promotability is enhanced by intelligence, and (3) intelligence is most clearly related to success in occupations requiring verbal skill (but even here the relationship is not close). The basic mistake which is too often made is to assume that because the *average* intelligence varies widely between occupations (e.g., 130 IQ for accountants and chemists, versus 85 IQ for miners and lumberjacks), the *minimum* intelligence required for success is the same as the average. Obviously this is not true.

A second and more satisfying way for the vocational educator to live with the relatively fixed intelligence of his students is to recognize that no one begins to approach the limits which his intelligence sets for his ability to learn. Sound education can enable the individual to approach this limit much more closely than he could without this learning environment.

MOTIVATION

Psychologists agree that motivation is extremely important in determining what an individual will or will not learn. But despite intense study, they have produced surprisingly little that aids the teacher either in recognizing motivations which exist (so that teaching can be structured to capitalize on these motivations) or in changing motivations (so that a student will want to learn essential ideas and skills). Perhaps the most helpful ideas have come from Abraham Maslow who suggests that there is a hierarchy of human needs, with each of the lower level needs having to be satisfied before a need at a higher level is effective in motivating a person to want to learn. From low to high, he lists needs as: (1) physiological, (2) safety, (3) belongingness and love, (4) importance, respect, self-esteem, and independence, and (5) information, understanding, beauty, and self-actualization (10, p. 80).

Most schooling assumes that the first four of these needs have been met outside the school, and that every individual is therefore ready for learning based on his needs for information, understanding, beauty and self-actualization. This assumption may be true for the middle or upper class student for the moment. But many students are concerned about the future. They wonder what type of education will satisfy their physiological needs when their parents no longer provide financial support. Preparation for a vocation will meet their physiological needs, and satisfy needs for safety, belongingness, importance, respect, self-esteem, and independence as well. With some prospect of these needs being satisfied through vocational education or through college preparatory education, they are in a position to begin to be concerned about their higher needs.

The future is not all that concerns students. While they are in school, many students, especially those from lower class homes and homes with one or more parents absent, have unmet needs within Maslow's first four categories, and hence cannot be motivated by the fifth category. Indeed, some students even have unmet physiological needs, for they are hungry, tired, poorly clothed, and inadequately housed. Such students are likely to view academic schooling in particular as being irrelevant. On the other hand, vocational education, especially cooperative education with its pay for useful work performed, offers a way to meet certain physiological needs; its small classes and work teams offer a sense of importance and belongingness; its emphasis on nonverbal content provides respect and self-esteem for the student with poor verbal skills, and its individualized instruction provides independence. With these needs met, the student may be ready for both vocational and non-vocational instruction which is designed to provide information, understanding, beauty, and self-actualization.

⌐ The need for safety (as Maslow defines it) is the only primary need to which vocational education does ⌒not⌒ make substantial contributions. Vocational education which is segregated by social class may indeed heighten the student's concern for personal safety, because it may put a student into an environment where threats to his safety from lower class students are much more common.

Two ways in which the school can modify the motivations of its' students are: by allowing the student to receive (at least for part of each day) instruction which appears to him to be relevant to his needs, and by providing extrinsic rewards for desired behavior. Properly designed vocational education appears relevant in its own right, and as the student learns that basic skills are required in the world of work, vocational education lends relevance to the study of basic skills. Both of these provide intrinsic motivation. Recently, the study of operant conditioning has emphasized the importance of extrinsic motivation, and has suggested ways in which it can be provided in the school. There are moral questions which inhibit teachers from using operant conditioning extensively to modify student motivations and behavior. Vocational education is relatively unique in providing both intrinsic motivation, and a considerable amount of perfectly natural extrinsic motivation through such rewards as the take home project, pay (in cooperative education programs), rank in the student personnel structure, and awards by out-of-school organizations.

PHYSICAL MATURATION

We know very little about the relationship of physical maturation to performance in vocational education. We do know that adolescent girls mature physically about two years sooner than boys. We also know that girls perform better than boys in general education and in the few areas of vocational education which encourage co-education. Fuzak (5, p. 53) found a high correlation between physical maturity, as measured by hand dynamometer scores, and boys' success in performance tests in junior high school industrial arts. We do not know whether this relationship holds for girls and for other types of subject matter. Nor do we know whether it holds in the senior high school and junior college. Since a few boys (though almost no girls) are still physically immature at age eighteen, it seems likely that physical maturity might be a factor in vocational education success. Certainly we need more information on these points.

If physical maturation is important for both sexes and for a broad variety of subject matter, the typical organization of a vocational education program would seem to be particularly unfortunate. Usually, vocational education, like history, is presented in chronological order. Those skills and processes which were discovered first are taught first. This means that skills which require a high degree of manipulative dexterity are taught early in the course, while the operation of machines, which requires less manipulative skill, is taught later. If physical maturation is important to success, this order should be reversed. (It should also be reversed because machine skills are easier to learn than hand skills.)

PHYSICAL CHARACTERISTICS

The ability to see small details, distinguish colors, hear high pitched sounds, lift heavy weights, be able to stand or sit for long periods of time, and other physical characteristics are important to success in certain occupations. Individual differences in these characteristics are rarely measured before enrollment in vocational education courses. So it is possible, for example, for a student who is partially color-blind to complete a year of instruction in printing and to be dismissed from the program as unsuitable, without knowing what caused his difficulty in matching colors. Each student should be informed if he has physical characteristics which will handicap him in an occupation, and be advised of the probability that his handicap will be serious.

Vocational Counseling

Guidance personnel, when they provide vocational counseling, have in mind two goals which are identical to two of the three goals of vocational education. Super and Crites state these as ". . . to help people make good vocational adjustments, and to facilitate smooth functioning of the economy through the effective use of manpower" (13, p. 1).

TESTS IN VOCATIONAL COUNSELING

The tests used are difficult to devise. They must be carefully constructed, using psychological models of the real world, then tried and revised repeatedly. During this process, data are accumulated on the test's effectiveness for different purposes. Because of the difficulties in constructing tests which are of real value in vocational counseling, it is rare for the counselor to devise his own tests. Rather, he selects from among the wide variety of tests which have been prepared for national distribution.

Tests may be roughly classified as aptitude and achievement tests, interest tests, personality and attitude tests, and proficiency tests. All of them have definite weaknesses. Aptitude can only be measured in terms of ability to achieve success on the test which is used. This in turn is based on past experience in the culture for which the test was built. Consequently, test results usually underestimate the ability of an individual who comes from a different culture. Interest test results are influenced by factors surrounding the testing situation. Applicants for a clerical job who take an interest test are likely to show higher clerical interests than they would if they were applying for a scientific job. Personality and attitude test results are seldom related to success on the job, in spite of the often repeated claim that personality is a major factor in job success. Proficiency tests are difficult to administer if proficiency involves skills which cannot be measured with paper and pencil. Despite these difficulties tests can be very useful, especially in two situations: (1) where a *group* is being screened for admission to training or to work, and (2) where an *individual* is sincerely interested in learning more about his interests, strengths, and weaknesses.

SCREENING FOR ADMISSION

If more people have applied than can be accepted for training or for employment, some method must be used for rejecting some and accepting others. Interviews, past records of success in similar situations, and test results are the most frequent devices used. A test which has relatively poor predictive ability (predictive validity) may still be useful in improving the batting average of the personnel man who must decide who will be employed. Gross errors can be made in individual cases, but if the proportion of successful employees is increased by use of test results, the personnel man is likely to continue using these tests.

The problem of the vocational teacher and counselor is more difficult. They must be concerned about both the individuals who are accepted and those who are rejected for training. Most tests having sufficient predictive validity for use with groups are not sufficiently accurate to provide assurance that each individual student is being treated fairly. Usually, all that can be said is that test results indicate the *probability* of success or failure in a particular training program.

The decision as to what should be maximized by the process of selection of trainees is extremely important, but is rarely considered. The success of a vocational education program is usually measured in terms of the success of the graduates. To maximize the success of graduates, the only students who should be admitted to the program are those who do not need the program. This technique has been used for years in elite colleges. Only those students are admitted as freshmen who already have the knowledge possessed by graduates of most colleges. This type of screening procedure assures the graduates' success even if the educational program adds nothing to their competence. Similarly, in vocational education some programs admit only students who have abilities and attitudes which virtually guarantee success in employment, even if the vocational program does nothing for them. From an educational standpoint, this type of evaluation and student selection is unacceptable. "Value added by education" should be the criterion of the program's success, and students should be selected who will gain most from the program, regardless of the level at which they start. We know little about methods of selecting those who will profit most from instruction, and this must be given high research priority in psychology and vocational education.

THE STUDENT AND HIS INTERESTS, STRENGTHS, AND WEAKNESSES

Fortunately, more is known about counseling students who want to learn about themselves. Here, the emphasis is on helping the individual to help himself. The first step is to help the individual to understand his interests and abilities. Interest tests are more useful in this situation than in screening for admission because the individual is free of immediate pressures as he states his interests. If the student has definite vocational goals in mind, tests can be selected to indicate his probability of success. If he does not have definite vocational goals, his interests can form the basis for selecting educational experiences which will help him explore occupations related to those interests.

The process of counseling individual students requires skill which is achieved only after specific training. The vocational teacher can, of course, provide answers to questions which lie within his field of expertise. Perhaps the best advice which psychologists provide to the untrained vocational counselor is: avoid telling people what occupations they should or should not enter. The vocational teacher can best work in cooperation with trained counselors, where his occupational knowledge and the knowledge he has acquired about his students can supplement their skills in counseling. Such cooperation assumes that the teacher has some familiarity with counseling techniques, and also assumes the availability of fully trained counselors. Too often the ratio of students to counselors is so high, and the availability of *well trained* counselors is so low that even the students who want assistance cannot be accommodated. No one has a good solution to the problem of the student who reaches late adolescence without realizing that he needs assistance in the process of vocational choice.

VOCATIONAL CHOICE

Super and Overstreet, in their study of ninth grade boys, point out that vocational choice is a process which extends over a period of time and is made up of a ". . . sequence of lesser decisions . . . which bring about a progressive reduction of the number of alternatives open to the chooser" (14, p. 141). This process begins at an early age and is accelerated if the student: comes from a home which provides a stimulating environment, has high verbal ability, is interested in the professions, gets good grades, and has parents who allow him to make decisions. These are precisely the characteristics of students who perform well in and enjoy the traditional school program with its emphasis on verbal ability and preparation for the professions. This is not likely to be a simple coincidence, but is probably cause and effect, for these are the middle class characteristics which dominate the schools.

The process of vocational choice is aided by practice in decision making of all types since vocational choice is itself made up of a number of decisions. The school would therefore be wise to provide opportunities for vocational decision making. So, contrary to the usual view, it is more important for a student to make vocational decisions than to make the *right* vocational choice. And it is essential that the right to change the decision be explicit.

There are two concepts of occupational exploration: (1) gathering knowledge and withholding any decision on goals, and (2) making a choice which may be changed if later knowledge makes the choice seem undesirable. The latter is preferable for two reasons. It is the best way to get commitment which leads to *apparent* relevance of academic subjects which should be learned but will not be learned by many students because these subjects appear to lack relevance. Also, it is education for change. If a student realizes that he can learn enough of the rudiments of three or four occupations to enable him to enter any one of them, he knows three things:

A. That he need not despair if his job changes or if he wants to change his job. He has proved that he can change.
B. That he has acquired a variety of skills and background knowledge which he knows to be common to several occupations.
C. That he has mastered some of the background knowledge and a variety of skills which are different in each of the fields he has studied, but which will be common to a number of other occupations which fall within his sphere of interest.

Most guidance personnel agree with Barry and Wolf that ". . . there is no justification for the separate practice of vocational . . . counseling." To separate each ". . . individual's concerns into the popular categories of personal, social, educational, and vocational with a special counselor for each is not only a complete absurdity, but dangerous and destructive to the individual" (2, p. 184). In one sense, this is a straw man, since no one proposes separate counselors for each of these four aspects of guidance. It is valid, however, in pointing out that vocational counseling must consider all aspects of the student's development. Despite the tone of their title, *(Epitaph for Vocational Guidance),* Barry and Wolf offer many positive suggestions for improving vocational counseling, and do not approve the too common trend of concentrating almost entirely on personal and educational counseling. Nor do they approve the use of untrained counselors who do not want to ". . . meddle with personality, and hence feel less meddlesome freely giving vocational advice, little realizing that this is the greatest meddling of all, for what a person does and becomes is a dynamic part of his personality" (2, p. 185).

Perhaps their greatest contribution, however, is their rejection of the assumption that the goal of vocational guidance is to persuade the student to make a final and unchangeable vocational choice. Vocational decisions should be made, but the individual should not be held to his decision.

> Any adult conversing with a youngster will sooner or later ask, 'What do you want to be when you grow up?' Depending upon his interests at the moment, the child will answer candidly in terms of the occupations with which he is most familiar. By the age of ten or twelve, he finds that adults are no longer pleased or satisfied with his changing answers, so he may protect himself by one of two devices: either he says honestly he does not know, or he reports some answer that has already brought approval from his parents or other adults. Many are the proud parents who state with conviction that their sons and daughters plan to become engineers, lawyers, or doctors. The youngster is virtually stuck with his decision, made not wisely, intellectually or knowingly, but rather on the basis of adult approval. It is no wonder that he views changing his mind as a mortal sin, for adults force him into this trap. (2, p. 186).

Not only parents, but teachers and counselors regard changing a vocational choice as a sin, and do everything possible to make such a change costly to the student. Vocational teachers are as guilty as the rest. But vocational education has occupational exploration as one of its goals in the high school, the junior college, and in adult education programs, and exploration assumes that change is desirable if the original goal proves to be unsound.

Therefore not only should the school provide a setting which encourages vocational decision making, but that setting should allow changes in vocational choice to be made without penalties, at least through the twelfth grade. Even in junior college, penalties for changes in vocational goals should be at an absolute minimum. Penalties may be severe after the adult acquires family responsibilities, so it is far better for changes to occur in adolescence, and preferably in an environment which encourages changes which have been carefully thought through. It is indefensible to require an eleven year old to make a vocational choice which is binding for life, but it is equally indefensible to encourage deferral of occupational choice until the student has left high school.

REFERENCES

1. Ausubel, David P., *Psychological Aspects of Curriculum Evaluation.* Paper presented to the National Seminar for Vocational Education Research. Washington, D.C.: National Science Teachers Association, 1964.

2. Barry, Ruth and Beverly Wolf, *An Epitaph for Vocational Guidance.* New York: Columbia University Press, 1962.

3. Coleman, James S., "The Concept of Equality of Educational Opportunity," *Harvard Educational Review*, XXXVIII (1968), 1-22.

4. Cronbach, Lee J., *Educational Psychology,* Second edition. New York: Harcourt, Brace & World, Inc., 1963.

5. Fuzak, John A., *The Role of Physical Maturation in Determining the Ability of Junior High School Boys to Perform Complex Finger Coordinative Activities in Industrial Arts, and an Index to Level of Ability.* Chicago: American Technical Society, 1958.

6. Gagné, Robert M., *The Conditions of Learning.* New York: Holt, Rinehart & Winston, Inc., 1965.

7. Hebb, Donald O., *The Organization of Behavior.* New York: John Wiley & Sons, Inc., 1949.

8. Klausmeier, Herbert J., "Psychomotor Abilities and Skills," *Learning and Human Abilities.* New York: Harper & Row, Publishers, 1961.

9. Locke, E.A., "A Closer Look at Level of Aspiration as a Training Procedure," *Journal of Applied Psychology,* L (1966), 417-420.

10. Maslow, Abraham H., *Motivation and Personality.* New York: Harper & Row, Publishers, 1954.

11. NSTA Curriculum Committee, *Theory into Action.* Washington, D.C.: National Science Teachers Association, 1964.

12. Roe, Anne, *The Psychology of Occupations.* New York: John Wiley & Sons, Inc., 1956.

13. Super, Donald E. and John O. Crites, *Appraising Vocational Fitness by Means of Psychological Tests,* Second edition. New York: Harper & Row, Publishers, 1962.

14. Super, Donald E. and Phoebe Overstreet, *The Vocational Maturity of Ninth-Grade Boys.* New York: Columbia University Press, 1960.

Part III ORGANIZATION OF VOCATIONAL EDUCATION

Chapter 10 ELEMENTARY AND SECONDARY SCHOOLS

There is virtually no vocational education in American schools below the ninth grade. The little that exists is found in large city schools for the chronic truants, the mentally retarded, and other students who for some reason have not secured enough academic credits to admit them to secondary schools, in spite of the fact that they have reached secondary school age. Little has been written about these programs and little is known about them outside the walls of the institution in which they are conducted.

Vocational Education in High Schools

There are three basic reasons for the fact that vocational education, when it is offered at all, usually begins in the high school:

A. Vocational education is understood by most educators to be highly specialized and hence not an appropriate part of the general education programs of the elementary school and junior high school.

B. Specialized vocational education is best offered close to the time a person will use this education in employment. It is almost impossible for a person to secure meaningful employment before age sixteen, two years after the typical student leaves the eighth grade.

C. There are few examples of integrated curriculum plans which bridge the gap between elementary and secondary schools. Thus, even pre-vocational education is nearly non-existent below the ninth grade.

HIGH SCHOOL CURRICULA

There are three principal curricula in high schools in the United States. The college preparatory curriculum enrolls almost 50 percent of the male students and 35-40 percent of the females; the general curriculum has almost 25 percent of the males and 20 percent of the females, and the vocational curriculum enrolls about 25 percent of the males and from 40 to 45 percent of the females (9, pp. 5-11 and E-2). These figures are based on Project TALENT questionnaires which asked high school seniors to state the curricula in which they are enrolled. The United States Office of Education (USOE) figures on the proportion of students enrolled in reimbursed vocational programs are slightly smaller but not too dissimilar except in the case of women. Over 85 percent of the female students who say they are enrolled in vocational curricula specify that they are in commercial or business curricula. Much of this instruction is not yet counted by USOE. On the other hand, students enrolled in homemaking, who are counted by USOE, are forced by the form of Project Talent questions to indicate that they are in the "general" curriculum.

Typical USOE figures show 25 percent of secondary education students taking vocational education courses at any one time. This figure is not as helpful as it might be, however. Not only does it fail to give a breakdown by sex, but since vocational courses in the secondary school range in length from four to one years (or even less), a count of enrollments provides no indication of the number of graduates. In another way, however, it supplements Project TALENT data very well. Project TALENT gives no state by state data. USOE shows that secondary education vocational enrollments by states range from 10.5 percent to over 50 percent. Generally, the south and border states have enrollments far above average, while low enrollments are found in the midwest. It is difficult to understand why enrollments should be high in Vermont, Utah, and New York when their neighboring states of Maine, Colorado, Connecticut, and New Jersey are among the lowest in enrollments (21, p. 20).

The definitions provided for the curricula by Project TALENT are realistic. The general curriculum ". . . does not necessarily prepare you either for college or for work, but consists of courses required for graduation plus subjects that you like." The college preparatory program gives you ". . . the training and credits needed to work toward a regular Bachelor's degree in college." Project TALENT subdivided the vocational curriculum into three parts: commercial or business (". . . prepares you to work in an office"); vocational (". . . prepares you to work in a shop or factory, or to enter a trade school, or become an apprentice"), and agriculture (no definition) (9, pp. 5-11).

The course content of these three curricula has more similarities than differences. In most schools half of the program is identical for all three. When tracking is done, it tends to be done on the basis of academic ability level, rather than on the basis of curriculum. The remaining half of the program for the general curriculum is usually made up of electives. Vocational and college preparatory students are required to take additional courses especially in communications, scientific, and mathematics areas, and have fewer electives. The typical vocational program requires that no more than one-fourth of the time in high school be spent in courses designed to prepare a student for a sizeable family of occupations. Small schools often have no general curriculum and offer only agriculture and home economics within the vocational curriculum. Suburban schools often have no vocational curriculum for males. In both small rural schools and suburban schools the college preparatory curriculum often enrolls 70 percent of the students.

VOCATIONAL EDUCATION PROGRAMS, ENROLLMENTS, AND GRADUATES

In 1964-1965, 16,332 secondary schools offered federally reimbursed vocational education. In the following school year the number decreased slightly to 16,023 (21, p. 27). These figures are misleading, since a school was counted if it offered even one class in one vocational subject. If one accepted this figure at face value, one would assume that vocational education was readily available, since there are only about eighteen thousand high schools in the United States. In fact, vocational education is not generally available except in agriculture and home economics (and in beginning typing and industrial arts, which often have vocational education value).

The United States Office of Education figures on total enrollment in federally reimbursed secondary school vocational education were slightly over three million in 1965-66 (21, p. 18). Almost half of this enrollment (1,280,000) is in home economics. The other large program is office occupations (798,000). The two together account for two-thirds of the enrollment. Most enrollment in these two programs is female. The same is true in health occupations (10,000), and it is nearly true for distributive education (102,000). The 510,000 enrollment in agriculture is heavily male and usually occurs outside the large cities. This leaves two programs, trades and industries (319,000) and technical education (29,000), having a total of 12 percent of the vocational enrollment available for males in large cities. Actually, the bulk of enrollment in even these two programs is outside the large cities. If you ask persons past the age of high school attendance about their secondary school vocational training, you get reports such as those shown in Table 10-1.

TABLE 10–1

Vocational Courses Taken	Males	Females
Typing	37%	73%
Bookkeeping	16	40
Home Economics		75
Shorthand		40
Agriculture	24	
Carpentry	30	
Machine Shop	30	
Metal Working	30	
Took a Vocational Curriculum		
Graduates	38	50
Dropouts	30	30

Source: See reference 13, p. 242.

There are no available figures on the actual number of vocational education secondary school graduates, though such data are now being collected and will soon be published. The total number of graduates could be estimated reasonably well, but what is needed is the number of graduates by occupational cluster.

CHARACTERISTICS OF SECONDARY SCHOOL VOCATIONAL STUDENTS

Except for the few exceptions noted below, data are not available on characteristics of students enrolled in each of the fields of secondary school vocational education. Lacking this desirable information, we can only look at the known characteristics of vocational students as a group. Obviously these data are quite incomplete.

1. Sex of Students. Vocational education is generally assumed to be a curriculum for males. That this is not true for high school seniors is illustrated graphically by the following table adapted from Project TALENT data.

TABLE 10–2

Percentage of High School Seniors Enrolled in Each Curriculum

	Curriculum	Males	Females
A.	General	24.8%	18.9%
B.	College Preparatory	48.2	37.8
C.	Commercial or Business	7.1	37.1
D.	Vocational (for shop or factory)	12.4	3.3
E.	Agriculture	4.1	.3
F.	Other	3.3	2.6

Source: See reference 9, pp. 5-11.

Adding percentages in the three vocational curricula C, D, and E yields 23.6 for males and 40.7 for females.

2. Academic Aptitude of Students. Female vocational students are not only more numerous than male vocational students, but they have on the average markedly higher academic aptitude, as shown in Table 10-3. Nevertheless, each curriculum had significant numbers of male and female students at every decile of academic aptitude.

TABLE 10–3

Percent of Enrollees Above Average (Median)
In Academic Aptitude

Secondary School Curriculum	Males	Females
General Curriculum	31%	35%
College Preparatory	69	77
Vocational	23	43

Source: See reference 9, p. E-2.

For males, the heaviest enrollment in vocational courses comes from students who are at the 40th percentile of academic ability. These students average two vocational courses (four semesters) in four years. Students in the lowest 10 percent of ability averaged less than one and a half year long courses, but even students in the top 10 percent usually took one such course.

For females, the pattern was similar. Those in the top and bottom 10 percent of academic ability averaged two semesters of commercial subjects, while the remaining 80 percent averaged four semesters (9, p. E-4).

TABLE 10–4

Ability Measures of Male High School Graduates of Vocational Programs (In Percentiles)

Ability Measure	White	Non-White
Verbal Knowledge	47.6%	40.1%
Perceptual Speed and Accuracy	47.4	45.1
Mathematics	43.2	52.2
English	36.9	36.4
Visual Reasoning	59.2	50.8

Source: See reference 10, p. 18.

Data in Table 10–4 indicate that vocational students have considerably greater ability in visual reasoning than in the other abilities which were measured. Since even the visual reasoning test items require reading ability and since both white and non-white vocational students are relatively low in English ability as measured by these tests, it is likely that actual visual reasoning ability is underestimated. It is interesting to note also that non-white male vocational students surpass their white counterparts considerably in mathematics ability.

3. Age of Students. It is very odd that no data are available on age of secondary school vocational students, for it could easily be collected. It is well known that relatively few fourteen and fifteen year olds are enrolled (agriculture and home economics enroll almost all of the students in this age range). Vocational enrollment increases rapidly from age sixteen to high school graduation, for the remaining vocational education programs enroll students primarily for the last year or two years of high school. Very few students remain in high school beyond age eighteen.

Since the largest number of students drop out of high school at age sixteen, most dropouts have not been exposed to vocational education. Yet 70 percent of the male and 90 percent of the female dropouts report having had one or more vocational courses (13, p. 244). Presumably they are counting, in the main, the often required junior high school courses in industrial arts and home economics, plus beginning typing, which had been taken by 50 percent of the female dropouts.

4. Dropouts. Combs and Cooley (5) report in their Table 13 that 51 percent of freshmen who later dropped out of high school wanted a vocational education curriculum, but only 23 percent were admitted to it. In contrast, 48 percent of freshmen who later completed high school (but did not go on to college) wanted vocational education, and 43 percent got it. At the time of leaving school, 67 percent of the dropouts were in the general curriculum, 4 percent in the college preparatory curriculum, and 23 percent in a vocational curriculum. Comparable figures for those who graduated from high school but did not attend college were 36 percent, 14 percent, and 43 percent. (These figures do not add to 100 percent, since some dropouts said they were in other curricula.)

5. Color of Students. Parnes has collected most of the data available on color and education. He found that 12 percent of white males fourteen to seventeen years of age who were in school were enrolled in vocational and commercial curricula as compared with 15 percent for blacks (14, p. 26). The big difference, however, was in the other two curricula, with 24 percent of the blacks and 46 percent of the whites being in the college preparatory curriculum, and 61 percent of the blacks and 42 percent of the whites in the general curriculum. (Enrollment in the vocational curriculum is almost certainly understated because Parnes did not include eighteen year olds, who are much more likely than fourteen to seventeen year olds to have vocational education available to them.) Parnes found that 24 percent of white males enjoyed practical arts subjects most, compared to 12 percent of blacks. Only 2 percent of whites and 5 percent of blacks disliked practical arts courses more than any other subject they had taken (14, p. 27). Of those males fourteen to twenty-four years old who had not completed high school and were not enrolled in school, 47 percent of the whites but only 25 percent of the blacks had obtained "vocational preparation outside regular school" (14, p. 23). Presumably this was through Manpower Development and Training Act programs and through training provided as a part of private employment.

The report of the Advisory Council on Vocational Education notes that there are no data on vocational education enrollments of minority group members. It calls attention to the fact that ". . . proportionally a high ratio of Negroes are enrolled in vocational schools which are de facto segregated" (21, p. 122). Schaefer and Kaufman quote from their earlier study which indicated that while Negro graduates of all curricula earned less than white graduates, the comparative disadvantage of Negro vocational graduates was less (16, p. 78). Almost one-third of non-white vocational graduates were employed as non-farm laborers five years after high school graduation, but only about half as high a proportion of white vocational graduates were non-farm laborers at a comparable stage in their careers. The proportion of non-white vocational graduates who were farm workers was approximately three times as high as for white vocational graduates.

Eninger found that Negro graduates of trade and industrial vocational curricula took twice as long as whites to find employment, and were half as likely to secure employment in the occupation for which trained. Negroes were less likely than whites to get help from the school in job placement, and relied more frequently on friends and relatives. They had less job security, less job satisfaction, and lower earnings (though not lower hourly wages) than whites. Negro graduates of vocational education programs were more likely to get higher education than whites who graduated from this curriculum (7, p. 19). Only 7 percent of Eninger's usable questionnaires came from non-whites. It is likely that the plight of non-white vocational graduates has improved in the past few years, but to what extent is not known. The overall rate of youth unemployment for Negroes remains far higher than for whites. Parnes found that unemployment rates for males sixteen to nineteen years of age who are not in school, by color and by high school curriculum were: whites, from the college preparatory curriculum, 1.6 percent; vocational, 3.2 percent; general, 6.9 percent: blacks, from the college preparatory curriculum, 4.5 percent; vocational, 11.1 percent; general, 13.9 percent. These figures mix graduates and dropouts (14, p. 75).

6. *Socio-economic Status of Students.*   Schaefer and Kaufman found that the fathers of over half of the vocational students (both male and female) were employed as laborers or craftsmen-foremen, while one-third of the fathers of college preparatory students were in these occupational groups. College preparatory students were twice as likely as vocational students to have fathers employed as professionals (16, pp. 74, 76). Using father's occupation as a measure of socio-economic status, it is clear that from low to high the ranking of curricula is: vocational, general, and college preparatory, with each being approximately equally spaced along the continuum.

7. *Student Attitudes Toward College.*   Unfortunately, Project TALENT data have not been tabulated in a way which allows differentiation of student attitudes by secondary school curriculum taken. Tillery and Donovan (20) indicate repeatedly that high school juniors who expect to dropout, to graduate from high school, or to graduate from junior college or post-secondary vocational school all have similar attitudes, and have quite different attitudes from students who expect to graduate from four-year colleges. For example, the males in the former group most frequently chose shop, drafting, and industrial arts as their most

interesting subjects, while females chose business, commercial, and secretarial subjects. Males who expect to take baccalaureates chose science, social studies, and history, while females chose English and speech (20, p. 58). Three-fourths of the former group would like to be in occupations other than the professions. For potential baccalaureates three-fourths chose the professions (20, p. 132). For the former group, the plurality of males would choose vocational, trade, and industrial subjects as college majors, and a plurality of females would choose business. Potential four-year college graduates chose majors spread widely through the professional fields. Less than 4 percent of males and 8 percent of females would choose liberal arts as a major regardless of their expected level of educational attainment (20, p. 142). All types of students agreed by a large majority that college is a place where you prepare for a job (20, p. 94).

8. Attendance In Post-Secondary Education.   Schaefer and Kaufman in their study of Massachusetts youth present the only data available on college-going rates for all of the major secondary school curricula. They found that 35 percent of vocational graduates and 41 percent of college preparatory graduates enrolled in post-secondary education. In marked contrast, only 9 percent of the graduates of the general curriculum went on to school (16, p. 68). USOE figures indicate that nationwide, 23 percent of secondary school vocational curriculum graduates continued full time in higher education (21, p. 31). Since the Massachusetts study included part-time enrollments, there may not be a sizeable discrepancy between the two figures.

Parnes was forced to collect his data in terms of census age groupings, rather than in terms of schooling completed. He found that for black males age twenty to twenty-four, those who had taken the general curriculum in high school were least likely to be in college, while those from the college preparatory curriculum were most likely to be in college. For white males, age twenty to twenty-four, he obtained poorer results for the vocational curriculum. College preparatory was high, with general and vocational curricula sending only 8 percent each to college (14, p. 44).

In the Schaefer and Kaufman study 51 percent of those males who took work at public technical institutes or junior colleges were graduates of the vocational curriculum, but for females, 59 percent were from the college preparatory curriculum. Seventy-six percent of those who were enrolled in company sponsored training programs were vocational graduates as compared with 12 percent from each of the other two high school curricula. Fifty-one percent of the males and 62 percent of the females who took work at private trade schools were college preparatory graduates as compared with 35 percent from vocational curricula and 10 percent from the general curricula (16, p. 69).

9. Status of Vocational Education in the Eyes of the Students. It is often reported that vocational curricula have low status in high school. Schaefer and Kaufman report that 33 percent of the high school graduates of the vocational curriculum felt that they had been looked down upon because of the course they took (as compared with 38 percent of the graduates of the general curriculum and only 7 percent of the college preparatory graduates). At the same time 77 percent and 87 percent of the vocational and college preparatory graduates would suggest that a young person starting high school follow their path. But only 39 percent of the general curriculum graduates would recommend it (16, p. 66). Even more striking is the fact that several U.S. Labor Department studies report that 95 percent of high school graduates say they had one or more vocational courses in school before they graduated (13, p. 244). Since no such enrollment is possible, one can conclude that some of these people either saw non-vocational courses as vocational or invented courses. In either case, graduates would seem to be investing vocational education with considerable status.

10. Placement. Placement of vocational curriculum graduates has been as low as 60 percent at times during the last twenty years, but the most recent figures show 80 percent of those available for employment placed in occupations closely related to the field of training. Placement rates varied by field of training from a high of 92 percent in health related occupations to 67 percent in agricultural occupations (21, p. 31). As would be expected, placement rates tend to be high in times of labor shortage and lower in times of labor surplus. Schaefer and Kaufman indicate that the secondary school was four times as likely to help find a job for vocational graduates as for graduates of other curricula (16, p. 66). The higher the level of education sought by high school juniors, the higher the desire for a job which allowed them to create something original; the lower the level of education sought, the more emphasis on a job which provided plenty of leisure (20, p. 138).

One year after the graduation of their high school class, among students who do not go to college, vocational graduates are earning the most money per year, followed by dropouts. Last in earnings come graduates of the college preparatory and general curricula (5, p. 352). Schaefer and Kaufman reported the same relationship among graduates and found that it continued to exist for the first three jobs held. Indeed, the wage of the college preparatory graduate who did not go to college declined relative to the graduates of the other curricula by the time of the third job (16, p. 75). This seems to indicate that while the secondary school college preparatory curriculum adequately prepares a student for college, it does not prepare him for employment success without college.

11. Earnings.   All studies of earnings of vocational graduates who do not go to college indicate that they earn more per year than graduates of general curricula or college preparatory curricula who do not go to college. However, one study shows college preparatory students earning slightly more per hour than vocational students eleven years after graduation. At two and six years after graduation, the vocational students were ahead in hourly earnings (7, p. 36). Almost all studies of earnings of high school graduates from different curricula considerably understate the true difference in amount of earnings. Most studies report hourly or weekly pay, but since vocational graduates are employed a considerably greater portion of each year, the yearly earnings of vocational graduates are considerably understated. Since vocational graduates work approximately 7 percent more of each year than graduates of academic programs (7, p. 33) their weekly or hourly earnings should be increased by this much to provide comparable yearly wages.

In many studies, a second factor which understates the earnings of vocational graduates grows out of the fact that vocational students have lower academic ability and lower socio-economic status than non-vocational students. Since earnings are related to both of these factors,

TABLE 10–5

Mean Weekly Earnings of High School Graduates by School
Program and Ability Quartile — 5 year Follow-up
(Males only)

	Ability Quartiles							
	Low		II		III		High	
	Mean	St. Div.	Mean	St. Div.	Mean	St. Div.	Mean	St. Div.
General	$104	45	$114	79	$120	88	$111	44
College Prep	98	34	116	39	112	41	116	30
Commercial	101	37	109	29	112	31	110	20
Vocational	106	34	121	45	121	38	124	43
Agriculture	98	39	107	56	105	43	159	75

NOTE: Includes individuals with no military service or full-time post-high
school education.

Source: Unpublished data from *Project TALENT* 5 year follow-up information on high
school graduates of 1960, from reference 10, p. 11.

TABLE 10–6

Mean Weekly Earnings of High School Graduates By School
Program and Socio-Economic Quartile—5 Year Follow-up
(Males Only)

High School Program	Socio-Economic Quartile							
	Low		II		III		High	
	Mean	St. Div.	Mean	St. Div.	Mean	St. Div.	Mean	St. Div.
General	$106	75	$111	41	$127	92	$117	35
College Prep	103	32	111	31	117	43	124	40
Commercial	101	38	108	28	114	33	116	24
Vocational	108	44	111	31	120	36	142	55
Agriculture	100	47	103	40	105	49	99	45

NOTE: Includes individuals with no military service or full-time post-high
school education.

Source: Unpublished data from *Project TALENT* 5 year follow-up information on high
school graduates of 1960, from reference 10, p. 12.

a fair comparison of earnings by school curriculum should match students who have similar academic ability and socio-economic status. This
is borne out by a comparison of earnings when either ability or soco-
economic status are held constant. The difference obviously would be
greater if *both* were held constant (see tables 10–5 and 10–6).

Clearly, the vocational students of high ability and high socio-economic
status have particularly impressive earnings. Unfortunately, they are
few in number. It is worth noting that earnings of students in commercial curricula (primarily females) are little effected by student
ability.

Vocational Education in Large Cities

Very few careful studies have been made of
vocational education in large cities. In addition to the scarcity of information, comparisons of vocational education in large cities with the rest
of the country are difficult because large cities have had a much higher
proportion of separate vocational schools and have had a higher proportion of black students enrolled in vocational education (while whites
tend to enroll in vocational education in about the same proportions in
large cities as in medium sized cities) (6, p. 7).

Separate Vocational Schools

No information has been found which indicates that vocational programs in separate vocational schools are in any way superior to vocational programs operated in comprehensive high schools. This might be due to inadequate information, but it is worth noting that, in large cities at least, the dropout rate from separate vocational high schools appears to be markedly higher than for comprehensive high schools. The Schrieber study found that the holding power of all large city high schools was 71 percent while that of vocational schools was only 51 percent (17, pp. 28 and 35). In view of the fact that dropout rates from general curricula are so much higher nationally than dropout rates from the vocational curricula, these data cast grave doubt on the desirability of maintaining separate vocational schools.

Every study of costs indicates that per pupil costs are higher in separate vocational schools than they are in academic high schools. This could be due to the fact that vocational education in any type of school costs more than non-vocational education, but one study conducted by the American Institute for Research shows average costs of non-vocational and vocational programs in comprehensive schools running about the same per pupil while per pupil costs in vocational schools were approximately one-third higher. Most of the added costs for programs in vocational schools appeared to be due to smaller class size, resulting from the operation of a greater variety of vocational education programs than is offered in the typical comprehensive high school. In contrast, Stromsdorfer, who studied both comprehensive and separate high schools, found vocational education costs to be approximately 50 percent higher than the costs of non-vocational instruction. Major factors in this difference in costs were not only the smaller size of vocational classes, but also higher equipment costs and higher salaries of teachers (19, p. 31). While the lack of data is unfortunate, the information which is available does not support the maintenance of separate vocational schools, for they appear to have higher costs, higher dropout rates, and seem to promote socio-economic segregation.

Shared Time Instruction

Very few parochial secondary schools have offered substantial amounts of vocational education. This is due not only to their difficult financial situation, but also to the fact that all federal and most state assistance to vocational education has been limited to programs which were under public control. There is an increasing tendency toward the development of "shared time" programs which allow students to receive religious instruction plus certain academic courses in the parochial school. They then move to classes under public control for vocational education and certain other school subjects which have not been operated effectively in parochial schools. The net result is almost certain to be a sharp increase in the occupational competence of sizeable groups of youths who up until now have been denied vocational education.

REFERENCES

1. American Institute for Research, *An Analysis of Cost and Performance Factors for the Operation and Administration of Vocational Programs for Secondary Schools.* Pittsburgh: American Institute for Research, 1967.

2. American Vocational Association, *The Advisory Committee and Vocational Education.* Washington, D.C.: American Vocational Association, 1969.

3. Burt, Samuel M., *Industry and Community Leaders in Education—The State Advisory Councils on Vocational Education.* Kalamazoo, Michigan: W. E. Upjohn Institute for Employment Research, 1969.

4. Burt, Samuel, M., *Industry and Vocational-Technical Education.* New York: McGraw-Hill Book Company, 1967.

5. Combs, Janet and W.W. Cooley, "Dropouts: In High School and After School," *American Educational Research Journal,* V, No. 3, pp. 343-363.

6. Cutright, Phillips, *Vocational Students, Teachers, and Schools in the United States.* Unpublished report based on data from the Equal Opportunities Survey. Washington, D.C.: U.S. Office of Education, 1965.

7. Eninger, Max W., *The Process and Product of T. and I. High School Level Vocational Education in the United States.* Pittsburgh: American Institute for Research, 1965.

8. Evans, Rupert N., "School for Schooling's Sake," *Transition from School to Work.* Princeton, New Jersey: Industrial Relations Section, Princeton University, 1968.

9. Flanagan, John, *et al. The American High School Student.* Pittsburgh: University of Pittsburgh, Project TALENT Office, 1964.

10. Froomkin, J., *An Analysis of Vocational Education in our Secondary Schools.* Unpublished. Washington, D.C.: U.S. Office of Education, Office of Program Planning and Evaluation, 1967.

11. Hamlin, Herbert M., *Citizen Participation and Local Policy Making for Public Education,* Revised edition. Urbana: College of Education, University of Illinois, 1960.

12. King, Sam W., *Organization and Effective Use of Advisory Committees.* Washington, D.C.: U.S. Department of Health, Education, and Welfare, Vocational Division, Bulletin No. 288 O.E.-84009, 1960.

13. Mangum, Garth, "Second Chance in the Transition from School to Work," *Transition from School to Work.* Princeton, New Jersey: Industrial Relations Section, Princeton University, 1968.

14. Parnes, Herbert S., *et al. Career Thresholds*, Vol. I. Columbus: Ohio State University Center for Human Resources Research, 1969.

15. *Projections of Educational Statistics to 1975-76.* Washington, D.C.: U.S. Government Printing Office, Catalog No. FS 5.210:100030-66, 1966.

16. Schaefer, Carl J. and Jacob Kaufman, *Occupational Education in Massachusetts.* Boston: Massachusetts Advisory Council on Education, 1968.

17. Schreiber, Daniel, *Holding Power of Large City School Systems.* Washington, D.C.: National Education Association, 1964.

18. Sinks, Thomas A. and J.E. Hess, eds. *Knowledge for What? The Purposes of Junior High School Education.* Danville, Illinois: The Interstate Printers and Publishers, Inc., 1969.

19. Stromsdorfer, Ernst W., *A Developmental Program for an Economic Evaluation of Vocational Education in Pennsylvania.* State College: Pennsylvania State University, 1966.

20. Tillery, Dale, *et al. A Study of Student Decision Making and Its Outcomes: SCOPE, Grade Eleven Profile, 1968 Questionnaire, Selected Items.* New York: College Entrance Examination Board, 1969.

21. *Vocational Education, The Bridge Between Man and His Work.* Washington, D.C.: General report of the Advisory Council on Vocational Education, Document No. FS 5.1280:80052, 1968.

Chapter 11 POST-SECONDARY SCHOOLS

Although community colleges have been in existence for over forty years, the predominant pattern for public education until recent years has been elementary schools, junior high schools, high schools, and colleges and universities. Vocational education in this structure was concentrated almost entirely at the secondary school level, while occupational education in colleges and universities was confined almost exclusively to the professions. Increasing educational demands of a number of sub-professional occupations led to an obvious need for vocational education beyond the high school. For many years this need was either ignored or was filled by private schools; most of which were designed to make a profit. This private school involvement in technical education (as the more sophisticated part of vocational education is often called) has been growing rapidly in recent years. But vocational education of all types in public post-secondary schools has been growing even more rapidly. It is estimated that a new community college is started some place in the United States each week, and a high proportion of these institutions are sold to taxpayers on the basis that they will provide significant amounts of vocational and technical instruction. Federal legislation strongly supports vocational education in these institutions.

Introducing Vocational Education
Into An Academic Community
College

Despite the fact that community (junior)
colleges usually are sold to voters on the basis that they will offer significant programs in three fields: vocational education, college transfer education, and terminal general education, the first program offered is
usually designed for college transfer students. In part, this is due to
student demand, since more students desire collegiate instruction than
can be accommodated in existing four-year institutions. These students
tend to come from families which are influencial in the community. An
equally important factor is the effect of limited finances and limited
space. College transfer programs frequently can be offered at considerably less cost per student than vocational programs, and the amount of
specialized space required is normally much lower. Since new community colleges are usually started before their buildings are constructed
and before adequate revenues are available, it is quite common for the
school to begin with a college transfer program. Naturally the president
selects a staff which is as competent to offer college transfer programs
as he can secure. He also seeks persons who are interested in and believe in the college transfer program at the community college level.

After several years of operation, new buildings are secured, and
the financial condition of the college permits expansion to include
vocational-technical programs and general terminal programs. By this
time, however, the existing faculty has established committees which
must approve new courses, counselors have been employed who are interested primarily in college transfer programs, buildings have been
built to accommodate college transfer programs, and the institution is
well on the road to becoming strictly a "junior college." In this atmosphere, the president, the board of trustees, or some state agency
attempts to mandate the development of a meaningful vocational education program. Typically, a confrontation takes place, and a compro-
mise is reached which allows the development of technical education
programs which are closely allied to the physical sciences and mathematics. Other vocational education programs are excluded on the ground
that they are too low level to deserve college credit.

This situation is exacerbated by feelings of insecurity on the part of
some members of community college staffs. They feel inferior in qualifications, working conditions, and status to staff in the public colleges
and universities which have been in operation for many years (though
they may not be at all inferior in salary). This induces the so-called
"ghetto complex" which causes them to try to be even more pure aca-

demically than the colleges and universities. Many technical educators support the views of their academic colleagues for essentially the same reasons. The upshot is that the community college may not serve the community at all, but instead serves the prejudices of the staff which was hired when the college began.

Technical Education

Many of the early educational programs for technicians were designed for the field of engineering technology. This has led to the mistaken idea that technical education is a type of education for certain engineering technologies. Now, however, there is general agreement that technical education is a level of education instead of a type of education, and that occupational education for the highest levels of sub-professionals in any occupational field is the proper province of technical education. Unfortunately, when some technical educators use the term "level of education," they mean that technical education is the only type of vocational education which should be permitted in the post-secondary school. This has the effect of denying the lower levels of vocational education to students who came from high schools which did not offer adequate vocational programs, as well as denying them to persons who decided after leaving high school that they needed vocational education.

Equally undesirable is the attempt to restrict high schools from offering technical education courses which prepare students to enter technical occupations or from offering upgrading courses for adult technicians. This has led to the curious anomaly of certain technical educators denying that instruction in drafting can be technical education, simply because drafting often is taught in the secondary schools.

Technical education is indeed a "level of education," but this refers to the fact that certain occupations require higher levels of education, rather than to the necessity for offering technical education only in post-secondary schools. Indeed, the level of education required for many occupations demands a technical education program which begins in the high school and continues for two or more years beyond.

Coordination of Vocational Education Programs Between the Secondary and Post-Secondary Schools

Many students who wish to enroll in vocational education programs in the post-secondary school have had no previous vocational education courses. Often they are graduates of a college preparatory curriculum, either because the type of vocational education they wanted was not offered by their high school or because they discovered relatively late in their high school career that they were interested in preparation for an occupation outside the professions. It is only right that these persons should be able to secure the type of vocational education they need in a community college or technical institute.

At the same time, however, we find students who have acquired an excellent secondary school background in a vocational field who desire further vocational education in a post-secondary school. Too frequently they are given no credit for this earlier instruction and are forced to repeat courses which they completed successfully in the high school. The best practical solution to this problem seems to be for the post-secondary school to administer proficiency examinations which would allow the student to establish credit in a post-secondary school course regardless of the way in which he acquired the necessary knowledge and skill to pass the examination. Some students would have acquired this skill in secondary schools, some through work experience, and some through private proprietary school instruction. The automatic awarding of credit as a result of completing a secondary school course seems to be unacceptable to most post-secondary school instructors. The community college expects senior colleges to award credit automatically for courses completed in the community college, but they seem to be unwilling to consider a similar arrangement with the high school.

Ideally, the curricula of the secondary and post-secondary schools should be arranged to complement each other. Then the student who made a decision prior to high school graduation to enter the higher levels of an occupational field could have a program which began in the high school, flowed without interruption into the community college, and, if he decided to go further, could lead naturally into a baccalaureate or even a graduate school program in that occupational field. Such an integrated system of occupational education assumes a career ladder extending from the bottom to the top of an occupational field. More importantly, it assumes that instructional personnel in all levels of education have respect for each other and are willing to work together for the good of the student.

Community Colleges and Technical Institutes

At the post-secondary school level, the community college theoretically is the rough analog of the comprehensive secondary school, while the technical institute is roughly comparable to the separate vocational high school. An examination of programs actually offered, however, reveals surprisingly minor differences. The technical institute usually offers a broader array of vocational curricula, a smaller proportion of college transfer courses, has more elaborate laboratories for vocational education, and has a higher proportion of students pursuing sub-professional vocational goals. The technical institute is most often headed by a person who has specialized in vocational education while the president of a community college almost always has been associated with college transfer programs. Both institutions send students on to college and directly into employment. Indeed, other than the difference in name, the chief difference seems to be in relative emphasis on curricula. The technical institute emphasizes vocational and technical curricula, and the community college emphasizes college transfer curricula, but neither is devoted exclusively to its principal interest.

Vocational Offerings of Four-Year Institutions

Increasingly, vocational education is offered by baccalaureate-granting colleges and universities. Martin reports that 40 percent of the 282 colleges and universities he surveyed offered less-than-baccaulaureate level vocational programs (15, p. 7).

Vocational education legislation prohibits the use of federal vocational education funds for occupational education at the baccaulaureate level or above. This has not deterred a large number of colleges and universities from offering occupational education programs for occupational education which would be eligible for federal aid if they were offered in the high school or community college. By extending the period of training from two to four years, and by offering a baccalaureate upon completion of the program, they have been able to substitute tuition payments and state aid for the relatively modest federal funds available for less-than-baccalaureate degree programs. A few such programs in engineering technology are reported by Defore and Foecke (6). Most of the growth in engineering technology baccalaureate programs has occurred in institutions which do not offer baccalaureate programs in engineering. It is possible in some cases that these really are engineering programs in disguise. Whether or not this is the case, it appears that graduates are being employed as engineers by companies who disagree with the trend in baccalaureate engineering education in the prestige institutions to eliminate almost all references to technology and to concentrate instead on science and mathematics. Whatever the cause, the effect is very clear. Four-year technology programs are growing rapidly and offer serious competition to two-year technician training programs and to standard engineering programs.

Motivation for four-year institutions to offer technician training is varied. In some cases, aviation technology programs are offered to support flight training and staff transportation services for professors. In other cases, strong support from a key executive or board member has led to the establishment of the program. In still other cases, entire state university systems have begun two-year technology programs as a means of delaying or preventing the establishment of state supported comprehensive community colleges. Four-year technician training programs most frequently are offered by former teachers colleges which desire a broadened curriculum and are prevented from establishing engineering colleges by the opposition of existing engineering schools.

Curriculum Development in Post-Secondary Education

Curriculum development in all of vocational education has been plagued by battles between subject matter specialists and administrators. The former attempt to get approval of specialized courses such as mathematics for carpenters while the latter attempt to consolidate classes to reduce high costs caused by small enrollments. In these battles, the needs of the student are often forgotten. Traditional studies of curriculum content have looked at individual occupations after the educational requirements of the occupation have been determined by means of occupational analysis (9), activities of employed workers (5), opinions of occupationally competent persons (14), opinions of supervisors of occupational specialists (21), or the teachers of the occupation (16). The items of content thus identified are combined more or less logically into courses, and the courses are fitted into a one, two, three, or four-year academic calendar. This procedure invariably results in unique occupational education courses for each occupational field. Too often, the only common elements in these specialized programs are the general education requirements of the institution offering the curricula.

Schill and Arnold (18) developed a method for determining logically the areas of instruction which are common and unique to different occupational programs. They looked at three technologies: chemical, electrical-electronic, and mechanical, and by asking technicians whether or not certain competencies were needed in their specific occupation, found that certain areas of instruction were unique to these three technologies and to each of their three combinations (electro-mechanical, electro-chemical, and chemical-mechanical). In addition, however, they found surprisingly large areas of instruction which were common to all of these six technological fields. The methodology they have used would seem to be applicable to all of vocational education and could result in elimination of much undesirable duplication of instruction.

Student Characteristics

We know considerably less about vocational students in post-secondary education than we do about high school students in vocational curricula. Graney points out that there is little but speculation about the technical student, but that even the speculation ". . . deals less with the subject of what technical students are than what they ought to be" (10, p. 88). Most studies of post-secondary education students have been concerned with criteria for admitting students, and hence have been concerned with predictions of success in different curricula. These studies have been of little value, since they seem uniformly to find that high socio-economic status, high secondary school grades, and high ability and achievement test scores are good indicators of success in all of post-secondary education. The implication seems to be that if students who score low on each of these criteria can be kept out, all will be well. This may make the task of the college teacher simpler, but it is hardly an answer for the student who ranks low in one or more of these characteristics.

Much more useful findings are those of Taylor and Hecker (20) and of Hakanson (11). Both of these studies indicate that students who do not succeed in the first post-secondary curriculum in which they enroll are likely to withdraw from college rather than to transfer to another curriculum. For example, Hakanson found that only 14 percent of the students who withdrew from college transfer programs enrolled in occupational education curricula. Almost all of the remainder dropped out of school. This finding suggests that community colleges should have both vocational and technical curricula available in the same occupational fields, so that students who are unable to succeed in a technical curriculum can move to a related vocational curriculum without having to change objectives sharply. For example, a student who has unsurmountable difficulty in a two-year mechanical design technology curriculum should be able to transfer to the one-year vocational drafting curriculum which has related occupational goals, but does not require such high mathematics achievement. Hakanson's findings also suggest that adequate counseling at the time of enrollment may be more important than has been thought, and may be even more important than counseling after the student has begun his studies.

This wedding of the student to the curriculum he desires may also explain why such a high proportion of high school freshmen who wish to be enrolled in vocational education drop out of high school when they are instead assigned to the general curriculum. The dearth of follow-up studies on the post-secondary vocational education graduates and dropouts is shown in the Sharp and Krasnegor study (19) which reviews more than forty follow-up studies of vocational education students. No national or regional follow-up studies for persons trained in technical institutes and community colleges could be found, and indeed, there are very few such studies even at the local level. The work of Hoyt (12) has promise of providing a great deal of information with regard to students both in public and private post-secondary education institutions. Another long-term study of students which is under way, though restricted to health occupations, is that of Kinsinger and Ratner (13).

Enrollments in Post-Secondary Vocational Technical Education

Less than 10 percent of enrollments in vocational and technical education comes at the post-secondary school level. This figure is misleading, however, because it does not show the very rapid growth of post-secondary enrollments in this field; it does not indicate the relative proportion of time spent by the student in vocational and technical programs; nor does it show the considerable differences by field of specialization. In 1960, there were only ninety-three thousand reimbursed post-secondary enrollments in vocational and technical education. By 1965, this figure had more than doubled to 207,000, and it doubled again in 1966. By 1970, enrollments should be at least four times those of 1965, and at least 100 percent increases may be expected each five years for the foreseeable future. Enrollments give an inadequate picture of the amount of instructional time and effort. Secondary school students spend from one-fourth to one-third of their school time in vocational education, while adults may be enrolled only a few hours per week and a few weeks per year. In contrast, post-secondary students usually spend over half of their school time in vocational and technical instruction during the one or two years they typically are enrolled in the program.

By far the largest enrollments in post-secondary vocational and technical education are in programs designed to prepare students for work in offices and other commercial fields. Programs designed to prepare persons for skilled occupations in industry and the construction trades and for technical occupations are large and rapidly growing. Preparation for home economics and agricultural occupations stands in sharp contrast. While these form the bulk of enrollment in secondary schools, they are by far the smallest in post-secondary education. Education for technical occupations in agriculture, however, is increasing rapidly in enrollment. Another program which is rapidly increasing in size, though relatively small in enrollment as yet, is distributive education. A larger program, but one which has been growing very slowly in relationship to society's needs, is the series of programs for the health occupations.

Competition Between Secondary and Post-Secondary Schools for Adult Education Enrollments

It has been noted that when a community college and a high school offer comparable adult education courses at the same time, in the same locality, enrollments in the program offered by the post-secondary institution tend to increase while enrollments in programs offered by the high school decrease. This may be an indication of the relative status of the two types of institutions, for some adults would much prefer to be able to say, "I am going over to the college for a course this evening," rather than to say, "I am going to the high school to study bookkeeping." This difference in status offers the post-secondary school an opportunity to attract adults who will not attend adult education programs offered by a secondary school either because they hold the high school in low esteem or because of past individual problems with a secondary school. At the same time, it offers an opportunity for the secondary-school educator to build highly desirable programs of adult education for persons who may feel that college programs would be too advanced or too difficult for them.

Conflicts between secondary and post-secondary institutions operating adult education programs in the same community seem almost inevitable. A combination of cooperative planning, joint advertising, and careful evaluation can (1) minimize undesirable conflicts which destroy public goodwill, (2) allow replacement of programs which are not meeting the needs of the community, and (3) develop programs which meet the needs of adults who previously have not been served. The adult and continuing education program of the community college in Fort Dodge, Iowa, has developed an ideal method of high school and college cooperation. Coordinators from each high school in the college district are employed part-time by the college, and develop programs which meet community needs regardless of the level of instruction.

Non-High School Graduates in Post-Secondary Schools

A number of community colleges have established programs which accept students who are not high school graduates. These programs range from remedial efforts, where an attempt is made to give the equivalent of high school instruction to high school dropouts, to an occasional program which accepts each student where he is and moves as far with him as is possible. When the Land Grant Universities were established immediately after the Civil War, many of them followed the same course of action. They set up preparatory schools for certain students and adopted a philosophy that instruction which met the needs of the students was far better than instruction which met the prevailing Eastern college notion of excellence. Most baccalaureate granting institutions discarded this philosophy long ago. But it has been picked up in part by certain community colleges, and a few have put it fully into effect.

REFERENCES

1. American Institute for Research, *An Analysis of Cost and Performance Factors for the Operation and Administration of Vocational Programs for Secondary Schools.* Pittsburgh: American Institute for Research, 1967.

2. American Vocational Association, *The Advisory Committee and Vocational Education.* Washington, D.C.: American Vocational Association, 1969.

3. Brick, Michael, *An Analysis of Selected Business and Technology Programs in High Schools and in Two Year Colleges and Institutes of New York State with a View Toward Initiating Articulation.* New York: Center for Urban Education, 1967. (ERIC ED 012791)

4. Burt, Samuel M., *Industry and Vocational-Technical Education.* New York: McGraw-Hill Book Company, 1967.

5. Christal, Raymond E., "Implications of Air Force Occupational Research for Curriculum Design," *Process and Technique of Vocational Curriculum Development,* Brandon B. Smith and Jerome Moss, Jr., eds. Minneapolis: Minnesota Research Coordinating Unit for Vocational Education, University of Minnesota, 1970.

6. Defore, Jesse J., "An Evaluation of Baccalaureate Programs in Engineering Technology," and Harold A. Foecke, "Four-Year Engineering Technology Programs in Perspective," in *Trends in Engineering*

Technician Enrollments and Graduates, John D. Aden, ed. New York: Engineering Manpower Commission, 1967. (ERIC ED 014298)

7. Evans, Rupert N., "School for Schooling's Sake," *Transition from School to Work.* Princeton, New Jersey: Industrial Relations Section, Princeton University, 1968.

8. Froomkin, Joseph, *An Analysis of Vocational Education in Our Secondary Schools.* Unpublished. Washington, D.C.: U.S. Office of Education, Office of Program Planning and Evaluation, 1967.

9. Fryklund, Verne, *Trade and Job Analysis.* Milwaukee: The Bruce Publishing Co., 1947.

10. Graney, Maurice, *The Technical Institute.* New York: The Center for Applied Research in Education, 1964.

11. Hakanson, John W., *Selected Characteristics, Socio-Economic Status, and Levels of Attainment of Students in Public Junior College Occcupation-Centered Education.* Berkeley: University of California School of Education, 1967. (ERIC ED 013644)

12. Hoyt, Kenneth B., "The Specialty Oriented Student Research Program: A Five-Year Report," *Vocational Guidance Quarterly,* XVI (March, 1968), 169-176.

13. Kinsinger, Robert E. and Muriel Ratner, *Technicians for the Health Field — A Community College Health Career Study Program.* Albany: New York State Education Department, 1966. (ERIC ED 011198)

14. Lescarbeau, Roland F., *et al. Development of a Curriculum to Meet Changing Manpower Needs of the Computer and Business Machines Industries.* Hartford, Conn.: Technical Education Consortium, Inc., 1968. (ERIC ED 022926)

15. Martin, Robert R., *Technical Education: Less-Than-Baccalaureate Level Programs in Higher Education.* Richmond, Kentucky: Eastern Kentucky University, 1968. (ERIC ED 019069)

16. North Carolina State Board of Education, *Court Reporting In Business Technology.* Raleigh: State Board of Education, 1966. (ERIC ED 013944)

17. Schill, William J., *Concurrent Work-Education Programs in the Fifty States.* Unpublished final report on USOE project 6-2851. Urbana: Bureau of Educational Research, University of Illinois, 1967.

18. Schill, William J. and Joseph P. Arnold, *Curricula Content for Six Technologies.* Urbana: University of Illinois Press, 1965.

19. Sharp, Laure M. and Rebecca Krasnegor, *The Use of Follow-up Studies in the Evaluation of Vocational Education.* Washington, D.C.: Bureau of Social Science Research, 1966. (ERIC ED 010072)

20. Taylor, Ronald G. and Donald L. Hecker, *Interest and Intellectual Indices Related to Successful and Nonsuccessful Male College Students in Technical and Associate Degree Programs.* Big Rapids, Michigan: Ferris State College, 1967. (ERIC ED 021127)

21. Vasek, Richard J., *A Comparative Analysis of Electronic Content in Public Post-High School Technical Institutes and Electronic Technology Requirements of Industry.* State College: Mississippi State University, 1967. (ERIC ED 015302)

Chapter 12 COOPERATIVE PROGRAMS

While the sharing of time between education and work is sometimes thought to be a new idea, it had its origins in England in the nineteenth century, when children employed in factories were required to attend schools on a half-time basis. Factory children learned as much as ordinary children, though they received instruction for only half as long each day. The report of the Inspectors of Factories for October 31, 1865, states,

> The reason of it is, I think, obvious. The labour of half a day is sufficient physical employment for a child . . . The change to school for the other half, and the interest taken . . . in new ideas . . . produces rest . . . whilst the discipline of labour carried into the school, absorbs all that time which a child at school from morning to night loses, in its vain efforts to relieve itself from the fatigues of school monotony (1, p. 107).

The available records do not indicate whether the school instruction was related to what was being learned on the job. Probably it was not.

Over fifty years ago the University of Cincinnati decided that engineers could be better educated if they spent part of their school career in employment and if the school program could be related to the things that the student had learned on the job. Twenty years later secondary schools in the South — perennially faced with low school budgets — made a virtue of necessity by adapting the cooperative education plan for high school students.

Despite strong opposition from vocational educators in the forties and early fifties, the program grew in secondary school enrollment from zero in 1930 to 117,000 in 1965-66 (7, p. 32) and to 190,000 in 1967-68 (6, p. 243). Some 2,500 of the 18,000 high school districts had 4,800 such programs in 1965-66. The number is certainly higher now, but no one knows how much higher. The approximate age of students by program may be inferred from Table 12–1.

TABLE 12–1

Percentage of Part-time Cooperative Students
by Program and by Grade Level

	Total	10th	11th	12th	13th-14th
Distributive Education	100%	0.2	15.9	79.3	4.6
Business/Office Occupations	100%	0	8.1	90.4	1.5
Agriculture	100%	0	21.3	78.7	0
Trade and Industrial	100%	0.9	41.4	57.7	0
Diversified Occupations	100%	0	26.2	73.8	0

Source: See reference 7, p. 61.

It is clear that most students are high school seniors, and that the involvement of community colleges education is minute. The above table does not cover four-year colleges. For some reason they have been much more active in cooperative education than have the two-year colleges.

The Advisory Council on Vocational Education which was established to evaluate the implementation of the Vocational Education Act of 1963 stated flatly that cooperative education had the best record of all vocational programs in terms of the proportion of students placed in the occupation for which they were trained. Studies of the economics of vocational education show higher rates of return on investment in cooperative programs than in other types of vocational education. (Capital costs for the school are lower, and since the student is receiving wages for the on-the-job portion of the program, the costs for the individual are lower.)

Congress has responded to this evidence by earmarking funds for cooperative education programs and by authorizing for the first time the use of vocational education funds to reimburse employers for the excess costs they incur through cooperation in the programs — a provision which should strengthen employer support if it is implemented. Until

Congress acted, the emphasis placed on cooperative education varied greatly from state to state. As late as 1966, one state reported only one such program, but Michigan had 632, nearly twice as many cooperative programs as any of the more populous states. Eight states had half of the programs.

Schill, in his 1965-66 study of cooperative work education (CWE) found that definitions of it were nearly identical in most states. Yet he found virtually no relationship between prevalence of the programs and various measures of state wealth or unemployment. The only reasonable explanation seems to be that boards of vocational education in some states have promoted cooperative work education programs, while in other states they have been apathetic to CWE or opposed to it. The net effect is that only about 15 percent of the nation's twenty-seven thousand public high schools and a considerably lower percentage of the junior colleges had CWE programs in 1966.

Cooperative work education involves cooperative arrangements between the school and employers, enabling students to receive part-time vocational instruction in the school and on-the-job training through part-time employment. The primary goal of CWE is to prepare the student for gainful employment. Cooperative work education should be sharply distinguished from work-study programs where the goal is to provide economic assistance which will allow the student to remain in school. The work which is provided seldom is relevant to the student's occupational goal. Work-study students undoubtedly learn some things on the job that are a valuable part of their education since any employment experience has some general educational value. The work-study program, however, lacks the structured and conscious relationship between work experience and educational goals which is the major strength of cooperative work education programs (5, pp. 119-120).

Cooperative work education goes under a variety of names. Distributive education (DE), office occupations (OO), part-time industrial cooperative education, and diversified occupations (DO) are some of the more common titles used for the federally funded programs. "Vocational cooperative programs" is a common generic title.

Schill found, however, that almost half of the schools operating CWE programs did not receive federal vocational education financial support for them. Little is known about the programs except that they include special CWE for mentally handicapped students, vocational rehabilitation programs, business education programs which the state chooses not to recognize, and programs in wealthy school districts which choose not to ask for reimbursement.

CWE is suitable for all fields of vocational education but is much more utilized for some types of occupations than for others. Cooperative distributive education has well over one-third of the enrollment in federally reimbursed CWE programs and almost twice the enrollment of the next largest subject field. Health occupations programs have clinical experience requirements which are in many ways analogous to CWE requirements. Yet these are not counted as CWE because there may not be a regular alternation between the in-school and on-the-job portions of health occupations education.

CWE invariably has a teacher-coordinator who advises students, identifies suitable training stations for them, teaches a class in the school which is closely related to the student's experience on the job, and evaluates the learning which occurs. In his "spare" time he builds better community relationships, adjusts all difficulties which arise in maintaining equitable relationships among parents, students, employers, unions, and sometimes runs evening classes to teach the on-the-job trainers (specified experienced fellow employees of the student) how better to teach the student.

Everyone who has studied the CWE program agrees that well prepared and able coordinators are the key to successful program operation. Ability to plan in advance, initiative, outgoing personality, and organizational skills are basic requirements. It is clear that successful coordinators are rapidly becoming the backbone of a new leadership for all types of vocational education programs at state and local levels.

Larger schools tend to operate multiple CWE programs with each coordinator specializing in a particular family of occupations. That is, a typical large school may have a distributive education coordinator, a coordinator of office occupations, a coordinator of industrial occupations, etc.

In nine states, smaller schools are encouraged to operate CWE programs under a single coordinator who is responsible for a broad range of occupations most frequently entitled diversified occupations (DO). The majority of state directors seem to feel, however, that if a school is not large enough to support separate cooperative programs, each limited to a traditional vocational service, it should not be allowed to receive state and federal funds. This attitude seems to be changing, however, and the 1968 Amendments should speed the change.

Advantages of Cooperative Work Education

Quick adaptability to changes in labor market demands characterizes CWE programs. By contrast, vocational education which is based on school operated laboratories can become quite out of tune with labor market demands, partly because most vocational teachers are prepared to offer instruction in only a relatively small family of occupations. If teachers have tenure and cannot be re-trained, the school has little flexibility in dropping outdated programs. Since CWE uses instructors on the job and since openings for training stations are closely related to opportunities for full time employment of graduates, CWE is quickly responsive to changes in the labor market. Moreover, training stations are most easily obtained in fields with the greatest labor shortages, and the coordinator is therefore more likely to use such stations.

The CWE program needs lower capital investment in space and equipment than does instruction in the school laboratory. CWE, indeed, requires little more equipment or space in the school than is called for in first rate classroom instruction in any subject. Highly specialized equipment which may quickly become obsolete cannot be afforded in the typical school vocational program but will be provided on the job because of production demands.

Cooperative work education stimulates desirable attitudes toward work. Work atmosphere is extremely difficult to reproduce outside of a real work situation, and the importance of promptness and regular attendance at work are much more demonstrable on the job than in school. Moreover, because of the difficulty of marketing goods and services produced within school laboratories, it is also extremely difficult in laboratory based programs to develop realistic attitudes toward speed, quality, and efficiency.

A student who performs effectively in CWE is very likely to stay on in full time employment after completing the school program. The employer knows the student's strengths and weaknesses, and the student has had ample opportunity to determine whether or not he likes and can succeed in a particular field of work and with that particular employer. As a result, typical placement rates are more than 80 percent in the occupation for which the student is trained.

If a suitable training station is available, cooperative education can be offered in a given occupational field for a small group or even for an individual. Other types of vocational education require at least ten students in a given occupational field before the program can be operated economically.

Overcoming Problems In Cooperative Work Education

CWE programs are not readily adaptable to some communities — those which are so small as to have a narrow range of available training stations, communities which have declining populations, or communities in which most employment is found in occupations which have little future. Cooperative programs are difficult to operate in establishments that have strong agreements with employees. If the employer has agreed that no new persons will be employed until all previous workers have been recalled, there will be times when CWE programs cannot operate in his establishment. If there is a tradition of employing only the relatives or friends of present workers, CWE will be sharply restricted for most students.

No figures are available as to the proportion of CWE programs operated in non-union or small establishments, but it is believed to be relatively high except in towns having near zero unemployment. Many CWE coordinators, however, have found it possible to negotiate bonafide apprenticeship agreements for CWE students. This arrangement eliminates many of the problems inherent in typical seniority provisions.

The number of students who could profit from CWE programs in any community is determined very largely by the birth rate which occurred there sixteen to eighteen years earlier. On the other hand, the number who can be accommodated in the program is determined in large part by the number of available employment opportunities at a particular time. Even minor economic recessions badly hamper CWE programs. In large cities, especially, it is not at all uncommon for each coordinator to have three or four students laid off and returned to the school for full time study several times during the school year. This requires the establishment of new sections of in-school vocational courses, the overcrowding of existing sections, or (worst of all) placing the student in several successive "study hall" periods.

In medium sized communities, there is often a closer relationship between the school and employer. Layoffs there are not such a severe problem since the employer frequently recognizes the injustice to the student who is dropped, and the burden that such layoffs place on the school. But even in small communities, prolonged economic recession inevitably will result in sharp curtailment in CWE enrollment. In such periods, rapid response to labor market demands appears as a disadvantage rather than an advantage for CWE.

Many problems posed by CWE programs can be overcome through careful planning and education of the school and community. A primary difficulty up to now has been the shortage of qualified teacher-coordinators. In the Vocational Education Amendments of 1968, however, Congress has authorized substantial funds for the development of teachers and other leadership personnel for vocational education. If a substantial portion of this professional development program is devoted to the preservice and inservice education of teacher-coordinators, much of the shortage in CWE coordinators can be overcome.

CWE has often been opposed by teachers who are accustomed to teaching in school laboratory programs and who are afraid that development of CWE will rob them of their students. Some schools have overcome this by restricting CWE to occupations that are not taught in school laboratories. Other schools have assigned students to vocational programs in laboratories until their last semester or last year of school and have used laboratory instructors as part-time teacher-coordinators. Still others have required the permission of the laboratory instructor before a student can be assigned to CWE in the occupation which the laboratory instructor teaches.

The traditional vocational education program has suffered from an attempt to turn out a year's supply of new full time employees during a single month. Naturally, there are not enough jobs to go around each June. Similarly, CWE has suffered from trying to find suitable training stations for all CWE students in a single month (September). Both problems could be eased by laboratory instruction which prepares students in advance of placement in CWE programs. The most able students would be available for CWE placement early in the school year, while less able students would continue in the school laboratory for longer periods. This arrangement could tend to spread the need for job placements more evenly over the calendar year (3). Some schools now conduct the CWE program on a twelve month basis. While this helps to hold a training station open by meeting the needs of the employer year round, graduation in June is still common.

Cooperative work education has often been opposed by individuals who think instruction must be given solely inside school walls. Every administrator who has operated a CWE program has had protesting calls from both teachers and laymen who do not understand why a faculty member should be off the school premises during school hours. The only solution to this problem seems to be a continuing program to educate the public about the rationale for CWE.

CWE programs may be affected by wage hours restrictions and youth employment safety regulations. The states which have tried hard to do so, however, have generally been successful in getting exceptions to state laws and to state administrative rulings. These exceptions allow special consideration for CWE students with regard to wages, hours, safety regulations, and other restrictions designed to protect youth from exploitation. The basic rationale is that through the teacher-coordinator the school makes certain that the student is involved in a bona fide education program and is not being exploited.

Some vocational educators in state offices make clear their opposition to CWE. Fortunately, these people are declining rapidly in number and in influence. It is still quite common, however, for states to have restrictive regulations prohibiting coordination which extends across two or more of the traditional fields of vocational education. This eliminates many occupations from CWE—for example, sales training for industrial supplies which cuts across distributive education and trade and industrial education. Some states have solved this problem by assigning the coordination to the teacher who is most competent to handle the major portion of the occupation. An equally oppressive regulation excludes from CWE those occupations which require less than two years for the "average worker" to learn. By definition, half of all students are below average in their ability to learn, so the "two-year" rule is really meaningless. All socially desirable occupations should be available to students through CWE. In some states still another type of arbitrary regulation excludes certain occupations such as radio announcing because they have not been a part of traditional vocational education even though they clearly meet all the criteria for inclusion.

Special difficulties are involved in the operation of cooperative programs in large cities. Travel time for teacher coordinators is one problem, since it is rarely possible to restrict students to employment in a particular geographic sector of the city. Other problems include a greater preponderance of employers who have tight seniority restrictions, and a greater proportion of teachers who feel that the working day ends promptly at three thirty in the afternoon unless they are paid at overtime rates. Despite all obstacles many large city school systems are operating CWE programs successfully. Other large city systems can best learn from these established programs how to develop cooperative programs of their own. Urban CWE programs will surely increase as a means to aid educationally disadvantaged and handicapped students—a major goal of the 1968 Amendments.

No one knows why CWE is much more prevalent in secondary schools and in four-year colleges than it is in junior and community colleges. Perhaps the "ghetto syndrome" is at work, with junior colleges feeling that they must be more academically pure in their educational programs than other, long established schools. Yet there are many valid reasons why CWE should be more successful in junior colleges than in secondary schools or universities. Certain community colleges such as The College of Du Page (county) in Illinois have installed CWE in each of their vocational and technical fields of instruction. Cooperative work education has had to compete with work-study which does not require the school to employ a teacher-coordinator or provide an organized educational program related to the students' work. Hence the educational costs are lower than for CWE. At the same time special appropriations have been available for work-study programs. This has led some school districts unwisely to adopt work-study programs which are not as educationally defensible but which require less local financial support. There is no reason why work-study funds cannot be used for CWE. Certainly the results would be educationally superior. It is to be hoped that congress will gradually phase out support for work-study in favor of additional support for CWE.

Cooperative programs have been hampered by a shortage of adequate instructional material of three basic types: (1) material for the general vocational instruction which applies to all of the occupations supervised by a particular coordinator; (2) materials directly related to each of these occupations, and (3) material which is suitable for developing on-the-job trainers. The Vocational Education Amendments of 1968 authorized seventeen million dollars over the next two years for the preparation of curriculum materials. Very high priority should be given to the development of instructional materials for the three phases of CWE.

In common with all vocational education, CWE suffers from that aspect of our culture which places a low value on employment in nonprofessional occupations. Most parents want their children to go to college because they believe this is the path to professional employment. They should be told that CWE does not block entrance to college any more than does any other type of vocational education. Indeed, many colleges give priority to students who have demonstrated that they are willing to work to get further education. Nevertheless, the primary goal of CWE should be to enable the student to get satisfactory, gainful employment upon completion of the program.

Some economists promise a long-term solution to the cultural values problem. They hold that as the supply of nonprofessional but vocationally trained employees continues to decrease relative to demand, wages for this type of employment will rise until people will reverse their attitudes. This wage change has already taken effect in many technical occupations where graduates of two-year programs are now employed at salaries higher than are paid to holders of Masters' degrees in many other fields.

A shortage of training stations caused by high costs to the employer has often discouraged efforts to develop CWE programs. No one denies that CWE training is costly to the employer. We have assumed that employers could recover added costs through having a better supply of well trained workers, or that they should contribute the added costs because of their sense of social responsibility. If CWE is to expand rapidly, it is unrealistic to expect employers to assume costs above those normally incurred in the training of other new employees. Actually a good case can be made for full payment to the employer of all the costs of training a CWE student. This is already being done in many manpower training programs.

Nevertheless, it would appear desirable at this stage to take only the step of paying for the added costs of CWE training. This type of payment is authorized by the Vocational Education Amendments of 1968. Guidelines for the implementation of this legislation should insure that the costs of applying for and substantiating these added costs are reasonable, relative to the amount to be claimed. It certainly would make no sense to spend two hundred dollars in applying for and substantiating added costs of training which amount to only three hundred dollars. The principal quality control should be certification by the school that the training program outline has been followed meticulously.

As is true of many other educational innovations, cooperative work education has been slow to gain acceptance. The research results make it plain that in the typical American community, and with a reasonable level of economic activity, CWE is a highly desirable vocational program. It offers instruction in occupations that cannot be touched by any other type of vocational education. On the other hand, CWE will not replace all in-school vocational instruction because of its sensitivity to short-term economic fluctuations, transportation difficulties in large cities, opposition from certain groups of employees, and because of age restrictions on employment in certain fields.

REFERENCES

1. Baker, Robert, *Reports of the Inspectors of Factories for the Half Year Ending 31st October 1865*. Cataloged under *British Parliamentary Papers*, XXIV, 1866.

2. Evans, Rupert, N., "Cooperative Education — Advantages, Disadvantages and Factors in Program Development," *American Vocational Journal*, XLIV, No. 5 (1969), 19-22 and 58.

3. Evans, Rupert N., "Training Time and Placement Time in Vocational Education," *American Vocational Journal*, XLV, No. 3 (1970), 16-18.

4. Evans, Rupert N., *et al. Education for Employment*. Ann Arbor: Institute of Labor and Industrial Relations, University of Michigan, 1969.

5. Levitan, Sar A. and Garth L. Mangum, *Federal Training and Work Programs in the Sixties*. Ann Arbor: Institute of Labor and Industrial Relations, University of Michigan, 1969.

6. Mangum, Garth L., "Second Chance in the Transition from School to Work," *Transition from School to Work*. Princeton: Industrial Relations Section, Princeton University, 1968.

7. Schill, William J., *Concurrent Work-Education Programs in the Fifty States*. Urbana: Bureau of Educational Research, University of Illinois, 1967. (ERIC ED 021049)

Chapter 13 **EMPLOYER AND EMPLOYEE GROUPS**

Vocational training conducted as a part of employment is most commonly sponsored by employers, though many apprenticeship programs and a relatively small amount of training provided to employed skilled workers are often sponsored by labor and management groups such as joint apprenticeship councils.

> The immediate objective is utility, whether it be the most effective methods of selling, the most approved processes of production, or just getting along with co-workers. But often there is idealism too, and a profound belief in education as a way of life . . . nevertheless, these broader concepts are usually by-products — not ends in themselves (2, p. 9).

". . . manufacturers will do as little or as much training as they need to produce their product and sell it on a competitive market—no more or no less" (12, p. 29). While certain employers undoubtedly do more training than would be required by their short run needs, and indeed, some companies provide training for disadvantaged workers (though they hold a belief that it is more of a service to the community than to themselves), the fact remains that the great majority of training offered by employers is limited to their immediate needs. It is a truism in industrial training that when corporate profits decline, the training department is almost invariably hard hit by economy measures and may be eliminated entirely. Moreover, there is a close relationship between the state of the labor market for different types of employees and the amount of training that is provided to these types of employees.

Belman and Bliek (1) found that large employers were much more likely than small employers to have training departments. This finding has been substantiated repeatedly, but almost all these studies suffer from an odd blind spot. They report the presence of a training function or report the presence of a particular type of training and do not identify the proportion of employees receiving training. A company having fifty thousand employees may have a training department and programs in a wide variety of different fields while serving a very small proportion of the employees. At the same time, a small company might not have a training department and might offer training programs of only two or three types, yet might be reaching a much larger proportion of its employees. In spite of great gaps in information about training offered by employers, there is general agreement that the larger the employer, the more likely he is to offer some formal training, and that with most companies, the size of the training program expands and contracts very rapidly in response to short run training needs.

Despite the fact that large employers are much more likely to offer formal training programs than small employers, it is by no means clear that the cost per employee trained is higher in large companies than in small. Economies of scale and the presence of internal labor market career ladders clearly seem to suggest that costs per trainee would be lower in large companies. Indeed, the very absence of definitive data on training costs may have been a major factor in securing almost unanimous employer support for passage of the British Industrial Training Act of 1964. This act, which set up industry training boards with authority to levy a training "tax" on all members of the industry, was hailed by both small and large employers as a means of distributing equitably the costs of training. Clearly, small employers felt that they were bearing an unreasonable proportion of training costs while large employers felt that quite the reverse was true.

One of the major factors leading to short-term goals for much of the training conducted by employers is the fear of competitive disadvantage. If an employer invests a substantial amount of money in training an employee only to have the trained worker leave to take employment with a competitor, he has suffered a dual disadvantage. He has lost the money that he has spent in training, and he has provided his competitor with a better trained employee than the competitor likely would have been able to recruit otherwise. In pre-1960

Japan, the employer did not have such a fear, because each employee tended to have a lifetime commitment to the enterprise. Or, under the levy-grant system of the British Industrial Training Act, whoever conducted the training would get paid for conducting it, with the cost being shared by all parts of the industry. The full cost thus could be passed on to consumers without competitive disadvantage among British employers.

The Goal of Training Offered by Employers

Training conducted by employers assumes the presence of workers who are capable of being trained. The section on Internal Labor Markets in chapter seven points out clearly the importance of "trainability" as an employee selection factor in most industries. Assuming that trainable workers are available, most training programs have one or more of four objectives:

A. Increased productivity
B. Increased promotability
C. Increased stability of employment
D. Increased safety

A. Almost all employers are extremely cost conscious, and one of the obvious major components of cost is productivity of each worker, from the president of the company down to the lowest level of unskilled worker. Productivity is influenced by skills, knowledges, and attitudes, and hence training programs are used to increase skills; to increase knowledge about the job, the company, the industry, and the economic system, and to change attitudes toward fellow workers and management. A single training program may have all three goals, but more commonly one goal is emphasized.

B. Programs to enhance promotability are heavily concentrated on supervisory and management personnel. Job rotation training, which familiarizes the supervisor with many different parts of the firm, and many other types of training are used. If a worker must be promoted because of his increased seniority, it is obviously advantageous to the employer to have him ready for the new position if at all possible. Even more important is the need to have supervisors and managers ready to step into posts of increased responsibility when the need arises.

C. When an effective employee leaves, a variety of costs are incurred. The employee must be terminated, and a new employee must be recruited, screened, and trained. Each of these steps is expensive. Job satisfaction is one of the major ways of reducing turnover, and training can be one factor which increases job satisfaction.

D. Poor safety records are expensive in terms of insurance costs and decreased confidence on the part of workers and of the community.

Not everyone in the employing firm has the same training goals. The first-line supervisor and his immediate superior are most interested in reducing costs in the supervisor's unit through increased productivity. The president of the firm, on the other hand, is most interested in finding managers who have a broad understanding of the firm, the industry, and the marketplace. This leads to differing emphases on selection of workers and on the training of workers once they are employed. The first-line supervisor tells the personnel department that he wants an experienced worker who can become productive with a minimum of training. The president tells the personnel department that he wants them to hire people who have a broad liberal education and that all necessary training will be provided by the company. Complaints about specific individuals who were hired are almost always registered by first-line supervisors rather than by presidents, so the personnel department often attempts to meet the goals of the supervisor, unless the president has recently instructed them to the contrary.

Selection of Employees and Training Needs

The selection of employees invariably is closely related to the need to provide training. If a worker can be lured away from an identical job in an identical industry (that is to say, if he can be recruited from a competitor), only a brief orientation need be provided by the employer. When there is a surplus of workers in a particular occupation, this is the method used by most American employers, from department stores to universities. With a surplus of capable workers, it is likely that a thoroughly trained employee can be found at a salary but little above that of a trainee. Since training costs money and since trained employees must be paid more than untrained employees, there is always an economic decision to make as to whether to spend money on the wages at which a trained worker can be recruited, or to spend money on training while paying lower wages. Eventually, of course, the broadly trained worker, whether trained inside or outside the firm, can command premium wages.

Some industries, such as steel, coal, and oil refining, have labor-management agreements which make it almost impossible to bring in trained workers. These agreements give preference in promotions to present employees, and virtually insure that each new employee will begin work on an unskilled job. As an opening occurs in a more highly skilled job, the most senior employee has a choice of moving into this job and is allowed to continue on it unless he is clearly incompetent. Such a promotion system places a premium on selection of new employees who are untrained but are highly intelligent. If they were well trained, they would not apply since they could get jobs elsewhere which utilized their skills. If they were not intelligent, they could not learn rapidly and thus would not be able to make a large number of major occupational changes successfully. For such a system to work, jobs must be designed so that intelligent workers can learn them rapidly once their seniority entitles them to begin learning.

Vocational education graduates are rarely welcomed in industries that promote entirely from within, unless they are so highly trained that they can be employed as technicians, and thus be exempt from the labor-management agreement. If employed as unskilled laborers, they are apt to become dissatisfied as they see less competent workers receive promotions and to look for employment which can use their skills immediately.

Types of Training

ORIENTATION TRAINING

The most common type of training offered by employers is orientation training. This training is designed to introduce the employee to the employer's business and to show how his duties are related to the goals of the entire establishment. For ordinary employees, it is seldom more than two days in length and may be conducted in a matter of a few minutes, but for management trainees it may last one to two years. Because of its uniqueness, orientation training must be offered by the individual employer, rather than by an outside agency, though public and private vocational education programs should and do offer orientation to an occupational field or to an industry.

Typical content for new hourly paid employees involves delivery of an identification badge or card, a welcoming speech by someone in the personnel department, a description of company regulations, safety and security measures, and a description of the suggestion system (2, p. 41). In unionized firms a copy of the union contract may be handed to the worker. Following a brief question and answer period, messengers escort each new worker to his place of work, and his first-line supervisor provides a specific introduction to the job.

A program of orientation for management trainees may involve several days of lectures and discussions about the company organization, history, and goals. After a welcome by a top company official, the trainees may be assigned to different departments or units of the firm, sometimes in different cities or even in different countries with a specific work assignment plus instructions to study and report on what they see. Periodically they may be brought back together for additional instruction and discussion. At the end of the orientation they will be assigned to a specific job, chosen on the basis of their interests and on the needs of the company.

SAFETY TRAINING

Companies which handle hazardous products or processes probably spend more man hours of training on safety than any other type of training program. A weekly safety meeting for all supervisors or even for all employees may be mandatory. A review of recent accidents in the industry, suggestions for improved safety practices, and "pep" talks with regard to competition in the latest safety contest are featured. The heavy economic penalties of a poor safety record provide the principal incentive for this type of training. Usually the same amount of training is provided to every employee in a particular department, regardless of his personal safety record. A few companies, especially in the transportation industry, provide special training in safety to those employees who have poor safety records. Companies which do not have such obvious safety hazards, and small companies regardless of their hazards, rarely devote much time to safety education programs.

MANAGEMENT TRAINING

Clark and Sloan found that in factories, management training was offered more frequently than any type of training except orientation. Foreman were most frequently expected to attend, for the higher a person's status in the company, the less likely he was to be required to participate. One of the problems in management training is that the teaching staff consists of company employees who are trainers either on a full or part-time basis, but "Status forbids a senior executive from regular participation in a class conducted by a subordinate" (2, p. 16).

Much of management training is not in the formal classroom. Distribution of weekly newsletters, inspirational booklets, and company reports is common. Little attempt is made to determine whether or not these materials are read. "Understudy" training is also quite common. Each supervisor is assigned the task of preparing one or more of his subordinates to take his place when and if he is promoted. Delegation of authority (but not responsibility), informal coaching, and close observation and evaluation of the trainee's progress is common. Some companies state flatly that they will not promote a supervisor until he has prepared a satisfactory understudy.

Job rotation is another commonly used supervisory training practice. It has, perhaps, been developed to the greatest extent in the military, where experience in a variety of different types of jobs is a prerequisite to promotion. The goal of job rotation is not only to acquaint the manager with many different aspects of the firm's operation, but also to observe his performance in situations requiring broadly different expertise.

Formal classroom instruction in the plant most frequently uses "conference" techniques where questions are proposed, and trainees are expected to discuss the questions. Content ranges from how to improve the quality of company products and services to ways of dealing with union officials. Occasionally questions of broad social interest are discussed, but rarely by first-line supervisors. Increasingly, mid-management trainees are being sent to university and trade association sponsored formal training programs where the conference method is supplemented by specific instruction by well prepared instructors.

When a company is expanding its employment of minority group members, management (and sometimes other employees) is given training on understanding minority group values and problems.

SKILL TRAINING

Instruction on how to perform a job efficiently is another common type of training. Its form and extent vary enormously, however, from a simple demonstration by an experienced worker to highly formalized training programs of four or five years in length. Its elaborateness is determined largely by the content of the job. The best measure of the simplicity of a redesigned job is in terms of the length of time required to learn it.

ON-THE-JOB TRAINING (OJT)

On-the-job training usually is a distinctly informal process. A brief job demonstration by a first-line supervisor or by a workman selected by the supervisor, followed by a period of trial and error learning, with occasional help from supervisors or from nearby workers characterizes the great majority of such training. If the performance is satisfactory, the on-the-job training may be terminated, and checks on quality and quantity of performance then will be handled as they are for any other worker.

In learning the content of more complex positions, the new employee often serves as a helper to a more skilled person, learning by observation and by trial and error under more direct supervision. The job may be subdivided temporarily, with a particular part being demonstrated, followed successively by practice, additional demonstrations, and additional practice. If the worker is expected to be competent in performing a variety of activities, he may acquire these through a planned program of job rotation or may learn new activities only when his presence is no longer required on an activity which he has learned earlier.

On-the-job training typically occurs during the process of production of goods or services, and it is the quantity and quality of production which indicates whether or not learning has occurred. Both the trainee and trainer occupy dual roles: the trainee serves both as a student and as a producer, while his instructor serves both as a producer and as an instructor.

The inseparability of dual roles and the informality of on-the-job training cause extreme difficulty in measuring its costs. Even where on-the-job training is more formalized, as in the armed forces, the formality often consists only of rotating the trainee through a variety of work experiences to be certain that he has been exposed to all of the tasks which he eventually will be expected to perform. There have been few serious attempts to measure on-the-job costs even in the military. Although the costs of OJT are not usually identified, they are real. Damage to equipment, low quality and quantity of production (both by the trainee and by the trainer), and wastage of material are common costs in production. Lost sales and dissatisfied customers are their counterparts for on-the-job training in service occupations. Costs of OJT are lowered by utilization of instructors who may be so poor in verbal communication that they could not teach in a classroom. The relevance of instruction is easily apparent, which tends to increase motivation. And instruction is sometimes provided on equipment which otherwise would not be in use, or by instructors who otherwise would be resting.

Undoubtedly most blue collar job skills are learned through training on-the-job (11, p. 437 and 8, pp. 43-45). For certain blue and white collar jobs, there is no alternative to on-the-job training. This is particularly true where workers desire to conceal from management the precise techniques used in production for fear that management will use this knowledge to increase work output. Where the cost of materials is high, where it is impracticable to assemble a group of workers simultaneously needing identical training, and where the cost of equipment is extremely high, on-the-job training is less costly than more formal training programs. Even where a group of workers needing similar instruction can be assembled, it is still common to use the method of OJT through a vestibule school which utilizes high cost material and high cost equipment in an area separated from the remainder of the production process, but with the output of the training program being fed into the production stream.

Skills which are transmitted through on-the-job training are rarely recorded. This leads to direct transmission of skills from a worker to his successor and to the changing of skills as the process of transmission is incomplete. This, in turn, leads to non-standard jobs as innovations are introduced without written record. These innovations may or may not be desirable in terms of increasing productivity.

When job skills are specific to a particular firm, present employees tend to have a monopoly on training if OJT is the method of instruction which is employed. Since on-the-job training is under the control of first-line supervision and other current employees, a worker who is not accepted by these current employees (for example, a minority group member) is unlikely to be allowed to learn the job, because he is subject to sabotage, harassment, and incorrect instruction. On-the-job training requires the approval and close cooperation of experienced employees. Since training is a process by which the supply of skilled labor is increased, it must be apparent to these current employees that an increase in the supply of skilled labor will not be detrimental to their own position. Otherwise they will not cooperate in the training process and will make it almost impossible for a newcomer to learn. Job security and promotions based on seniority help to insure that the newcomer is not an active threat to existing employees.

A second method of insuring against too active competition from new workers is the restriction of entry through labor organizations. The craft unions, such as those in the building and printing trades, rely heavily on this method of protection. By controlling entry to the occupation, they find it much less necessary to rely upon seniority as a control device. Hence, employers are much freer to assign workers from unions having close entry level restrictions than they are workers from industrial type unions which rely much more heavily upon seniority. In either case, proposals for change in the allocation of scarce jobs among the internal labor force through training will almost certainly lead to conflict, and if labor union officials appear to countenance such proposed changes, their positions as leaders are likely to be in jeopardy.

TEACHING SPEED AND ACCURACY IN JOB PERFORMANCE

On-the-job training is very much concerned with the development of necessary speed and accuracy of performance. The process of acquiring the necessary speed and accuracy can be described for each individual learner as a learning curve which relates output of satisfactory product or service to length of time on the job. The curve showing the amount of satisfactory product eventually levels off. If it levels off at or above the standard required for the job, the worker is said to be trained. It it levels off below the standard required, additional training efforts may be employed or the worker may be transferred or discharged.

One of the hazards of on-the-job training is that it has a potential for permanently lowering work norms. Particularly during periods when there is a tight labor market and employment standards are relaxed, new workers may have difficulty in meeting old job standards. Since these job standards are rarely written, but are generally transmitted through the on-the-job training process, they are almost certain to be lowered unless new employees can meet them quickly. Similar problems are involved in the use of on-the-job training to develop behavioral traits such as promptness, regular attendance, and acceptance of criticisms from management. Reductions in behavioral work trait standards during the training period are likely to be incorporated as a permanent feature of the work setting.

FORMALIZED SKILL TRAINING

Formal training is emphasized in employment much more frequently during tight labor markets than when adequate numbers of employees are readily available. In part this is a reflection of economies of scale which permit personnel to be assigned temporarily to full time training duties and to the presence of enough trainees to establish a "class." Classroom training in basic mathematical and verbal skills, blueprint reading, and other generalizable, standardizable skills can be organized. When the labor market is loose, these skills can be obtained through a process of selection from the available labor supply and are unlikely to be taught within the plant. In the armed forces, where inadequate pay for technically trained personnel produces a perpetually tight labor market, training is carried on continually, and training standards appear in written form. This is in marked contrast to the situation in most industrial employment where training is a sometime thing and rarely is carried on long enough or intensively enough to result in written training standards.

GENERAL EDUCATION

Clark and Sloan (2) found that general education was the least frequently offered of any type of employer sponsored training. Even so, the programs classified by employers as being "general education" often sound remarkably specific, e.g., "accounting machine applications," "aircraft flutter and transient loads," "applied electronics," "engineering report writing," "automatic box-loom fixing," plus certain avocational subjects and elementary school and high school subjects which most people would accept as "general education". Some employers who reimburse workers for college fees will pay for general courses required for a degree, but others restrict payment to courses approved in advance as being useful on the job.

Decision Making in Employer Sponsored Training

Two major decisions are necessary once it has been decided that employee performance is not satisfactory. The first decision is whether to recruit or train. Since little is known about the costs of recruitment, and even less is known about the cost of training, this decision is very often made on non-economic grounds. The presence of skilled, experienced personnel who can be recruited almost always tips the decision in favor of recruitment. If skilled, experienced employees are not available on the labor market, or if management is prohibited from employing them, training will be instituted. The starting of such training often is not as a result of a formal management decision, but is done by first-line supervisors who are forced to institute on-the-job training in order to meet quantity and quality quotas. Formal training programs such as vestibule schools or classroom programs, on the other hand, almost always require high level management decisions.

PURCHASING OR PROVIDING TRAINING

If a decision is made that present or prospective employees need training, a second level decision must be made as to whether to purchase this training outside the company or to provide it internally. Sometimes a combination of these methods is used. The army, navy, and air force provide training for officers in service academies and officer candidate schools, and they purchase training in reserve officer training programs in universities. A large bakery may provide training on-the-job and through formal courses, but it may also purchase training from the American Institute of Baking, which operates a school supported by the industry. General Motors operates its own college, but it also purchases college training for some of its employees. It trains service personnel through a large network of regional service schools, but it also subsidizes vocational training programs through gifts of equipment, instructional materials, and low cost teacher training.

Training may be purchased from a variety of sources. Trade associations very frequently have training programs available which may be offered inside or outside the place of employment at a relatively modest cost. Local high schools and community colleges are frequently anxious to provide training programs at even lower costs.

The availability of vocational education in high schools and colleges and the availability of training services offered by the vendors of equipment often lead employers during tight labor markets to contract for vocational education to be conducted off the job. It is characteristic of these programs that they are initiated by the employer rather than by the training agency and are so closely related to the employer that they appear to be extensions of his internal training activities. In almost every case, they are designed to provide instruction which is specific to the needs of the employer rather than to provide basic or general vocational education.

This procedure is in marked contrast to the public statements of most employers that they desire broad general and vocational education programs. Perhaps an explanation lies in the fact that an employer who is recruiting new employees desires to employ people who have had general and vocational education which is broad enough to include the specific skill requirements of his firm, but when contracting for the training of his current employees, he does not wish the instruction to be so broad as to include the specific requirements of other employers. Broader training would be more expensive, and might lead some employees to seek employment elsewhere. Decisions to provide training rather than to buy it are almost always swayed by such factors as a desire to provide an instructor who "knows our situation," fear of letting outsiders know company secrets, and the desire of workers to have training offered on company time on company premises in order to minimize their personal costs.

Almost invariably, employers prefer to operate their own training program if their size will permit it. With the training directly under their control, no time is spent on instruction which they regard as superfluous. Second choice is usually training offered by a trade association which is at least partially under their control. Only in the event that these two methods are inadequate do they purchase training from outside educational institutions. Usually, if the training program in a large company must be reduced in size, purchased training is discontinued first. Conversely, purchased training often expands most rapidly when the internal training facilities are fully occupied and additional training is needed.

When training of known high quality is provided at no added cost to the employer, a different set of values is employed. Typists are usually trained in public schools, with all or part of the cost (including foregone earnings) being borne by others. This makes it extremely unlikely that an employer will offer training in typing, unless the number of graduates from outside training agencies is completely inadequate to meet the demand. Even then, he first is likely to ask the public schools to increase their output.

Some vocational training, however, is so poor in quality that its output is not desirable even if it is free of cost to the employer. If graduates of a program cannot be placed in employment even in times of shortage of employees, the program must be improved or be terminated. If graduates of a program are placed during times of shortage of employees, but cannot be placed when the labor market is loose, however, this is not necessarily an indication of poor quality vocational education. Often this is due to employers searching for employees of higher verbal intelligence than the students who are enrolled in that vocational program. High placement rates of school graduates, regardless of the state of the labor market, is a common sign that the vocational program is refusing to serve some of the students who most need its help.

Advantages and Disadvantages of Employer Training

Training offered by employers has numerous advantages. Instruction is almost always relevant and timely in the eyes of the trainee. It is offered in a setting which appears to be relevant to trainee goals. It seldom requires the purchasing of expensive equipment specifically for training. The products and services produced during the process of training are readily sold as regular products of the company. Length of training is not constrained by artificial lengths of class periods, semesters, or school years. Disadvantages are few but important. The business of the employer is to produce products or services other than training, so training is a by-product which inevitably receives less attention than the prime goal of the firm. Not only the training but the trainee is a means to an end. In an educational institution, no one would think of expecting a trainee to continue indefinitely practicing a skill which he has already learned. Instead, he would be instructed in a new skill. If this process were followed in employer sponsored training, the company would quickly go bankrupt. The cost of training to an employer can only be recouped by a period of heightened productivity following training. Unless the employee is needed to perform some other process, he can expect to continue practicing indefinitely the processes which he has learned most thoroughly.

It is obvious that in many cases human talent is developed more effectively in a production setting than in a school which is removed from contact with employment realities. On the other hand, it is certain that the development of human talents in an employment setting is often accidental and is almost always subordinate to a production goal.

Training by Organized Labor

Training sponsored by labor organizations has many of the characteristics of employer training. Workers and union officials must be oriented to the goals of the labor organization. Officials must be developed through on-the-job training and through formal educational programs. As with big companies, big unions also are more likely to have sophisticated training programs. Indeed, the AFL-CIO operates a college which in many ways is as sophisticated as those run by General Motors and by International Business Machines.

Apprenticeship training may be sponsored by employers, by labor groups, or may be jointly sponsored. In any case where labor organizations are involved, they regard the apprenticeship program with an almost sacred reverence. Attempts by outsiders to modify the program in any way are regarded with suspicion. In one way, this high regard for apprenticeship training is misplaced. No more than 250,000 persons in the United States serve as apprentices at any one time, and in view of the fact that dropout rates are rather high, and programs average four years in length, no more than fifty thousand workers could complete apprenticeship programs each year. This amounts to about 2 percent of the yearly additions to the labor force. Even in the construction trades and in certain metalworking crafts, where apprenticeship in the United States is concentrated, apprenticeship rarely provides more than a tenth of the new skilled craftsmen.

On the other hand, the person who completes an apprenticeship program is in a very favored position. He is better prepared than any other skilled worker in his field and usually has many positions from which to choose. About a third of the apprentice graduates become supervisors; a third enter technical positions; and a third work directly in the occupation for which they are prepared. This latter third provides a sizeable share of the leadership of organized labor. With these facts in mind, it is easy to see why labor guards jealously a program which provides upward mobility for their sons and leadership for their movement.

While the history of apprenticeship is well known (7), current programs have not been studied intensively. A forthcoming report from Professor Alfred Drew of Purdue University should add greatly to our knowledge of this field. Enough is known, however, to make clear that a far smaller portion of the skilled manpower in the United States is provided through apprenticeship than in any other Western industrialized nation. In most other countries, workers in many more occupations, from waiter to technician, are trained through apprenticeship than is the case here. Instead, we tend to rely on OJT which lacks a definite program of job rotation through each of the activities requisite for skilled performance. Moreover, it usually lacks the formal education in the theory and practice of the occupation which accompanies on-the-job training in a well structured apprenticeship program.

Education in the Armed Forces

Education in the Armed Forces has numerous parallels with education sponsored by any other type of employer. And, since records of armed forces training are much more complete than records of other types of training by employers, we turn to them to note substantial changes in training by employers during our country's history. Three general principles seem to have pervaded the training programs in the military:

1. The greater the level of technological advance, the greater the amount of formal schooling provided to cope with these technological changes.
2. Following the introduction of a technological innovation, which requires employees who have new job skills, the first response is to provide a completely inadequate quantity of such training. This is succeeded by a period in which the quantity of trainees is sharply increased and the curriculum is made up of a combination of general education and specific education. This in turn

is followed by a sharp curtailment of the curriculum, eliminating many of the general education elements.
3. A shortage of funds is followed almost immediately by sharp curtailment in formal education programs.

In 1802, the United States Military Academy was established with a curriculum that emphasized engineering. This subject was outside the academic pale of the universities, but it was obviously successful, for not a single fortification designed by West Point graduates was captured by the enemy during the war of 1812. During this same period the Navy depended upon skilled manpower from the Merchant Marine and supplemented their skills by on-the-job training. Its lack of regard for formal instruction is conveyed in an order of 1802 which required the chaplain of each ship to instruct officers ". . . in writing, arithmetic, navigation, and whatsoever may contribute to render them proficients" (quoted in reference 3, p. 16). Very likely the chaplain was the only person on board who could write, though his qualifications for instruction in navigation almost certainly left a great deal to be desired.

In 1814, the first steam powered warship in the United States Navy was constructed by Robert Fulton, but it was not until thirty-one years later that the United States Naval Academy was established, with a curriculum which emphasized steam engineering. The first army airplane was purchased in 1909, but training for aviators lay dormant until 1916. The first army motor truck experiments began in 1904, but when fifty thousand motor vehicles were purchased at the start of World War I, there were no trained technicians for maintenance and repair. The time lag between the introduction of new technology and the preparation of personnel to cope with it continues to decrease. At present, the armed forces are leaders in an attempt to design educational programs which will produce technicians almost simultaneously with the introduction of new technology.

Formal Schools in the Military

In spite of having the best organized and probably the largest system of on-the-job training of any employer, the United States military finds a need for a great deal of formal education. Much of this education is provided through specialized schools operated by the military, but a considerable amount of formal training is acquired through contracts with colleges, universities, private trade schools, and schools operated by vendors of equipment. The level of training ranges from basic literacy education to education at the post Ph.D. level. A brief catalogue of a few of the major training installations in the Army gives some flavor of the scope of training provided.

Army Medical School (1893)
Army Ordnance School (1902)
Army Quartermaster School (1910)
Army Artillery and Missile School (1911)
Army Infantry School (1918)
Army Chaplain's School (1918)
Army Chemical School (1920)
Army Finance School (1920)
Army Armor School (1940)
Adjutant General's School (1941)
Army Language School (1941)
Army Intelligence School (1941)
Army Information School and Army Transportation School (1946)
Army Strategic Intelligence School (1947)
Army Schools for Arctic and Jungle Warfare (1948)
Army Command and Management School, Helicopter School
    (1954)
Army Civil Affairs Military Government School (1955)

Although they were relatively late in establishing formal schools, the Navy and the Air Force now provide more such training per employee than the Army does.

Two major facts emerge from this brief recital. First, no new major schools were opened between 1920 and 1940. The amount of money spent on formal education declined much more rapidly during this period than did total appropriations for the military. Secondly, as the rate of technological advance has increased during recent years, the rate of establishment of specialized schools has similarly increased.

Size of the Military Training Effort

Technical training in the military is undoubtedly the largest vocational and technical program maintained by any single establishment anywhere. At any one time between 10 and 15 percent of the personnel of the armed forces in the United States are receiving formal instruction in a school. Over four thousand resident courses are offered which prepare people for almost twenty-five hundred separate jobs. Since most courses are less than a year in length, it is likely that the number attending formal classes during any one year is considerably higher than 10 to 15 percent, and may approximate the number of persons who enter and leave the armed forces each year (approximately 20 percent). "If all these schools were placed on one contiguous campus, the area covered would probably exceed that occupied by the three largest cities . . . in the United States—New York, Los Angeles, and Chicago" (3, p. 1). In addition to those enrolled in formal courses in resident centers, nearly one million students are enrolled in the more than twenty-five hundred correspondence school courses offered by the armed forces.

THE RELATIONSHIP BETWEEN MILITARY TRAINING AND SUCCESS IN CIVILIAN LIFE

As is the case with training offered by an employer, all or almost all of military training is designed to enable the trainee to better succeed in military life. Although there have been limited experiments, such as "Project Transition," there has been no sustained attempt to design military training which will enable a person better to succeed in civilian life. Inevitably, of course, there is some value in civilian life for many types of military training, and a great deal of civilian value for a very few types of training. Basic training in the military is sometimes accepted by colleges in lieu of health and physical education courses. Language instruction, typewriter repair, medical instruction, certain of the broader electronics training courses, air traffic control, and certain clerical trainings have very close parallels in civilian occupations. The most striking example of transferability is found in the fact that a very high proportion of commercial airplane pilots received their initial technical instruction and experience in the military. On the other hand, instruction in anti-submarine warfare, cryptography, mine warfare, artillery gunnery, and the like, has little or no relationship to civilian occupations employing sizeable numbers of people.

Even in cases where there is some relationship between skills taught in the military and skills needed in civilian occupations, the number of people trained may bear no relationship to civilian needs (though it certainly will have a close relationship to military manpower needs). For example, very few people are employed in civilian life as hunters. One of the qualifications of many soldiers is the ability to shoot well. The number of people trained to shoot well in the military is quite unrelated to the number of people needed in this civilian occupation, for obvious reasons.

THE NEED FOR TRANSITION EDUCATION BETWEEN MILITARY TECHNICAL TRAINING AND CIVILIAN TECHNICAL NEEDS

Retirements from the military occur at relatively early ages except for the very few officers who reach the highest levels of command. Many career officers and enlisted men retire at forty to forty-five years of age.

The great majority of enlisted men leave the armed forces before they are thirty. Most of these persons have acquired some skills which would be useful in civilian life. If they go to college, arrangements have been made for them to receive college credit for relevant formal education received in the armed forces. Few such arrangements have been made for credit in apprenticeship, in vocational and technical education programs, or in occupational licensure.

Manpower Planning

With the exception of the military, very few of even the largest and most sophisticated employers in the United States engage in manpower forecasting or planning for any part of their labor force, and those few who do engage in manpower forecasting do it almost entirely for their management personnel (6). When the employment office of a company reports that the labor market is tightening, it receives approval to begin advertising for employees, to make contacts with school systems and with public employment services, and to ask current employees to suggest names of friends who might be interested in employment. If the market continues to tighten and insufficient applicants for employment are recruited by these means, the employer then turns to paying bonuses to employees for referrals, pays visiting and moving costs for recruits, activates training and apprenticeship programs, contributes instructors, equipment, and even money to local schools for vocational education, and contacts ethnic groups and civil rights organizations to secure referrals of recent arrivals in the community.

Skill shortages also lead to decisions to allow engineers to proceed with implementing their natural biases in favor of job simplification and the substitution of equipment for labor (the strength of these biases of engineers is constant and independent of labor scarcities, but funds to implement these biases on a grand scale are often dependent upon shortage of skilled personnel).

Davis and Canter (5) point out that when new equipment is being designed, it is relatively easy to see what tasks must be performed to operate the equipment. However, the combining of these tasks into jobs depends upon other work which is being performed nearby, attitudes of union officials, and qualifications of the labor force, and usually must wait until the equipment is in operation. Even minimum job qualifications are almost impossible to foresee, since the new equipment has been operated and maintained by over-qualified engineers. During the process of installation of a new technology, as operators assigned to jobs change, the jobs automatically change to take into account the capabilities of the new operators. Enterprises attempt to mold men to jobs, not jobs to men, but in practice men frequently mold jobs.

REFERENCES

1. Belman, Harry S. and J.E. Bliek, "Training Departments in Business, Industry and Government," *Journal of the American Society of Training Directors*, XII, No. 9 (September, 1968), 45-53.

2. Clark, Harold F. and Harold S. Sloan, *Classrooms in the Factories*. New York: New York University Press, 1958.

3. Clark, Harold F. and Harold S. Sloan, *Classrooms in the Military*. New York: Teachers College, Columbia University, 1964.

4. Clark, Harold F. and Harold S. Sloan, *Classrooms in the Stores*. Sweetsprings, Missouri: Rocksbury Press, 1962.

5. Davis, Louise and Ralph Raymond Canter, "Job Design," *Journal of Industrial Engineering*, VI (January, 1955), 3.

6. Doeringer, Peter B., *et al.* "Corporate Manpower Forecasting and Planning," *Conference Board Record*, V, No. 8 (1968), 37-45.

7. Douglas, Paul Howard, *American Apprenticeship and Industrial Education*. New York: AMS Press, Inc., 1921.

8. *Formal Occupational Training of Adult Workers*. Manpower/Automation Research Monograph No. 2. Washington, D.C.: U.S. Department of Labor, 1964.

9. Hansen, Gary B., *Britain's Industrial Training Act, Its History Development and Implications for America*. Washington, D.C.: National Manpower Policy Task Force, 1967.

10. Mesics, Emil A., *An annotated bibliography on industrial training: training in organizations, business, industrial and government*. Bibliography Series Number 4. Ithaca: New York State School of Industrial and Labor Relations, Cornell University, 1960.

11. Piore, Michael J., "On-the-Job Training and Adjustment to Technological Change," *Journal of Human Resources*, III, No. 4 (Fall, 1968), 435-449.

12. Smith, Paul W., of Western Electric Company quoted in Dunlap, J.T., ed. *Work Force Adjustments in Private Industry — Their Implications for Manpower Policy*. Manpower/Automation Research Monograph No. 7. Washington, D.C.: U.S. Department of Labor, 1968.

Chapter 14 VOCATIONAL EDUCATION CONDUCTED BY OTHER AGENCIES

When we think of vocational education, we usually think of school programs, or of education conducted by employer and employee groups. Undoubtedly the major part of vocational education is provided by these institutions, but a number of other agencies and groups also contribute markedly to vocational education. There is virtually no literature on vocational education of this type.

ORGANIZATIONS SELLING PRODUCTS OR SERVICES

A very extensive part of vocational education, but one about which little is known, is that conducted by organizations which are interested in selling products or services. These educational efforts are particularly intensive when the product or service is so new that formal schools have not yet had an opportunity to incorporate it into their curricula; where the demand for this education is so geographically dispersed that it is impractical for formal schools or even employers to provide instruction; or where vocational educators and employers have failed to provide adequate training (in quantity or quality) for whatever reason.

These training services are expensive, but are justified on the ground that the product or service will not continue to be sold unless its performance is satisfactory. And the only way in which its performance can be guaranteed to be satisfactory is to have capable persons who know how to use it or adjust it and repair it. Even where vocational education is not included as a part of the sales or franchise contract, many manufacturers and franchisers are willing to provide training to user organizations, with free or nominal tuition, simply upon request. As a means of expanding the availability of qualified personnel, many such schools allow vocational instructors to enroll with no tuition payment on the assumption that as they acquire the necessary skills, they will pass them on to their students.

FACTORY SCHOOLS

Quite often the manufacturer, franchise owner, or other purveyor of a product or service will organize a school adjacent to the headquarters of the firm. This allows ready use of personnel in both production and instruction roles and allows students to see the production of goods or the development of promotional materials firsthand.

Where a relatively expensive product is involved or where large quantities of even inexpensive products are sold, the buyer may receive as a part of the purchase contract an agreement to train a certain number of his employees in the factory operated school. Examples of products which include training as a part of the sales package include: computers, digital controlled machine tools, airplanes, and locomotives. Sellers of franchises for hotels, food retailing establishments, and many other service establishments provide a similar type of training in a central school. Often, this training is mandatory, and sometimes re-training at specified intervals (such as once each year) is also mandatory. At least one large manufacturer of automobiles requires personnel from a prospective franchise holder to be trained at a central location before a franchise may be transferred.

Organizations selling petroleum products often require the manager and key personnel of automotive service stations to receive training in the central school. Often, this central school may also be a factory operated service station, which allows personnel to receive not only classroom instruction but also supervised on-the-job training for brief periods of time. In the automotive industry, the critical shortage of skilled repairmen has led to the establishment of regional factory schools which provide a site for training conducted by subsidiaries of the parent corporation.

CLINICS FOR SERVICEMEN

One of the difficulties with factory schools is that it is necessary for the trainee to leave his place of employment often for a week or more and travel to some central training area. In order to reach more effectively the persons who need training, many organizations have developed mobile training units which travel from town to town, advertise the availability of training, and attract trainees for sessions as short as an hour. Types of organizations which use mobile training include manufacturers of fertilizer, electronic equipment, and automotive equipment. Indeed, almost any manufacturer of a new product who finds he cannot attract students in sufficient quantity to a centralized school is likely to consider seriously the desirability of setting up mobile training units. Often these training units serve not only a training function, but also a sales function, for as people see equipment and services demonstrated, they are often willing to invest in them, particularly if they are assured that additional training will be available as needed.

TECHNICAL INFORMATION BROCHURES

A great deal of vocational training is carried on through printed material which is distributed to users. Ordinarily this method of training works best when the persons to be trained have some familiarity with the product or service, but need to be introduced to important modifications in it. As in the case of training clinics, technical information brochures serve both a sales and a training function. Indeed, the sales department is often responsible for the preparation and distribution of technical information brochures. In some organizations this leads to conflicts in design of the information to be distributed, since sales personnel usually wish to stress advantages of the product or service, while personnel from engineering and training departments wish to call attention to key problems which can be circumvented through adequate training. Advertisements, especially in trade journals, also serve a vocational training function. Usually, however, advertisements are under control of the sales department, and training content is usually incidental to the sales purpose.

University Affiliated Groups

COOPERATIVE EXTENSION

Although the cooperative extension service was organized in land grant universities to provide educational services to farmers, it recently has expanded its goals to provide services to city dwellers as well. It has always had a goal of increasing the total well-being of the men and women it serves. Programs range from instruction in art and music to an understanding of better means of marketing home produced goods and services, but a high proportion of the instruction given has been related to increasing occupational competence. A major reason for the success of these programs has been that efforts have been made to determine the needs and interests of the clientele to be served.

UNIVERSITY EXTENSION

Most university extension programs began as a way of carrying the standard credit instructional programs of the university off campus. This still continues to be a major goal of persons who operate university extension programs, but they have learned many things from cooperative extension. Today, the educational programs of cooperative extension and university extension are remarkably similar, and indeed several universities have acted to combine the two. The image of university extension is that its programs serve only professionals and businessmen. While it is true that these groups ask for and receive a great deal of assistance, a glance at total university extension programs will show that they serve people from almost every walk of life. Programs designed to raise occupational competency, however, tend to be confined to professional and business occupations.

Y.M.C.A.'s and Y.W.C.A.'s

The Young Men's and Young Women's Christian Associations, while established for religious purposes, have developed a wide range of educational programs to meet the needs of their clientele. As is the case whenever the needs of the student are taken into account, a sizeable portion of the educational program is devoted to increasing occupational competence. By meeting the needs of people through inexpensive well planned occupational education programs, and by being accessible as a result of having large facilities in inner cities, many Y.M.C.A.'s and Y.W.C.A.'s have built adult education programs which are models of effectiveness.

Opportunities Industrialization Centers

The Opportunities Industrialization Center (OIC) movement began in Philadelphia in the late fifties as a means of increasing the options of blacks. Unlike cooperative or university extension services or Y.M.C.A.'s, the OIC program is designed by blacks for blacks. This concept of self-help has appealed to white business men and to the federal government, which have provided financial assistance. At the same time, the sense of controlling their own educational and occupational destiny has appealed to blacks. The OIC program is not entirely occupational, though this forms its major emphasis. Instruction in fields such as black history is designed to instill racial pride, and some OIC groups operate social programs which involve the entire community. Opportunities Industrialization Centers have spread across the country. While some have failed, largely due to deficiencies in local leadership, others have succeeded very well. As is the case with secondary school vocational education, OIC's programs attract more female than male trainees.

Professional and Trade Associations

Most professional associations and associations of employers and employees maintain occupational education programs. These range from correspondence school instruction and short-term seminars, to formal instruction in association operated schools with the course of instruction lasting a year or more. Traveling lecturers, magazines devoted to education of the members, closed circuit television instruction, and mailed brochures bringing members up to date on recent occupational developments are part of the program of many such groups. The size and scope of these programs have never been tabulated, but it is certain that few people realize their magnitude.

Role of the Federal Government

Aside from its support of vocational education activities conducted by secondary and post-secondary schools for in-school youth and adults, the federal government has financed a variety of other training programs for non-professional occupations. These other programs have been well described by Levitan and Mangun (1), and by Venn (2).

VOCATIONAL REHABILITATION

The oldest of these programs, vocational rehabilitation, began in 1920 to meet the need for re-training persons who had been physically disabled as a result of industrial employment. It was gradually expanded to include medical, financial, counseling, and all other types of services needed to return the disabled to employment. At the same time, its clientele was expanded to serve those whose handicaps were the result of birth defects and all types of accidents. Most recently it has stated that it can serve anyone who has a physical or mental disability which is a handicap to employment, if rehabilitation services are likely to make him employable.

Like vocational education, vocational rehabilitation requires the participating states to match federal funds, and allows the states wide discretion in the ways in which services are provided. A further similarity is that both programs have tended to serve an upper-lower class clientele and to provide inadequate service to lower-lower class persons. Two of its strongest points have been the quality of training provided to its counselors and its willingness to purchase quality service for its clients from any agency which can provide the assistance which is needed (1, pp. 277-331).

MANPOWER DEVELOPMENT AND TRAINING ACT AND "POVERTY" PROGRAMS

In 1962, there was fear that technological change would cause unemployment among heads of families. The MDTA was created to ease this dislocation. Within a year, however, it was plain that youth and minority group members had far greater problems, so programs were designed to meet their needs. Many of these took the form of federal grants to neighborhood groups, public and private schools, and employers who provided similar services and competed for students and for employment slots.

Unlike vocational education and vocational rehabilitation, few MDTA and "poverty" programs operated through state agencies. Most were directed from Washington, and funds were sent to program operators with no intermediaries. Programs were started or stopped on short notice, with little relationship between funding level and quality of program. Costs per trainee were high, ranging up to ten thousand dollars per trainee per year (in the early years of the Job Corps). One reason for high cost was that, unlike vocational education and rehabilitation, MDTA and poverty program trainees were paid to go to school. This was justified on the grounds that it made no sense to pay people more to accept public assistance (welfare) than to receive training which could remove them from welfare rolls. But stipends to trainees were not the only element of high cost. Food, housing, and medical costs were a far larger proportion of Job Corps costs than were trainee stipends. Costs of training were high because teachers and administrators had to be paid extra to serve in programs which were temporary. Costs per trainee were inflated markedly by the practice of admitting a specified number of trainees to a program to last, say, forty weeks. As trainees dropped out or were placed in jobs, the instructor might have only two or three trainees by the thirty-fifth week. The teacher's salary and overhead such as rent remained almost constant, sending costs per trainee up sharply.

One reason for funding programs on a short-term basis was refusal to recognize that training programs for unemployed and underemployed adults would be needed for many years. Failure to plan for the institutionalization of such programs increased costs and lowered staff morale. This failure to plan was justified by claims that stopping a project and starting new funds only after a delay of indefinite length allowed local program operators to discharge incompetent instructors. In practice, however, the more competent the instructor, the less likely he was to tolerate a one to three month period without pay. In one case, thirty-four of thirty-five instructors took non-teaching jobs within a month.

SKILLS CENTERS

A major step toward institutionalization was taken with the establishment of Skills Centers which were funded on an annual basis. Unlike earlier manpower and anti-poverty training programs, Skills Centers could accept trainees whenever a training slot was open; trainees could change from one occupational goal to another if the first choice proved to be inappropriate, and trainees lived at home (which lowered costs and increased trainee morale).

One group of Washington policy-makers feels that private industry will be more effective than non-profit groups in providing training to the unemployed. In spite of clear evidences of fraud in scattered cases, it seems likely that the private sector will be encouraged to expand its training efforts through a combination of persuasion and payments of approximately three thousand dollars per trainee per year, through the Job Opportunities in the Business Sector (JOBS) program and similar plans. It seems likely that the major impact of MDTA and anti-poverty programs has been as a force for change in institutionalized training programs. Not only have they demonstrated new methods and demonstrated that a new clientele can be served, but they have also shown a need to shift from matching the *best* person to an existing job to preparing *each* person to fill a suitable job (1, p. 9).

Coordinated Planning For Manpower Development

Through the Manpower Development and Training Act, the federal government has moved more and more strongly to emphasize its concern for developing the full potential of disadvantaged and handicapped persons. Because the unemployment rate is so extraordinarily high for disadvantaged and handicapped youth (higher than for the general population during the depths of the depression), the first efforts were directed toward skill training for immediate employment. It was quickly found that basic educational deficiencies, primarily in reading, needed to be remedied simultaneously.

In its efforts to do something quickly to solve these serious problems some eighteen different federal agencies set up a variety of competing and overlapping programs. Most of these have had little relationship with the formal school structure because: (a) there was a general feeling by those in charge that the schools had had their chance and had failed; (b) the formal school structure was not attractive to many of the potential trainees; and (c) most school people were not interested. Soon there were so many programs, with different requirements, different benefits, and starting and stopping at such irregular intervals, that no one could possibly know where to send a person who needed help.

The first attempt to remedy this situation on a nationwide basis was the Cooperative Area Manpower Planning System (CAMPS). This involved state and federal agencies for the first time on a large scale basis, and brought the various agencies together to tell each other what they were doing. Unfortunately, most agencies chose not to tell what they were planning for fear that some other agency would steal their plans. State wide plans often consisted of agency plans stapled together into one document. One wag referred to this as "coordination by staple." Schools, in particular, have contributed and received little from CAMPS. They have been represented by state educational officials or in the large cities by central office staff. Most program planning and implementation, however, is done at the local educational agency level. These local people do not want state and central office staff to speak for them.

CAMPS was an attractive concept, but it is failing because no one wants to give up his autonomy. Due to the inadequacies of CAMPS, decisions on the life and death of federal manpower programs continue to be made in Washington, on grounds which appear to governors, mayors, and community action groups to be capricious. They are asking for control, and it appears likely that they will get it effective in 1970-71. Governors, mayors, and organized groups representing minorities are apt to be even less tolerant than Washington bureaucrats of the failures of schools to help solve pressing problems of manpower development. Secondary schools which have high dropout rates and community colleges which have little or no remedial work, little or no vocational education, or do not agree to accept students who lack high school diplomas are apt to be particular targets.

REFERENCES

1. Levitan, Sar A. and Garth L. Mangum, *Federal Training and Work Programs in the Sixties*. Ann Arbor, Michigan: Institute of Industrial and Labor Relations, University of Michigan, 1969.

2. Venn, Grant, *Man, Education, and Manpower*. Washington, D.C.: American Association of School Administrators, 1970.

Chapter 15 TEACHER EDUCATION AND LEADERSHIP DEVELOPMENT*

One of the principal reasons for the failure to do more for youth with special needs is the shortage of broad gauge administrators to plan programs, and a shortage of teachers and supportive personnel who know what to do. These shortages illustrate the major problem which faces vocational education: inadequate emphasis on the preparation and upgrading of educational personnel.

The Labor Market for Vocational Teachers

Any study of supply and demand for vocational teachers must consider the labor market for this field. Table 15–1 represents the first attempt by the United States Office of Education (USOE) to identify the demand for various types of vocational education personnel. The first two columns are "actual", while the remaining figures are generally based on an assumption of annual increases of 7

---

*This chapter is adapted from Evans, R.N., "Teacher Education in Vocational and Technical Education" to be published as part of a University of Wisconsin text edited by Dr. Gerald Somers.

TABLE 15-1

Actual and Projected State and Local Administrative and
Other Ancillary Personnel in Vocational Education

STATE LEVEL	Fiscal Year					
	1965	1966	1967	1968	1970	1975
Directors or Supervisors	336	360	372	385	425	530
Assistant Directors or Supervisors	370	414	420	430	470	650
Area Supervisors	303	298	340	380	460	740
Youth Specialists	38	28	50	75	90	145
Teacher Trainers	52	56	58	60	68	90
Itinerant Teachers	141	177	185	190	210	235
Research Specialists	19	58	62	65	70	90
Guidance Specialists	36	51	65	70	85	95
Curriculum Specialists	37	52	54	60	70	90
Work-Study	31	28	25	—	—	—
Other	111	135	135	135	150	200
Sub-Total	1,474	1,657	1,766	1,850	2,098	2,865

Institutions						
Teacher Trainers	1,571	2,145	2,359	2,480	2,640	3,150
Total State	3,045	3,802	4,125	4,330	4,738	6,015
LOCAL LEVEL						
Directors or Supervisors	2,729	2,936	3,106	3,275	3,950	5,675
Guidance Specialists	874	962	985	1,000	1,050	1,200
Curriculum Specialists	162	123	135	142	160	200
Work-Study	72	607	450	—	—	—
Other	271	313	310	310	350	450
Total Local	4,108	4,941	4,986	4,727	5,510	7,525
Total State & Local	7,153	8,743	9,111	9,057	10,248	13,540
Teachers	109,136	124,729	146,000	163,000	213,000	350,000
Teachers in Teacher Education Programs						
Preservice	33,771	38,774	50,500	56,000	73,500	121,000
Inservice	35,280	38,317	51,500	58,000	75,800	124,000

Source: See reference 1, p. 4.

percent per year for local and 5 percent per year for state employees. Apparently the zero figures for work-study personnel are based on the fact that congressional authorization for work-study was to have expired in 1968, though why this was assumed to result in zero local employment is unclear. Certainly the assumption was faulty.

Since data on the actual vocational staff employment by type of teacher are available only for 1965 and 1966, it would be dangerous to extrapolate to future years on the basis of changes in these two sets of figures. It does seem remarkable, however, that state employed research specialists who went up 200 percent in one year are assumed to increase only 5 percent per year thereafter. Indeed, it is almost certain that Research Coordination Units alone employed more state research specialists in 1968 than are predicted for 1975. Similar comments might be made about the 40 percent gain in teacher trainers and state curriculum specialists, particularly since the trend away from local curriculum development in favor of state and national curriculum and program development has been apparent for some time.

A form for collection of data on teachers is being used on a trial basis in three states. If this trial is successful, we may have, for the first time, information about the background of and subjects taught by vocational teachers whose salaries are reimbursed by one division of USOE. Unfortunately, no information will be collected about preparation for teaching except the name of the college major field, and then only if the teacher has an academic degree. This study, and indeed all planning for vocational teacher education programs suffers from a far more serious defect, however. There is a large overlap in the labor markets for vocational staff and for the staffs of many other manpower programs. This labor market overlap occurs for teachers, administrators, and other educational personnel employed by:

A. Manpower Development and Training Act programs, especially institutional programs such as Skills Centers

B. Office of Economic Opportunity occupational programs

C. Job Corps

D. Opportunities Industralization Centers

E. Vocational education in federal prisons (and in a few state prisons)

F. Private trade schools, many of which operate training programs under contract to the federal government, as well as programs supported by tuition

G. Training programs in private business and industry

H. Armed forces occupational programs

I. Baccalaureate technical programs

Educational personnel for the above programs (and this is not an exhaustive list) are interchanged regularly. They come from much the same sources, and shortages or surpluses of personnel in one area quickly affect the others. Who should pay for training these persons, and who should forecast demand and supply? USOE seems to be saying that these programs belong to someone else and should not be considered in planning.

There is still another very large area of labor market overlap. There are about fifty thousand industrial arts teachers, five thousand non-vocational home economics teachers, and thirty thousand non-vocational business education teachers, plus an unknown number of former teachers of vocational and practical arts, some of whom are available for vocational teaching under certain conditions. Vocational education planners deny the transferability of many of these teachers, but in practice, state departments of vocational education "lower" standards when needed, to allow enough of these people into the fold to solve educational manpower shortages temporarily. Indeed, the availability of this pool of people who can be used in an emergency explains in large part how forty thousand teachers could be found between 1964 and 1966, though vocational teacher education programs expanded very little during the same period.

The process works in this way. Non-vocational practical arts teachers usually have a baccalaureate degree, but less occupational experience than vocational teachers. They teach courses such as beginning typing, general metals, and general home economics which are prerequisites to reimbursable vocational courses. Compared to vocational instruction, equipment is less adequate; students are younger (most commonly age thirteen to sixteen); many more classes are taught per day, and class sizes are larger. For these reasons, vocational teaching is often considered to be more desirable.

Public school teachers are employed for approximately nine months per year, so most male teachers and many female teachers get summer jobs outside education. Practical arts teachers usually look for employment in occupations which are related to their school work, and over a period of time, can accumulate considerable occupational experience. When vocational teachers are in plentiful supply, state boards of vocational education discount this summer employment. They seem to feel that full time commitment to an occupation is better preparation for vocational teaching than short-term employment of people who feel they really are teachers and only temporarily are business or industrial employees. But when there is a shortage of vocational teachers, this objection is waived.

Another sort of interchangeability exists. Particularly in the midwest, certain teachers spend half of their time teaching vocational courses and half of their time teaching non-vocational courses, usually in the practical arts. The former requires occupational experience, and the latter requires baccalaureate teacher education. Such teachers can and do move to full time teaching in vocational or in non-vocational fields, depending on supply and demand. Less mobile teachers (from both fields) often regard such dual allegiance with suspicion, feeling that a person should be fully committed to one field or the other.

If shortages in vocational teaching become severe enough that salaries and working conditions are considerably improved, other pools of people become available for full time vocational teaching. Examples include full time industrial employees who also teach part-time in vocational programs (these are eagerly sought because their expertise is known), agricultural and home economics extension workers, employees in industrial training departments, and rank and file workers and supervisors. Usually, however, expansion in demand for vocational teachers occurs at the same time or later than expansions in opportunities in private employment.

Still another device to meet shortages of vocational instructors is to employ teachers in a full time day school program and to pay them extra for teaching evenings and weekends in part-time vocational programs for adults. This not only provides extra hours of teaching service, but it also raises total salaries, making teaching positions more attractive. No one has conducted a thorough study of the effect of long continued overtime on the quality of instruction, but it may be assumed to be deleterious.

Flexibilities of the type described above work reasonably well for teachers. Unfortunately, there seems to be no ready way of similarly enlarging the pool of vocational administrators. Shortage of administrators have occurred each time the vocational program has expanded, but the shortage during the sixties has been especially severe because administrators, even more than teachers, have been in demand for occupational education programs of all types. Fifty percent increases in salaries offered to both teachers and administrators have been common as new occupational education programs have tried to get off the ground by luring experienced staff from public school vocational education.

Administrators are responsible not only for program and facility planning, but also for in-service education of teachers. The combination of a shortage of administrators and recruitment of an untrained teaching staff has created a real crisis in in-service teacher education. Realistic planning for development of educational personnel for vocational and tchnical education must take into account the entire labor market for these personnel. We can no longer afford to assess needs and plan educational development programs based on the public school segment of the market for vocational teachers and administrators.

Supply and Demand for Teacher Educators

Nationally, in 1966, there was one teacher educator per fifty-eight teachers. The range by states was from one to twenty-five to one to three hundred. Three-fifths of these teacher educators are part-time, and in every field except agriculture and office occupations, part-time teacher educators predominate. ("Part-time" usually means that the teacher educator is employed fulltime, but spends part of his time in activities not considered reimbursable by his state, e.g., teaching general education courses. "Full time" may not mean full time spent in educating teachers, since certain research curriculum development, and similar activities may be reimbursable.) The proportion of teacher educators to teachers was only one to seventy in 1965, and probably was even smaller in previous years. Unfortunately, no data are available to indicate long-term trends in this ratio.

Teacher educators are experienced vocational teachers or administrators, most of whom have done advanced graduate work in the field. They are employed by universities or by state departments of vocational education to conduct pre-service and in-service programs of teacher education, to develop curriculum materials and tests, to operate experimental programs, and to conduct research. For that portion of their time spent on state approved vocational activities, state and federal funds are used to pay a portion (often half) of their salaries. Travel and other expenses may also be reimbursed. Requirements for approval of teacher educators are written into the state plan, and often are similar to requirements for state supervisors, though the duties of these two types of positions are dissimilar. Social scientists and educational specialists in such fields as evaluation, who could add much to research and instruction in vocational education are excluded almost universally by state plan requirements. Universities add their own requirements, most frequently the earned doctorate. Persons who possess this combination of requirements are rare and are in great demand. Data on the production of teacher educators are not available.

Interaction of Supply-Demand and Certification

Measurement and prediction of supply-demand relationships in teaching are difficult because employment standards are lowered when the supply of teachers is scarce and are raised (gradually on paper, and rapidly in actual practice) when the supply is plentiful. Because of working conditions, the supply of a given type of teacher may be plentiful for a wealthy suburb at the same time it is scarce for an inner-city school or a poor rural school. Most states have some type of emergency teacher certification which allows almost anyone to teach in most subject fields, so employment standards effectively are in the hands of the local school district. These standards tend to be high if enough prospective teachers feel working conditions are good in that district, and tend to be low if the district cannot recruit better teachers.

In vocational and technical education, however, the state typically controls the number of new teaching certificates, which places power to control "quality" more in the hands of the state than in the hands of the local district. Most states refuse to certify a vocational or technical teacher until requested to do so by a school which wishes to employ him. This enables the staff of the state board of vocational education to suggest better qualified individuals who might be available. (In practice, this can be a powerful tool for conformity—you get recommended for a better job only if you are on good terms with your state supervisor.) In contrast, teachers outside vocational education usually are certified upon completion of a prescribed program of study and experience. The local school district can then select from among the pool of certified applicants, some of whom may be poor, indeed.

The practice of limiting vocational certification to teachers who are or are about to be employed has an additional effect. If the state's pool of potential vocational teachers increases in any one subject area, the real requirements for certification will be raised until they may actually reach the requirements specified in the state plan. Refusal to issue certificates until they are required for employment prevents formation of a pool of certified people who might be less qualified than those who could be certified later.

Certification of vocational teachers usually is handled by the state board of vocational education instead of by the certification board operated by the state department of education. Even in states where junior colleges have been declared a part of higher education and hence exempt from teacher certification, the state board of vocational education usually retains authority to approve or reject vocational and technical teachers by approving or withholding reimbursement of salaries. As in the case of the secondary schools, this can be used as a tool for assuring conformity.

All teachers are expected to know their subject matter and how to teach it. Mastery of the art and science of teaching usually is assumed if a certain pattern of courses has been completed. For vocational teachers, depending on state and institutional requirements, this theoretically may require full-time teachers to complete the equivalent of from two to forty semester hours of prescribed courses and require part-time teachers to complete from zero to thirty semester hours of similar courses. In practice, however, some vocational teachers are allowed to teach for twenty years or more with no teacher preparation whatsoever. More commonly, vocational teachers get an initial minimum of training and teach for twenty years or more without updating.

Methods of determining subject matter competency are more varied. For agriculture and home economics teachers (often including agribusiness and gainful home economics) the usual requirement is completion of a baccalaureate degree with a prescribed pattern of specialized college courses. No occupational experience is required beyond that which would be acquired by growing up on a farm or in the home, though in the better colleges the trend is toward requirement of occupational experience in gainful employment. In some states, teachers of technicians and office occupations teachers may also be approved as teachers on the basis of collegiate course work, but most states expect them also to have had at least brief occupational experience.

Health occupations require certification as a practitioner of the subject taught or certification at the next higher level. Occupational experience for all teachers is regarded as being important, but this experience need not necessarily be in the occupation taught. Dentists teach or supervise the instruction of prospective dental hygienists and dental technicians, but registered nurses teach prospective registered nurses. Registered nurses also teach prospective practical nurses. No one seems to know why these differences exist, though they may be related to the relative lengths of time the occupational fields have existed, and hence to the presumed availability of qualified teachers from the occupation.

Most distributive educators (who educate for occupations involved in the distribution of goods and services) and trade and industrial educators must have had work experience in the occupational field in which they are teaching. This requirement is usually stated as so many years beyond the learner period. In practice, the range of occupational experience required is from approximately eighteen months (in a college cooperative education program) to six years. The length of the "learner period" is elastic, depending on supply and demand for teachers.

It is generally agreed that the number of years of experience does not correlate well with the criterion of competence, but only three states have used occupational competency examinations extensively. Even they require a number of years of experience prior to taking the examination. Large school systems often do not depend on state certification, but establish their own certification or other approval procedures, occasionally using local advisory committees.

Development of Educational Personnel for Vocational Education

In a very real sense, in the entire United States and Canada there are only three or four programs for the development of vocational education personnel. Rather, there are programs for the development of agriculture instructors, or distributive education instructors, or home economics instructors, etc., with faculty members and students alike rarely talking to their counterparts in the rest of vocational education. The preparation of administrators and teacher educators is in a similar state. If you want to hire a vocational educator, probably the best you can do is to hire the best trade and industrial educator, or business educator, or similarly specialized person you can find and try to make a vocational educator of him on the job.

This situation arose because the vocational education acts before 1963 had not been vocational acts at all, but rather, acts for the support of education in agricultural occupations, in home economics, in industrial occupations, in health occupations, and in occupations related to the distribution of goods. As a consequence, teacher education programs for each of these specialties were established as separate departments, often in separate colleges within one university, or even in separate parts of each state. In some states certain institutions of higher education wanted no part of these new teacher education programs, and in some states the state board of vocational education thought higher education could not do the job, so certain teacher education programs have been operated by the state board or have been contracted for outside the state. The result of this fragmentation is that variations in recruiting practices, teacher education programs, and teacher certification practices are tremendous. These variations exist, not only from state to state, but also from one occupational field to another within each state. Indeed, the latter variations are generally greater than the former.

Where professional education courses are provided, they are almost invariably segregated by occupational field. Thus in the same university it is possible to find seven different professional courses duplicated in as many as six different departments. Some states specifically exclude from enrollment in these courses anyone who has not been approved in advance by the state office.

In junior colleges, area vocational schools, comprehensive high schools, in the United States Office of Education, and increasingly in state departments of vocational education, there are needs for a variety of educational personnel who are qualified to study, to plan, and to administer a broad range of vocational education. With rare exceptions, there are no programs to prepare or upgrade these leadership personnel.

There seems to be no question that better means are needed for coordinating programs of vocational education personnel development. A few universities have established departments of vocational, technical, and practical arts education, usually within a college of education to maximize interaction with other teacher education programs. The influential Gordon and Howell, and Pierson reports, which recommended in 1959 that colleges of commerce and business administration drop business education or transfer it to colleges of education, have helped this move considerably. Other universities have established vocational teacher education coordinating councils which operate across departmental or college lines. A unified department of vocational and technical education tends to:

A. Eliminate undesirable duplication of courses or units of instruction on topics such as program development, research, philosophy, history, administration, and evaluation of instruction. Using certain of these courses as a common core with individual projects in each student's field of specialization will save staff and money and provide more well rounded instruction.

B. Provide better education of planners, researchers, teacher educators, and above all, administrators and other leaders who can see the field more broadly.

C. Permit development of programs for general administrators who cannot take several different courses in vocational and technical education, but who need a broad knowledge of the field.

    D.   Facilitate joint development of programs for occupations which cut across two or more content specialties. This need is particularly acute for emerging occupations, which rarely coincide with traditional fields of instruction.

    E.   Allow more efficient allocation of resources. As needs for vocational teachers change, it is easier to shift staff to meet needs. Moreover, specialists (e.g., in international education and postsecondary education) can be developed to serve all fields.

Advocates of the status quo say that such a program would produce individuals who would have nothing to teach. This is not correct. What we need are people who have something to teach, and who know why and how they should teach it. What we need is teacher specialization tied together with a common core of courses and other experiences which also makes them vocational educators and educators, period. The problem is most difficult in states which have assigned different occupational fields to different institutions. This makes the preparation of broad guage vocational education personnel very difficult. Indeed, some states have gone so far as to approve vocational home economics teacher education programs in small colleges which have no real home economics program. This makes it likely that preparation in even this one field will be inadequate.

Even where teacher education programs for all occupational fields exist in one university, the problem of coordination is not simple. Consider, for example, the frequent situation where 25 to 50 percent of the graduates of a college of agriculture are preparing to be vocational agriculture teachers, and where from 50 to 75 percent of the entering freshmen in the college of agriculture are graduates of high school vocational agriculture programs. Such a college may find it difficult to view vocational agriculture as a program designed to prepare students for employment immediately after graduation from high school or junior college. Rather, it is likely to see vocational agriculture as a preparatory program for entrance to colleges of agriculture. And, it may not wish to share control of a program involving such a high proportion of its students and its graduates.

Undoubtedly, the coordination of programs for vocational education personnel would be hastened by federal action giving preferential fund allocation to combined or coordinated programs. Since federal action was largely responsible for the development of fragmented programs, this would seem to be poetic justice. The amendments of 1968 suggest such preferential treatment, but action has been anemic. Indeed, there has been practically no federal support for any type of vocational education personnel development since the days of the 1917 Smith-Hughes Act. Some federal actions definitely have hampered development of strong programs. Consider these facts:

A. Only in vocational and technical education must college teachers of a subject be approved by the state. (This was instituted to keep colleges from hiring academics who were not interested in vocational education, but almost all states are also unwilling to approve educational specialists or economists, sociologists, and other social scientists who could contribute much to the program.)

B. Vocational education is the only field obviously related to national defense which was excluded from the teacher education sections of the National Defense Education Act.

C. Only vocational education has a sizeable program of federal assistance to state and local educational agencies without a parallel program of scholarships, fellowships, and internships to prepare the personnel to enable the program to succeed. (Such a program was envisioned in 1968, but no appropriations have been forthcoming. The small amounts allocated from Education Professions Development Act funds have been inadequate.)

D. Vocational education is the only educational field whose professional organization suggests that if we do get a program of financial aid for education personnel development, selection of persons to receive fellowships, scholarships, and internships should be in the hands of the state, rather than being determined by the employing school or the institution where training would be received.

Why should vocational education be so far behind in the development of education personnel? There seem to be four reasons.

First is the problem of mobility of teachers, combined with state by state financing. The state director of vocational education gets a lump sum of money from the federal government. Almost all of this money is spent on subsidizing high school and junior college vocational programs. Three percent of it must be used for one or more of some seven purposes, including teacher education. Any one of the seven purposes could use all of the 3 percent, and the state director has urgent demands for all of his money. If he can steal good teachers from another state, he can save teacher education money. But even more important is the fact that if he pays for collegiate teacher education for a competent individual, he knows that this will increase the likelihood of that teacher moving out of state. Often, he decides he had better spend his money on something other than teacher education.

Second, the state director is likely to be a victim of nostalgia. In the "good old days" a vocational educator began as a teacher, moved to the state department, and then to the USOE as a supervisor, then to a local directorship, state directorship, and eventually, he might become director of vocational and technical education in the USOE. Programs were not changing rapidly then, and this job rotation plan was reasonably satisfactory. The group was small and tightly knit. Everyone knew everyone else, and no one outside really mattered. But this system has broken down. Local schools pay more than state offices, so teachers do not want to move to a state job. Local schools reward college credits with pay increases, which brings colleges into the picture and somewhat diminishes the authority of the state director. Moreover, the director may wonder why he should pay colleges for teaching courses they ought to be teaching anyway, especially when their staff is paid better than his.

Third, universities are much more interested in preparing teachers who will send students to higher education than in preparing teachers who will send students directly into employment. College entrance requirements are not geared to the tradesman who wants to learn to teach. Universities tend to resent direction and control by the state board of vocational education, unless they are adequately paid to accept it. They cannot understand why the state board, which spends almost all of its money to bribe local schools and junior colleges to offer vocational programs, should object to paying the university to conduct vocational teacher education programs. Moreover, they are accustomed to the federal government paying almost all of the direct and indirect costs of non-vocational programs it wants to support, and they see no reason why federal funds channeled through the state should pay only a half or a third of actual costs. For all of these reasons the gap between needs and offerings tends to be greater for vocational teachers than for other teachers.

Fourth, there is an element of self-protection in not training too many education personnel. The need for teachers of elementary education, and indeed for all of general education is closely related to the number of youth in a particular age range. Not so with vocational education, for it expands with amazing rapidity (and would contract as rapidly if it were not for teacher tenure and educational lobbyists who press for continued federal funds). The reason for this is that demand for vocational education has been tied, not to the number of students needing education, but rather to the number of job vacancies for youth and adults. When there is a job market of constant size, vocational education is expected to supply only replacements due to death, resignation and retirement. When there are shortages of workers, vocational education is expected to supply replacements plus personnel for expansion. When there is a surplus of workers, vocational education is supposed to die temporarily until natural replacements use up the surplus. This is what economists call acceleration, and, of course, vocational teacher education is particularly susceptible to this problem. Indeed, it suffers from double acceleration.

In short, many people in vocational education are afraid to train many teachers for fear there will soon be a decrease in demand. After all, most of them can remember from 1952 to 55 when the president was saying federal aid for vocational education should be abolished, and he was joined then by many of the same interest groups who now support vocational education expansion.

It would appear obvious that vocational education, as an integral part of the educational system, should provide education for the good of students and society, not for the good of employers alone. Certainly there is a close relationship between these needs, but the educational philosophy involved is markedly different. One result of gearing vocational enrollments to the number of people who need it would be that we could minimize the effects of acceleration, and could prepare teachers on a more regular basis without fear of flooding the market for teachers.

Programs of Pre-Service Development

The states report that in 1966, there were thirty-eight thousand persons involved in pre-service vocational teacher education programs. Unfortunately, no data are available to indicate for which types of positions people are being prepared, so we cannot tell whether or not they are being prepared for positions for which the need is greatest. In states for which detailed information is available, there is a very high negative correlation between the number of teachers being prepared for each field of specialization, and the number of teachers needed in each of these fields.

Moreover, the length of these programs and the rate of progress in completing them is unknown. Consequently, yearly output cannot be computed. It is likely that some of these thirty-eight thousand persons were taking one course or attending one conference, and it is almost certain that some people were counted more than once. Apparently there are no plans to gather national data on teacher education programs beyond the total number of trainees and the number of teacher educators by occupational field.

Types of Pre-Service Programs

There appear to be two basic types of pre-service teacher education programs, which differ in the way in which the prospective teacher learns the subject matter he later will teach. Type

I assumes that the subject matter will be learned during the course of employment in the occupation which is to be taught. Type 2, on the other hand, assumes that all or most of the subject matter to be taught will be learned in a school. Both of these types have sub-types. Type 1a assumes that what is learned on the job is learned as a by-product of employment. An advocate of type 1a believes that the desirable sequence of experience is from worker to teacher, and that a person who plans to be a vocational teacher, and secures work experience to that end, is missing an identification with the working group which is essential to successful vocational teaching. An advocate of type 1b, however, feels that more efficient learning occurs if the prospective teacher approaches work experience with plans for learning as much about it as he can because he wants to be an effective teacher. Prospective teachers who follow plan 2a learn their content in a school which is at the same level as the type of school in which they expect to teach. Type 2b teachers, on the other hand, learn their content in a school which is at a higher level than that at which they expect to teach.

Instructors who follow type 1a teacher education programs often begin as workers, then teach part-time in evening school, and then become full-time teachers. Teacher education may be provided concurrently with or preceding either of the last two steps. Type 1b instructors include industrial arts teachers who leave teaching temporarily to gain work experience which will allow them to earn additional money and to become more effective industrial arts or vocational teachers. Sometimes this experience is gained through part-time or summer work. Cooperative teacher education programs which provide both college classes and work experience in a baccalaureate program are also of type 1b.

Most persons who follow pattern 2a teach in basic courses in industry, private trade schools, or the military. This type of instructor is so common in the military that a special term "pipeline instructor" has been coined to describe him. Two or three of the most able students graduating from a technical training course are retained in the "pipeline" and become instructors after receiving a brief teacher education program. Occasionally, financially embarrassed institutions of higher education retain some of their advanced seniors to teach freshmen, but usually without benefit of teacher education. Some technical education programs in community colleges encourage their best graduates to stay in the "pipeline" to teach, or encourage them to return to teaching after a brief employment experience.

Most academic teachers receive all of their preparation in programs of type 2b. They learn in a college what they are to teach in an elementary, secondary, or post-secondary school. Teachers of teachers and teachers of teachers of teachers usually follow this same pattern of pre-service instruction.

In 1964, the International Vocational Training Information and Research Center published a volume entitled *Training of Vocational Teachers*. This document reported a conference involving twelve European countries. It noted that vocational education was expanding rapidly, was moving away from premature specialization, and was recognizing that knowledge had now become as important as manipulative skill. As is our case, the Europeans noted that there was a great shortage of qualified instructors.

They identified three groups of countries. One group recruits teachers who have acquired skill through long experience in employment (Type 1a). The second group of countries sees teacher training as a continuation of the vocational training system, with able students continuing on and becoming teachers (Type 2a). A third group of countries sees teacher training for vocational education as being parallel to the training of teachers for general education (Type 2b). Programs of type 1b were not mentioned.

Observation of the vastly different types of pre-service teacher education used in the country for the different subject matter fields within vocational education leads one inevitably to the conclusion that we are several countries in one. Until this time, it has been nonsense to talk about *the* philosophy of preparing teachers and administrators of vocational education in this country. We have several contradictory philosophies and must resolve these philosophical problems before we can talk knowledgeably of a single method of preparing staff for vocational and technical education.

In this country, patterns of pre-service education for home economics, agriculture, office occupations, and distributive education are closely parallel to baccalaureate programs for non-vocational teaching (Type 2b). Portions of the program are allocated to general education, to specialized education in the subject to be taught, and to courses in pedagogy. Students often begin teaching immediately after college graduation. However, as gainful employment occupations in home economics and agri-business occupations in agriculture gain importance, occupational experience outside the home or farm becomes essential and is beginning to be required. (Type 1a or 1b).

Office occupations teachers may begin teaching non-vocational business education courses, but begin to teach vocational courses after they have acquired occupational experience in summer employment or in full-time leaves from school teaching (Type 2b plus 1b). Distributive education teachers have little opportunity for non-vocational teaching, so they often go directly from college to full-time employment in the distribution of goods or services for several years and then begin to teach (Type 2b plus 1b). If they have not acquired teacher education courses as an undergraduate, these may be included in a masters degree program following occupational experience (Type 1a).

TABLE 15–2

Types of Pre-Service Programs	Content Learned in	Primary Identification While Content is Being Learned
Type 1 a	Employment	Worker
Type 1 b	Employment	Prospective Teacher
Type 2 a	School	Prospective Worker
Type 2 b	School	Prospective Teacher

Teachers in health occupations ordinarily follow a sequence of health professions education and occupational experience before beginning to teach, and then receive teacher education concurrently with teaching (Type 1a). Trade and industrial teachers are much less likely than teachers of other vocational and technical subjects to have a baccalaureate degree. The most common sequence is: high school graduation, several years of occupational experience, part-time teaching, teacher education, and full-time teaching (Type 1 a). Often the last two steps in this sequence are reversed. An increasing proportion of vocational industrial teachers, however, are coming from the ranks of industrial arts teachers who acquire occupational experience after college graduation (Type 2b plus 1b). If the trades and industries teacher does not have a bachelor's degree he usually is allowed to teach only the subject in which he has occupational experience. This contributes to inflexibility in the school program once he has acquired tenure.

In all undergraduate vocational and technical programs, increasing use is being made of cooperative work-education to provide occupational experience prior to completion of the baccalaureate degree (Type 1b). These programs usually require from five to six years for completion. Unless special incentives can be supplied, however, there is little inducement for the student to choose a five-year vocational teacher education curriculum when he can complete a practical arts non-vocational curriculum in only four years, and find employment after graduation at the same salary.

Canada has developed an excellent pattern for teacher education for trade and industrial and technical teachers which involves payment of a stipend to a skilled worker or technician to induce him to attend college for a year. The stipend is nearly equal to a skilled worker's wage (five thousand dollars) and is paid by the federal government, the province (state), and the school in which the student will teach.

In this country, much teacher education which should be offered pre-service is done in-service or not at all. Teacher shortages force employment of completely untrained teachers, and weak state departments are reluctant to insist on in-service training for them, particularly in fields where teacher shortages continue to be severe. If they insisted on teacher education, the teacher might quit, and local school officials would be offended.

Pre-service programs for vocational administrators are notoriously lacking. Administrators for vocational programs have been developed in sizeable numbers at only three periods during the history of the program in this country: from 1917 to the early twenties, during the early forties, and again since 1963. These were the three periods of rapid program expansion, due almost entirely to sizeable infusion of federal funds. In each of these periods the majority of training was by trial and error on-the-job, supplemented by short-term training conferences and summer programs at universities. In recent years, the largest single source of local directors of vocational education has been the industrial arts teacher who acquired enough occupational experience to be certified as a co-ordinator of a part-time cooperative program. If he succeeded on this latter job, he had learned the needs of his community, had been accepted by its leaders, and in effect had completed an internship and screening process. Both of these processes were unplanned, but still were far more effective than other methods of training and selection which were available.

A pre-service program incorporating a carefully planned internship would be most appropriate for developing administrators and other leadership personnel. The lack of stipends for trainees and the shortage of comprehensive training programs covering all of vocational education have been substantial deterrents to the development of pre-service programs for administrators.

Programs of
In-Service Development

The United States Office of Education has asked the states to indicate the numbers of vocational teachers enrolled in in-service teacher education programs. Replies indicate that about 30 percent of teachers are enrolled in any one year, but almost certainly some people are counted more than once. Unfortunately, no information is available as to the length and quality of such programs. They almost certainly range from one day professional meetings to programs carefully planned and extending over several years.

Responsibility for in-service education programs usually is assumed to be on the shoulders of the local school administration. Unfortunately, however, the greatest need for in-service education comes at a time when programs are expanding and new teachers are being added. This is also a time when local administrators are overburdened with other tasks, and, indeed, when the demand for administrators is so great that new administrators are placed in very demanding positions for which they often are unprepared. This seems to argue for: (1) leadership by state offices of vocational education and universities in providing itinerant in-service program leadership, (2) funds to support local proposals for in-service education, and (3) fellowship and institute programs which will allow certain functions of in-service development to be carried out on a state-wide or regional basis.

At present, probably the greatest amount of in-service education is accomplished on a purely voluntary and individually planned basis. The teacher decides that he has certain deficiencies which should be corrected. He then maps out ways of correcting these deficiencies through such means as:

A. Reading periodicals and books about teaching or about the subject being taught.
B. Securing part-time employment during the week or during the summer.
C. Attending schools conducted by business or industry.
D. Visiting local business and industry.
E. Attending technical meetings or meetings of educational personnel.

All of these methods may be effective. Unfortunately very few schools reward participation in them, though an effective administrator will certainly work to facilitate such in-service education by serving as a counselor to the teachers and by serving as a facilitator (arranging for employment, getting teachers appointed to committees so that their expenses will be paid for attending conventions, etc.).

Employers of vocational teachers generally do reward successful completion of college credit courses. Some of these courses are very valuable in improving the quality of teaching, but many are too general or are offered in such remote locations or at such times as to be of little utility.

Too often they are chosen on the basis of accessibility. Credit courses offered during the summer force the teacher to choose between spending five hundred dollars or more on tuition and extra living expense, or earning four or five times as much on a job (which may or may not be related to the subject taught). Naturally, summer institutes with stipends for participants are much more attractive to teachers. To date, the scope of summer institutes has been such that no more than 2 percent of vocational teachers could be enrolled. Academic year institutes, which allow more extended study, have been even more rare. The scarcity of institute programs has been such that only the best qualified applicants could be enrolled, and those who need the instruction most are excluded.

One of the more effective in-service education programs conducted by universities is the "first-year teacher" follow-up conducted in agricultural education in a few states. New teachers are visited regularly on the job by university teacher educators. Those who are encountering unusual difficulties are given individual help, and all meet together periodically at a regional center to share ideas and experiences and to get further help from the teacher educator.

Another type of credit course or institute is considerably less expensive, yet works well in heavily populated areas. Instruction is offered in a central location in the evening or on Saturday. Participants live at home, but the instructor may travel a considerable distance. Instruction may concentrate on technical or on professional aspects of the teacher's job. Small stipends to compensate teachers for loss of part-time employment occasionally are provided.

One of the most promising in-service educational devices has been developed by certain post-secondary institutions such as Oregon Technical Institute of Klamath Falls and Parkland College of Champaign, Illinois. This program calls for year round employment of all professional staff and assignment during the summer to activities which are most needed for the personal development of faculty members and administrators. Staff members may be assigned to curriculum development, attendance at college institutes or other summer programs, employment in the occupation being taught, etc. Canada uses an extensive sabbatical leave program for these same purposes.

The great majority of institutions, however, find it economically or politically impractical to employ staff on a twelve month basis or to grant many sabbaticals. The employing institution should have a major voice in determining which of its staff most need fellowship support for study in colleges or for work with business and industry which will allow them to keep up to date.

Improvement of Staffing in Vocational Education

Six steps for improving the quality of staffing in vocational education seem desirable:

1. Base pay on merit and on supply and demand, rather than on hours of education and seniority.
2. Eliminate certification, if it cannot be substantially modified.
3. Limit teacher tenure to ten years, with renewal or notification of nonrenewal near the end of this period.
4. End discrimination by sex in the employment of teachers.
5. Make pre-service education the primary responsibility of the university, with substantial involvement of local and state education agencies.
6. Make in-service teacher education the primary responsibility of the local educational agency, with substantial involvement of universities and state departments of education.

1. Pay based on merit and on supply and demand rather than hours of education and seniority. On the average (and of course there are frequent exceptions) teachers who have served approximately five years are at peak effectiveness. Teachers with less experience and teachers with more experience are, on the average, considerably less effective. No one knows for sure whether this is caused by some of the more effective teachers leaving after a few years of teaching, or whether it is a matter of stagnation. Certainly there is no evidence to suggest that in every case, the longer a teacher has taught, the more he should be paid. Similarly, we know that there is no relationship between the number of hours of college courses a teacher has had and his effectiveness. It is clear that many people who are completely inadequate as teachers return again and again for additional courses in an attempt to have something that allows them to feel superior. Under our present salary structure such insecure individuals are rewarded with additional salary increments. The objection may be raised that merit pay has been thoroughly explored and discarded on the basis that judgements of merit cannot be made accurately. Many colleges do make such decisions and have made them for over a hundred years. No one seems to disagree that the top and the bottom 5 percent or so of teachers can clearly be identified. They should be rewarded in accord with this identification.

Equally important is the matter of pay based on supply and demand. A recent case occurred in a community college which had an outstanding program in industrial electronics. Graduates of this two-year program regularly started employment at salaries above those earned by the majority of the junior college faculty. Salaries of each of the two instructors were some two thousand dollars less than they had received in industrial employment, but were the highest two salaries on the whole junior college teaching payroll. This led to a considerable amount of hostility on the part of some of the academic teachers, but the decision of the college administration seemed exactly correct. To attempt to employ teachers of all types at the same salary schedule will insure that most teachers in fields which are in short supply will be less competent than those teachers who are in plentiful supply. There is no justification whatsoever for providing lower quality education to those students who happen to want to specialize in areas where they are badly needed while at the same time providing superior education for people in fields where they are less in demand.

2. End certification if it cannot be substantially modified.   Recently a local director of vocational education said in a private conversation, "I can employ better teachers for my evening school staff than I can for my day school staff solely because the evening school staff does not have to be certified." This is a sad commentary on the state of certification. College teachers are not certified. Because there are many poor teachers in college, some people have suggested that certification would be in order for them. Why are they poor teachers? Almost invariably it is because they do not know how to teach.

At the secondary school level, where certification is almost universal, we also have many poor teachers. They may be poor because they do not know how to teach, because they do not know what it is that they are supposed to teach, or both. Few college teachers are poor because they do not know their subject matter. Certification, which is supposed to attest both to subject matter and instructional competence, has obviously failed in many cases. Two possible improvements suggest themselves.

A.   Have colleges certify teachers upon graduation, have the effectiveness of these teachers reviewed periodically by the state, and take away college authority to certify teachers in a particular field if the graduates of that institution fail to perform satisfactorily.

B.   Instead of certification, have the state approve local proposals, program by program, with qualifications of the instructors being part of the package. Have this followed by a post-audit by the state with termination of program approval for poor performance.

3. Limit teacher tenure to ten years with notification of renewal or non-renewal near the end of this period.   Teacher tenure has had many worthwhile effects. Unlimited teacher tenure has had many bad effects as well. A requirement for renewal of tenure at the end of ten years would force a periodic look at faculty competence. At present, we look at faculty competence only at the time of hiring and at the end of a short probationary period. Unfortunately, too many teachers stop professional improvement at the end of their probationary period, though they may go on teaching for forty more years. Stated negatively, if vocational education is to survive, it must find some way of getting rid of its deadwood. To put it in a more positive sense, it should be the responsibility of every administrator to build, in cooperation with each staff member, an individualized staff development plan covering five to ten years. If it works, the teacher should be retained. If it does not work, he should be released.

One way of insuring that there will be staff development is to use as a key criterion for employment of any administrator, his past record of developing staff members. Many industries have a standing rule that no administrator can be promoted unless he has developed someone who is capable of taking his place. This does not mean that a person who was developed as a replacement would be chosen as the successor, but it does emphasize the role of the administrator as a developer of staff, and refuses promotion to those who fail to perform in this role.

4. End discrimination by sex in the employment of teachers.   In vocational and technical education men teach men, and women teach women. There are a few exceptions, mostly in the clerical and sales fields, but the general statement certainly holds. Indeed, there are some who go so far as to say that all instruction in "women's occupations" should be provided by women. The occasional female teacher of drafting can testify to the discrimination she faces in professional meetings of drafting teachers. We need to take special steps to recruit teachers (and students) of the minority sex in each of our vocational programs, for exactly the same reason that we need to recruit black students and teachers in predominantly white institutions.

5. Preservice education should be the primary responsibility of the university with close cooperation of local and state education agencies.   Many excellent ideas for an effective pre-service education program will be found in B.O. Smith's *Teachers for the Real World* (3). This is a delightful book. He has a section on "Why Teachers Drop Out." Here he mentions our blind confidence in the value of pooling personal experiences in group discussion in teacher education and suggests that this is valuable only for therapy. He suggests that student teaching should be eliminated and replaced by a carefully structured series of simulated and real experiences, followed by a genuine internship, under supervision, which avoids the make-believe character of much of our student teaching. He has a good section on "Bringing the Teacher Trainer Up-to-date," which would be applicable to many of the people in our field. Throughout the book Professor Smith emphasizes close relationships among the university, the local educational agency, and the non-educational community. His section on "Differentiated Teacher Roles" suggests that teacher aides could be recruited from the community. An example of this is the program in Edmonton, Alberta, where an educational specialist works with four craftsmen to provide the best possible instruction for technical students in the printing trades. This is a way of using teacher aides from the community in an excellent pattern of differentiated staffing.

Universities can provide excellent professional training. They can do this job better than institutions which are designed for other purposes, but they can perform effectively only if they work closely with the groups which use their product.

6. In-service education should be the primary responsibility of the local education agency with close cooperation of universities and state departments of education. The most effective pattern of in-service education is one which involves employment of the teacher for twelve months with summers devoted to building strengths and remedying weaknesses. Depending upon the long-term professional development plan which has been prepared for each teacher, summers may be spent in employment, in curriculum development, in further education, or in a variety of other needed activities. Every professional development plan should include the opportunity to visit other schools for brief periods of time. It is amazing how parochial most teachers really are. They have no idea of the strengths and weaknesses of programs in comparable schools in other communities, and have little knowledge of employment opportunities outside their own community.

Another highly desirable activity would be a regular exchange program with employers, not only to upgrade the knowledges of the regular teacher, but to acquaint key individuals in business and industry with what is actually going on in the schools.

A third major feature of each professional development package should be attendance at and participation in professional meetings. There is a tendency to have the same people year after year on the same programs. Half of the participants might well be required to be new each year. This would not only improve the competence of the people participating, but it would add a freshness to professional meetings that is badly needed.

The Identification of Leaders

Potential leaders need to be identified as well as to be trained. Too often the identification process has been left to chance. At the local level, vocational education leadership potential is rarely surveyed until an administrative opening has occurred through death, resignation, or expansion of the program. Then the local school officials try to identify an individual who can be immediately promoted and later trained. As was mentioned in the chapter on cooperative programs, a likely candidate will be the cooperative education coordinator, because the job of this teacher is most like that of the local director of vocational education. Since no one has been selected and trained by design, the person best trained by accident is often selected. At the state and national level, a wider choice of candidates may be available. A great deal depends on the salaries which can be paid to new supervisory staff, and whether or not selection and tenure depend on membership in the political party in power. Low salaries and a requirement of political loyalty obviously decrease the pool of potential candidates.

Regardless of the size of the pool, it is still necessary to identify the best candidates for promotion. Except in the largest cities this is not a great problem for internal promotion at the local level since every insider is likely to be known. Recruitment from outside the system is a different matter. Individuals have made themselves noticeable by appearing on convention programs, by writing, by taking additional college courses, by passing certification examinations, by performing favors for leaders in the profession, and the like. Excellent recent performance in any of these roles helps to bring the individual's name to mind when a current leader is asked to recommend someone for another leadership role.

Recently, the federal government has attempted to improve this process by asking for nominations for fellowships and stipends which allow these potential leaders to receive additional training through university courses and internships. This should markedly expand the pool of potential leadership, for it serves the dual function of identification and training.

Technical Education Teachers

Technicians are aides to professional workers, and technical education is designed to develop technicians. Technicians are needed in every major field of business and industry, and every field of vocational education has a responsibility for conducting technical level education. Technical programs, however, generally require specially prepared teachers.

Most of the earlier comments in this chapter apply to technical education as well as to vocational education. There are, however, certain aspects of the development of technical education personnel which deserve special mention.

The majority of technical education programs are offered in junior and community colleges and other post-secondary institutions, though a few programs begin in the secondary school. About 4 percent of youth reaching age eighteen each year could be accommodated in existing post-secondary technical education programs. Facilities for such programs are expanding at a considerably more rapid rate than staff and students. This reflects a desire on the part of governing boards to expand their offerings, but they are understandably reluctant to employ unqualified instructors. Students, too, are reluctant to enroll in technical programs with mediocre instructors. Given a choice between such a program and a college transfer curriculum, they often will choose the latter, for they know that credits from college transfer courses are accepted at face value even if instruction is mediocre, while employers carefully evaluate skills and knowledges possessed by the graduate of the technical curriculum. Both students and employers know that mediocre instructors are not good enough, if the technical education graduate is to be acceptable in his occupation.

There are very few teacher education programs designed to prepare staff for technical education. In some cases vocational and technical teachers are taught together for professional courses, e.g. teachers of engineering technicians are grouped with trade teachers. Some of this is desirable; indeed all vocational teachers need some courses in common. But technical education, particularly in the junior college, has problems for which teachers need special preparation. Traditional vocational teacher education programs hardly recognize that the community college exists.

The National Science Foundation has supported a few institutes for teachers of engineering technology. But usually, technical teachers receive no teacher education. Indeed, they often have had no formal education as technicians, but have learned the occupation on the job, supplemented by science and mathematics courses which appeared to them to be useful.

As technician education programs have become more common, an increasing number of teachers of technicians are found to have received training as technicians and to have supplemented this training with on-the-job experience. Most of the persons who begin technician training do not graduate from the two-year program, however. They take all of the technical courses, but avoid the general education courses, and hence are not eligible for a diploma. As in some types of vocational education, given a choice between a technician instructor who has only academic training and one who has only successful occupational experience in the subject to be taught, most institutions choose the latter. One exception is the frequent use of graduate engineers to teach basic mathematics and science courses for technicians. In engineering technician training, the American Society for Engineering Education is exerting pressure, through its accreditation procedures, for more emphasis on academic preparation of all instructors.

Summary

1. A major reason for the failure of vocational education to do more for "youth with special needs" is the shortage of broad gauge administrators to plan programs, and a shortage of teachers and supportive personnel who know what to do.

2. There is a distinct shortage of programs and instructional personnel to upgrade adults so as to provide room at lower and intermediate levels of employment for youth and for unemployed and under-employed adults.

3. Data on vocational teachers and teacher educators are conspicuously lacking. The USOE plans to collect information on subjects taught, degrees held, etc. for teachers reimbursed under the Vocational Education Amendments of 1968, but no plans exist to collect information on preparation for teaching, nor will data be collected on teachers in non-reimbursed occupational programs.

4. The labor market for vocational teachers has never been defined, and predictions of supply and demand neglect the fact that teachers and administrators can and do move from employment in one occupational education program to another and from public to private employment and vice-versa.

5. Certification for vocational teachers is often restricted to the number of teachers employed. Requirements for certification are raised when there is a surplus of teachers and lowered when there is a shortage.

6. Teacher education programs and certification practices are even more diverse from one vocational field to another than they are from state to state.

7. Teacher education programs in separate fields of vocational and technical education badly need coordination. There are virtually no vocational teacher education programs, but rather programs for developing subject matter specialists in isolation from each other. They now exist frequently in separate departments, colleges, and even in separate parts of a state. This fragmentation makes it difficult to prepare teachers who have a full understanding of education for the world of work, and has been particularly harmful to the preparation of administrators and other leadership personnel.

8. Vocational teacher education suffers greatly from acceleration effects, since the need for teachers expands very rapidly as the need for

skilled workers expands even slightly. Prediction of the need for vocational teachers depends greatly on whether we continue to educate for immediate manpower shortages, or whether we follow the suggestion of the Vocational Education Amendments of 1968 and serve the needs of students who should have vocational education.

9. Vocational education leaders have paid remarkably little attention to the education of teachers because of shortage of funds, mobility of teachers, and fear of training too many teachers. Universities, likewise, have not done enough, largely because they are interested primarily in college bound students and their teachers. Even less attention has been paid to the development of vocational teacher educators.

10. Certification practices and state approval of teacher educators have tended to exclude educational specialists and social scientists who could aid in the study of vocational programs.

11. Expansion of vocational and technical education has been slowed by a shortage of qualified teachers, and the development of new programs has been hampered by an extreme shortage of administrators and other leadership personnel.

REFERENCES

1. "Actual and Projected State and Local Administrative and Other Ancillary Personnel in Vocational Education." Unpublished planning document. Washington, D.C.: The Division of Vocational and Technical Education, U.S. Office of Education, March 15, 1967.

2. Arnold, J. P., "Applying Differentiated Staffing to Vocational-Technical Education," *Journal of Industrial Teacher Education*, VII, No. 1 (1969), 13-20.

3. Smith, B. O., *Teachers for the Real World*. Washington, D.C.: American Association of Colleges for Teacher Education, 1969.

4. Smith, H.T., *Education for the World of Work*. Kalamazoo, Michigan: W.E. Upjohn Institute for Employment Research, 1963.

5. "The Need for Vocational and Technical Educational Personnel," *The Education Professions 1969-70*. Washington, D.C.: U.S. Office of Education, Superintendent of Documents No. HE 5.258:58032-70.

6. *Training of Vocational Teachers*. Geneva, Switzerland: International Labor Office, 1964.

Part IV THE FUTURE OF VOCATIONAL EDUCATION

THE FUTURE OF VOCATIONAL EDUCATION

Almost every country in the world has more college graduates than can be employed as professionals. This is true in both underdeveloped and developed countries. In many of these countries, the availability of a well educated but significantly underemployed minority has serious political consequences. In some countries this has created so much of a problem that special efforts are made to recruit these people into government employment. But this does not seem to be a solution which is feasible either economically or in terms of maintaining the self-respect of the embittered college graduate.

There is also a severe surplus of unskilled manpower in all except a few nations whose labor supply of certain age groups has been badly disrupted by past wars. This surplus probably exists even in countries which have too few workers of any other type, but is concealed by the political necessity of employing every able-bodied person no matter how inept. (The British have a good term for such incapable personnel: "dilutees.") On the other hand, virtually every nation in the world has had a long continued shortage of skilled workers, clerical workers, sales personnel, and health personnel at every level. Indeed, there are severe shortages of capable workers in almost every occupation which

267

requires more than a year for the average person to master it, but which requires less than a baccalaureate degree for entrance. Shortages of workers in occupations which require skills may be masked temporarily by economic recession, but they become apparent again the moment that normal economic activity returns. These are the occupations which produce the goods and services the world needs in the qualities, quantities, and at the prices people can afford to pay. These are the occupations for which vocational education could prepare people. But there has been too little vocational education, and a large proportion of occupations have no public vocational education at all.

As shortages of skilled personnel have increased, and as surpluses of college graduates have increased, normal economic forces are in the process of inverting the pay structures for these two fields. In community after community beginning firemen, policemen, truck drivers, and persons in other occupations for which little or no vocational training has been provided start at higher salaries than school teachers, city planners, architects, lawyers, and persons in many other professional occupations for which four to six years of occupational training has been provided by society. Trends indicate that soon the average salaries will follow the same course that starting salaries have taken. Not only are wages changing, but working conditions are improving as well. Skilled workers who are in short supply can and do demand working conditions which are the equal of those provided to white-collar workers in every respect.

These changes seem to signify a new era of status for the well qualified nonprofessional, and consequently a new status for the vocational education instructor who can meet society's needs. On the other hand, it seems likely that the vocational instructor who turns out unqualified graduates will be subject to closer scrutiny that has ever been true in the past and will have to increase his efficiency or lose his justification for continued employment.

Public Versus Private Vocational Education

Public awareness of the importance of vocational education is almost sure to be accompanied by public willingness to spend public funds on vocational education. The availability of substantial finances, however, almost certainly will increase the competition for those finances. Some private industry which was not at all interested in training personnel except for a small proportion of their own needs leaped at an opportunity to train workers on the production line when federal payments for training disadvantaged workers reached three thousand dollars per trainee per year (though other employers were not interested even at this price). The expansion in private-for-profit vocational schools was phenomenal following the passage of the GI Bill for veterans and the Manpower Development and Training Act for disadvantaged workers. Where there is a job to be done, and money to be made, the private competitive industrial system of the United States responds rapidly.

The chief deterrent to efficient vocational education in the private sector has been the fact that business and industrial corporations have had production as their primary goal, while education played a distinctly secondary role. In the private vocational school, however, education is a primary goal. A few proprietors have sought for quick profits and have given a bad name to some of the remaining schools which lacked the advantage of a long established reputation. But the principal problem of the private vocational school has been the high cost of recruiting students. Cost of advertising, sales commissions, and the cost of collecting unpaid tuition have in a number of cases amounted to more than the cost of providing instruction and job placement.

Private vocational schools rapidly are being bought and established by large organizations which can recruit students more efficiently. Not only can advertising dollars be spent more effectively on a chain of business education schools stretching from coast to coast than on a school operating in a single locality, but unsuccessful applicants for jobs in the parent corporation can be referred to the school with promise of further consideration after they have completed training successfully. Not only will the parent corporation be able to earn a profit on tuition charged, but it will have first pick of the better quality graduates.

It is difficult to predict the outcome of such competition between public and private vocational schools, but the beneficiary of such competition should be the student, provided that society insures that the competition is conducted in a way which protects the consumer of vocational education.

Who Should Receive
Vocational Education

As blue-collar jobs become more attractive, and as the status of vocational education rises, it seems likely that the proportion of students seeking vocational education will increase dramatically. In the past, when vocational educators have been faced with more applicants than they could educate, they have responded in almost every case by accepting those applicants who least need vocational education services: the persons with highest verbal intelligence, with highest grades in school, and with influential parents. This type of selection makes the teacher's task easy, but it is questionable whether it has served the best interests of the total student body.

The supply of vocational education services should be increased to the point where all students who want vocational education can be admitted. Data from several studies indicate that half of high school freshmen want vocational education, but only one-fourth of them can be accommodated. The proportion of students who want vocational education is almost certain to increase more rapidly than the supply of available instruction. With substantial increases in state and federal support, this long-term imbalance between supply and demand can gradually be overcome. But where there are temporary unavoidable discrepancies between demand and supply of vocational education, we need a measure of "value added by vocational education" which will enable us to determine which students will receive the greatest benefit from vocational education as compared with other educational or non-educational programs. Those students who will benefit most from vocational education are the ones who should be admitted.

A Major Change in Emphasis

Until 1963, federal legislation directed vocational education to meet the needs of the labor market. Students were to be admitted only if they could profit from the instruction then being offered. Local advisory committees dominated by labor and management were strongly recommended. Prior to 1946, instruction could be offered only for occupations which required a long time to learn (and were in short supply). The 1963 Act changed this philosophy to one of meeting the needs of individual students, but most vocational education continued business as usual.

In 1968, Congress made it clear that it was not making an idle suggestion in 1963. Twenty-five percent of appropriations were set aside for vocational education for the disadvantaged and the handicapped effective with the 1969-70 school year. Earlier expenditures from vocational education funds for these two groups certainly did not exceed 5 percent. This new requirement almost certainly will raise the proportion of vocational students with below average academic ability since the mentally handicapped and many of the disadvantaged are well below average in verbal skills. It almost certainly will not decrease the number of above average students, since total appropriations are increasing markedly.

The primary effect on post-secondary schools could come from additional encouragement of vocational students to attend college. While very few vocational teachers have ever discouraged students from attending college, state and federal officials have discouraged publicity on the numbers of students attending college. It is a general public impression, as a result, that it is impossible for vocational graduates to attend college. Almost certainly this false impression will change, and it may change dramatically if present studies find, as they well may, that if academic ability level is held constant, a higher proportion of vocational graduates attend and succeed in post-secondary schools than do the graduates from the college preparatory curriculum.

Development of
Parallel School Systems

Most other nations have separate, parallel systems of secondary education for vocational and for college preparatory students. Educational reform in these countries concentrates on developments similar to our comprehensive high schools. But at various times and places, separate systems have existed in this country as well: the National Youth Administration (NYA) schools which ended in the early forties and the Wisconsin system which existed for half a century are two examples of such programs which have been totally or partially abandoned. Most of our large cities built separate vocational high schools, but these are gradually being phased out, largely because they became racially segregated.

This does not mean that the concept of separate parallel schools is dead. Rosen expresses the prevailing point of view of the Department of Labor when he says, "The time has come for us to recognize that the good vocational schools are capable of making an important contribution in developing the supply of our skilled workers. However, the only way they can really carry out this function is to separate out those students who need special treatment by developing a new institutional arrangement so that they can be taught in separate schools" (5, p. 10). Job Corps centers and, more recently, Skill Centers have been set up to provide this "special treatment" which has not been available in most public schools.

The most rapidly growing organizational structure in vocational education is the area vocational school. It serves principally small city and rural areas which will not or cannot consolidate secondary schools to achieve the two thousand to four thousand student enrollment which seems necessary for a fully comprehensive high school. The area vocational school has a potential for encouraging school consolidation by making people aware for the first time of the services which can be provided by a full scale vocational program. But it could postpone consolidation by providing certain of these services without requiring the trauma of closing small high schools.

Both of the above solutions, one sponsored by the Department of Labor and the other by the United States Office of Education, have numerous advantages. These advantages seem completely outweighed, however, by one tremendous disadvantage; they segregate students by socio-economic level. Data are not available on the effect of these patterns of school organization on the rate of attendance in post-secondary education. It is likely, however, that both types of segregated occupational education will decrease the college-going rate.

Another type of parallel school system, the private vocational school, has considerable potential for competition with community colleges. Schaefer and Kaufman report that a survey of twenty-five hundred private vocational schools indicates that only 7 percent of them will accept persons who do not have a high school diploma (primarily barber and beautician colleges). Median length of a program was one year, and median cost was over six hundred dollars (6, pp. 92 and 100). In view of the small proportion of private vocational schools accepting high school dropouts, this source of training is not likely to be an important factor at the secondary school level.

One argument in favor of specialized educational institutions for college transfer programs and for vocational and technical education is that only in this way will administrators be selected who will allow and encourage full development of this specialized program. All other arguments are spurious. Sufficient size to operate programs effectively can be obtained in either specialized or comprehensive institutions. School esprit de corps can be developed, and an adequate tax base can be provided for either type of institution.

It seems likely that the administrator is indeed the key to the success of technical institutes, area vocational schools, and other specialized segregated vocational school organizations. But the administrator is important in a different way than is generally assumed. Study after study shows that general education administrators in comprehensive institutions place a higher value on vocational education than do vocational educators in these same institutions. If the vocational educator were being held back by the general educator, such a difference in values could hardly be found to exist.

There is no question but that there is a grossly inadequate supply of adequately prepared administrators for vocational education. Thus, is seems likely that the more capable vocational administrators are being attracted to positions where pay and working conditions are most attractive to them. The administrative head of a separate vocational school is almost invariably paid more than the head of a vocational program in a comprehensive school organization, even though the qualifications and duties are not too dissimilar. Moreover, the head of such a specialized school has a freedom of action which is not accorded to the high school vocational director who must report to a high school principal or even to an assistant superintendent for secondary school education. Similarly, the head of a technical institute has greater freedom of action than a dean of occupational education who must report to an official two or three steps down the administrative hierarchy in a comprehensive community college. This suggests that the more able vocational administrators are more likely to be attracted to separate vocational institutions, while comprehensive institutions are able to attract persons who are willing to accept poorer working conditions and who are in the main less competent. Twin remedies for this situation would seem to be: (1) greatly expanded programs of development of vocational education administrators so that the supply of competent personnel is somewhere near the demand, and (2) improved working conditions for capable people in vocational education in comprehensive institutions so that these positions will be considerably more attractive than they have been in the past.

The fatal defect of most school organizations which separate vocational and general education is the fact that such an organization results in segregation of student bodies by social class. Middle and upper-class students will attend the college transfer school, while lower class students will attend the vocational school. This pits class against class, limits social mobility, and, in accord with findings of the Coleman Report, results in decreased rates of learning in the lower class institution.

It seems likely that as the supply of well prepared vocational education administrators is increased and as the findings of the Coleman Report become part of the conventional wisdom, separate institutions for vocational and for college transfer programs will decrease sharply in both number and proportion, and comprehensive institutions at every level will become the norm.

In contrast, imagine the effect of widespread application of the system reported in the *Wall Street Journal:*

The local school board has proposed a conversion to an 'integrated two-track' system, with the present white high school providing college preparatory work and the present black high school offering vocational training. Students would be selected for one or the other on the basis of achievement tests. White school officials are hoping such a system would deposit most whites in the college prep school and funnel most blacks to the vocational school (3, p. 1).

Cyclical Changes in Demand for Vocational Education

The cyclical changes in demand for vocational education have had an important effect upon the development of effective programs for the education of vocational education administrators. When vocational education was seen as having a single objective of meeting the manpower needs of the nation, it was inevitable that as the manpower needs of the nation increased on a short-term basis, the demand for vocational education increased sharply, and as the level of economic activity decreased, vocational education was expected to lie dormant for an extended period of time. This made the development of educational programs for administrators almost impossible, and made programs for teacher education almost as difficult.

Now, there seems to be general agreement that vocational education should assume the additional objectives of increasing the options of the individuals it serves and of lending intelligibility to general education. Moreover, there is understanding, in at least some quarters, that we should serve long-term manpower needs of society rather than the short-term fluctuations from month to month. All of these changes suggest increased stability for vocational education which will allow long-term planning and the development of competent personnel to meet the needs of students, both youth and adults.

Education of Women

Until comparatively recently, secondary school occupational education for women has been confined almost exclusively to homemaking and clerical occupations. Today these two programs have two-thirds of the total enrollment in reimbursed secondary school vocational education, and perhaps 90 percent of the female enrollment. This has been somewhat reasonable since most women become homemakers and since 70 percent of the women high school graduates who do not go to college are employed as clerical workers (4, p. 243). It has, however, provided very few opportunities for women to break out of these two rigid molds. In community colleges, nursing and business education provide most of the opportunities for vocational education for women. For some reason, after an initial surge, the rate of increase in health occupations has been relatively low, but enrollments in business education are large and expanding.

The most rapidly expanding occupational programs for women have been distributive education (DE) and home economics wage earning occupations. DE covers the occupations related to the distribution of goods and services. It enrolls some men, but women make up the bulk of its enrollment of over one hundred thousand students. Home economics wage earning occupations cover a variety of fields, including child care, foods, and textiles. They cover both production and service occupations.

More and more women are enrolling at the secondary school level in occupational education courses which were at one time the exclusive province of men. Men are rarely welcomed into "women's" occupational courses, however. Beyond question the amount of secondary school occupational education for women now exceeds that for men, but its breadth is increasing far too slowly. As this breadth of opportunity continues to grow, it should further reduce the dropout rate for women and thus increase their rate of attendance in college.

Cooperative Work-Education

The future should see cooperative work-education greatly expanded in size, with major expansions coming in community (junior) colleges. Work-study programs should rapidly be converted into cooperative education so that educational and employment goals are coordinated. Truck driving, heavy equipment operation, and similar occupations which require large capital and operating costs are quite suitable for cooperative education. Addition of courses in such fields would broaden markedly the typical school offerings. In small schools which cannot afford specialized coordinators for each of several occupational fields, the trend is likely to be toward approval of a coordinator who can serve vocational education needs in all fields.

Coordinated Planning for Vocational Education and Manpower Training

The chapter on training offered by other groups has a section on the need for coordinated planning. There is a feeling on the part of some vocational educators that their field should not be included in a state-wide or metropolitan area-wide coordinated plan. There is an attempt to justify such exclusion on the ground that vocational education has objectives in addition to meeting the manpower needs of the nation. This is true, but Manpower Development and Training Act programs also have additional objectives, such as alleviating poverty and providing basic general education, so the differences are more apparent than real. General education, vocational education, and MDT are all part of the same education continuum which ranges from the very general to the very specific. These three types of education are not points on the continuum. Rather, they are ranges, and the ranges overlap considerably. If vocational education is excluded from comprehensive manpower development planning and coordination, the effect is almost certain to be the development of two separate, parallel school systems — one for college preparation, and the other for occupational preparation. Such separation is undesirable because it promotes socioeconomic segregation and thus hampers the education of the poor. From a selfish point of view, separation leaves vocational education with no home. It would be completely unwelcome in the college preparatory school and largely unwelcome in the occupational education schools operated by the Department of Labor, as can be seen in the many countries which operate such dual systems. So, on educational grounds and on the ground of self-preservation, vocational education has every reason to support comprehensive high schools and community colleges. Vocational educators must insist that these schools include manpower development and training type activities for youth and adults, and insist that in-school vocational education be coordinated with manpower development activities in the private sector.

Local, State, and National
Advisory Committee Development

The earliest proponents of vocational education in the schools recognized that if school administrators and teachers attempted to set up vocational education programs without advice from employers and employees, two major problems would probably occur:

1. Programs might be established which did not meet local manpower needs.
2. Employers and employees, not having been involved, would regard vocational education as "their program" rather than as "our program."

The establishment of local advisory committees worked very well for both purposes in the early days of vocational education. Local surveys of employment needs were undertaken, and programs were established to meet local needs. Having been involved from the inception, both employers and employees tended to be satisfied with the results.

Two types of committees usually were established: a general advisory committee which was concerned with the entire vocational education program, and a series of occupational advisory committees, one for each occupational program. These committees generally worked well so long as manpower shortages existed in the local community. But in city after city, when economic recession or changing employment patterns appeared, conflicts arose in local advisory committee meetings. Some representatives of employees could see no need for the school to continue to turn out vocational graduates when experienced adult workers were unemployed. Some employers could see no need to spend tax money on keeping the program up to date, or even on the relatively high cost of maintaining the program as it was. Some school officials were reluctant to accept advice if it was contrary to the desires of the professional staff, or to close classes, re-assign, re-train or dismiss teachers on tenure. These conflicts came to the surface most frequently in advisory committee meetings so the majority of vocational educators simply stopped calling advisory committee meetings, tightened their belts, and waited for the next manpower shortage to bring them added support.

Recently there has been a resurgence of interest in advisory councils (1). In part, this is due to recurring manpower shortage, but it is also due to the studies of S. M. Burt (2) which helped to convince Congress that advisory committees should be mandated at the state and national level. Over one thousand persons now serve on such committees in addition to the one hundred thousand estimated by Burt to serve on some twenty thousand local committees.

State and national advisory committees add an important dimension to vocational education. Manpower shortages and surpluses can be assessed more accurately by persons removed from local pressures. One reason is that a shortage of persons in one occupation in one community is often cancelled by a surplus in another community. Educational needs for occupations employing only a few people in any one community can best be assessed at state and national levels. But an even more important reason is that administrative and legislative decisions affecting vocational education are made more and more by state and federal governments. These decision makers need advice as much as do decision makers at the local level.

The developing social consciousness of employers and employee groups is likely to lead them to accept all of the goals of vocational education instead of concentrating only on the goal of meeting manpower needs. This augurs well for continued usefulness of advisory committees.

Elimination of the General Curriculum

The general curriculum in the secondary school has so little to commend it that it is sure to disappear. Both the vocational and the college preparatory curricula are expanding slowly, and this expansion comes at the expense of the general curriculum. Elimination of the general curriculum will result in higher rates of college attendance, since it has by far the highest dropout rate of the present three high school curricula and has by far the lowest rate of college attendance by its graduates.

In the long run, the vocational and college preparatory curricula should merge and form a single basic curriculum for the secondary school based on general education (not the "general curriculum"). This will require deleting as well as adding courses for it is clear that most high schools now require certain mathematics, physical science, and foreign language instruction that is not needed by all citizens.

Some very interesting programs which could lead to a single secondary school curriculum are underway. Some of these are the Industrial Arts Curriculum Project at Ohio State, the American Industries Project at Stout State University, the Enterprise program at Southern Illinois University, the Richmond, California Plan, the Ziel program at the University of Alberta, and Project Feast of San Francisco State College. Other programs which could have similar effects include the institution of a requirement which demands (1) that students develop a saleable skill as a prerequisite to high school graduation, and (2) that action be taken by most of the major national curriculum projects to revise their materials so that they will be usable by all students rather than just by those who plan to go to college. Many of these programs have as a goal the integration of knowledge about the world of work, occupational preparation, and the rest of general education. All have as a goal the preparation of all high school graduates for life outside the school, as well as for post-secondary specialization. It is too early to predict the direction of the single curriculum which may result, but it is apparent that many people are working hard to bring it to reality.

Specific Versus General Vocational Education

The issue of whether or not vocational education is too specific has been raised constantly since its inception. Too often the argument has generated more heat than illumination because those who say vocational education is too specific tend to rely on assumptions rather than facts. Vocational education has almost never been so specific as to warrant the frequently made charge that it prepares individuals for a single occupation. On the other hand, in response to demands from general educators, it occasionally has become so general as to have practically no occupational relevance.

Relevance to the needs of youth and of society is a far more important test than is a measure of generality or specificity. Almost certainly, irrelevance is caused most frequently by instructors who are out of touch with the world of work. Equipment, texts, materials, and instructional organization can all contribute to a lack of relevance, but most of these deficiencies can be overcome by a competent instructor. It is to be hoped that a combination of improved evaluation techniques and greatly increased emphasis on teacher education programs for vocational instructors will lead to the elimination of the teacher as a major cause of irrelevance.

A charge of too great specificity is usually accompanied by a statement that occupations rapidly become obsolete; hence, it is charged that vocational education will be of no value a few years after it is completed. A variation of this theme admits that vocational education may be of value but claims that since no one knows which occupations will survive, each student should be prepared for all occupations. Undeniably, if a form of vocational education could be devised which prepared all students for all occupations, it would be a great boon to society. But it has not been devised, and it is unlikely that it will be devised. The difficulties involved in preparing a person for all skilled occupations are roughly comparable to the difficulties of devising a single graduate school program which would prepare students for all professions.

Barring some miracle which would produce a universal vocational education program, the best assurance of continued usefulness of vocational education is the provision of well prepared teachers. It is a well known fact that within one occupation, obsolete practices exist for years alongside the most modern practice. A capable instructor will be several years ahead of the generality of practice in the occupation he teaches, and simply because he is ahead of general practice, he can provide his students with competencies which will insure that their skills and knowledges will be obsolete much less quickly than is true for the occupational field as a whole.

There is, however, one side of the question of generality of instruction on which most vocational educators have a blind spot. Because they have suffered for many years from inadequate resources to accomplish the tremendous task which faces them, they tend to be jealous of the resources that they have and to be wary about sharing these resources with other parts of the school system. Vocational education, and indeed all of education, is hampered greatly by the fact that education about the world of work begins so late in the student's educational career. It does no good to complain that general educators should recognize that education for the world of work is a basic part of the education needed by everyone. They have not seen this in the past, and they are unlikely to deal with it effectively in the near future. The only plausible remedy is to use vocational education funds to prepare curriculum materials and to train classroom teachers in their use so that an understanding of the world of work can be a part of the educational program from early childhood education onward. This will make the task of vocational education easier when students arrive at the point that they are ready for more specific occupational instruction. But equally important, the general citizenry will in the long run become aware of the importance of vocations to the national welfare and will insist that increasing educational resources be devoted to their development.

Level of Vocational Education

Youth and adults who need and want vocational education have suffered because of controversies as to the level at which vocational education ought to be offered. General educators who desire more time for their own instructional program have been almost unanimous in demanding that vocational education be postponed until after high school. They have been joined by certain technical educators in the community colleges who feel that education for occupations below the level of technician is worthless and should be eliminated both from high schools and from community colleges.

So long as emphasis was placed on meeting the needs of the labor market, it was logical to postpone vocational education until just prior to the time when the student would enter the labor market. This was particularly true for programs which emphasized the development of specific skills, because such skills become obsolete more quickly than do general principles. In spite of the changes suggested in the preceding section, vocational education necessarily has a considerable tie to the labor market, if for no other reason than that to date it has been evaluated only on the basis of the success of its graduates in employment. If the thirteenth and fourteenth years of education become nearly universally accepted, almost all vocational educators will do all they can to get specific skill training moved to that level.

It is generally true, however, that middle class people, including vocational educators, want a different type of education for their children than they prescribe for the "disadvantaged." Just as the prescription for early childhood education for the lower class is "drill, drill, drill," while the program for the middle class is "breadth and creativity," so it is that the middle class prescribes vocational education for the lower class students in the high school. We should not be sure that the "disadvantaged" will accept such discrimination. The most likely solution should seem to be expanded enrollments in vocational education for the disadvantaged (both high school graduates and dropouts) in community colleges, where almost everyone (regardless of class) is pursuing an occupational or professional goal.

If we assume that the more specific types of vocational education should be provided close to the time when the graduate will use them in his employment, there is no question that as the average age of leaving school increases, the average age of the vocational education student who is receiving specific instruction will also increase. At the same time, if we assume that all students who need and want vocational education should have it available to them, it is crystal clear that we must continue to offer vocational programs in the high school for the foreseeable future. Moreover, for those students who are likely to drop out at the age of compulsory attendance, we must insure that vocational education programs are provided to at least some students prior to age sixteen.

The high schools of the nation have access to almost every youth, and they are accessible to almost every adult. Post-secondary education institutions, however, are attended by considerably less than half of our youth and, because of their geographic dispersal, are practically inaccessible to a high proportion of adults. To argue that vocational education programs for either youth or adults should be conducted only in post-secondary education institutions is completely unrealistic for the foreseeable future. Vocational education programs suitable to the needs of the student are needed and will be needed for the foreseeable future, at every level of education and for every age of student from early childhood to retirement from the labor force.

Curriculum Development

In some ways, vocational education has had an embarrassment of riches in text material. Specialized trade magazines, extremely specialized books on industrial processes, highly specific catalogues and sales brochures, motion pictures designed to sell products or services, and a wealth of other materials have been available. Moreover, in many cases they have been available at low cost, and vocational educators have been urged in no uncertain terms to accept them. On the other hand, until comparatively recently, there have been very few texts designed specifically for vocational education instruction. Unlike the English teacher or the foreign language teacher, the vocational educator rarely has, even today, a choice of more than one or two suitable texts, and in many occupational fields he has none.

Even worse is the fact that there have been no large scale curriculum development projects designed to prepare a course of study, select or develop instructional aids, prepare examinations, and train teachers to use these revised curricula in any field of vocational education. The closest we have come has been the federally supported work in industrial arts curriculum development in two university centers. In contrast, the physics course, which enrolls no more than 5 percent of high school students, has had over ten million dollars of foundation and federal money spent on the development of curriculum materials. A similar expenditure on the development of curriculum materials for orientation to the world of work in the elementary school, which would reach every student, could produce far greater results. Not only do we know more about developing curriculum materials than we did fifteen years ago when the new physics course was begun, but the new physics course replaced a series of old physics courses which were reasonably satisfactory, while the development of curriculum materials for orientation to the world of work would meet a pressing need which is now not met at all satisfactorily.

The development of sound curricula to meet the needs of the occupational fields covered by vocational education will be an extremely time consuming and expensive task. It is unlikely that a competent job can be done for less than three million dollars per occupational cluster. Yet it can and must be done if vocational education is to be maximally effective. The present system of curriculum development, where twelve states operate independent curriculum laboratories, investing ten to twenty-five thousand dollars per curriculum, duplicating each other's services, and in many cases being unable to distribute their products beyond the borders of the state, is grossly inefficient. It must be replaced by federally supported curriculum development projects, adequately funded, and with only enough duplication of effort to give the teacher a choice of two or three excellent curriculum packages which can be modified to meet regional needs.

Vocational Education in Developing Countries

Vocational educators from the United States have provided instruction in a number of developing countries around the world. In addition to teaching in the classroom, they have worked to develop appropriate curricula and establish vocational education institutions. A few vocational educators have even become proficient at securing funds for such endeavors. In the course of this employment, vocational educators from the United States have learned a great deal, much of it through trial and error. One of the things they have learned is that similar teams of vocational educators from such countries as England, Japan, Germany, and Russia are on similar missions. In some countries, teams from all of these nations have been in active competition.

Valuable as this type of vocational education foreign assistance has been for the development of the vocational educators involved, it is not a realistic long-term approach to the development of vocational education abroad. In the long-term, vocational education must be provided by individuals who share the culture of the students being educated. This is true for two reasons. One is national pride, which demands that key educational positions be staffed by nationals of the country for whom the training is given. The second reason is goals and methods in different cultures are so diverse and even contradictory that an outsider not only has difficulty in communicating, but may indeed be suggesting solutions which are entirely inappropriate or even offensive to the culture in which he is teaching.

The only serious attempt to solve this problem has been the assignment of "counterparts" from the country being served. In addition to carrying on his assigned role as a teacher or administrator of vocational education, the American (foreign) expert has been expected simultaneously to train his counterpart to succeed him. In practice, this counterpart system has not worked well. Sometimes this has been because the wrong persons were assigned as counterparts, but equally often it has been because the American vocational educator was more interested in doing the work himself than in training his replacement.

These considerations suggest the following remedies:

A. Most Americans have little appreciation of cultures which exist outside this continent, and indeed have little understanding and appreciation of values held outside the American middle class persons from his particular section of the country. As vocational educators are forced to work with lower class leaders who demand respect, these attitudes may gradually change. Another step toward the understanding of other cultures would be full scale American participation in international conferences of vocational education. At present, these are regarded as unimportant, and only token American representation is sent, if any is sent at all. Generally, those persons who are selected to attend are bureaucrats who are felt to deserve a vacation from the conflicts within the federal office of education. Substantial representation by persons who regard international conferences as a professional opportunity instead of as a vacation would teach us much and might teach foreign vocational educators some things as well.

B. Most of our foreign assistance in vocational education should be transformed into teacher and administrator training activities conducted on a part-time cooperative basis here and abroad. A staff of educators in this country who had had meaningful foreign experience could conduct an educational program for foreign nationals who would spend half of their time working on a college campus and half of their time in observation and participation in vocational education institutions in this country. After perhaps a year of such instruction, the locale of training could be shifted abroad, with foreign educators being developed through formal instruction which supplemented actual work as a teacher or administrator in schools or in training programs conducted by business and industry.

The Future of Vocational Education

The years ahead call for more and better vocational education. This book has tried to describe some of the dimensions of "better." If even a small proportion of the events predicted here come to pass, there will be more work for vocational educators than we can accomplish. As we recruit others to the task, we need to remind them and remind ourselves that our goals are to serve students, youth and adult, by helping to meet the manpower needs of the nation (and of the world), increasing individual options of students, and lending intelligibility to all of education.

REFERENCES

1. American Vocational Association, *The Advisory Committee and Vocational Education*. Washington, D.C.: American Vocational Association, 1969.

2. Burt, Samuel M., *Industry and Vocational-Technical Education*. New York: McGraw-Hill Book Company, 1967.

3. "Integrating Teachers," *Wall Street Journal*. (January 30, 1970), 1.

4. Mangum, Garth, "Second Chance in the Transition from School to Work," *Transition from School to Work*. Princeton, New Jersey: Industrial Relations Section, Princeton University, 1968.

5. Rosen, Howard, *Job Training of Blue Collar Workers: Implications for Vocational Guidance*. Unpublished speech. Washington, D.C.: Office of Manpower Research, Manpower Administration, U.S. Department of Labor.

6. Schaefer, Carl J. and J. J. Kaufman, *Occupational Education in Massachusetts*. Boston: Massachusetts Advisory Council on Education, 1968.

INDEX